# The India Traveler

# The India Traveler

Overland 1973
Returns and Reflections 1983, 1997

Bharat Darshan

**Marjorie A. Kircher**

**Gottlieb Press**
Portland, Oregon

www.theindiatraveler.com



ISBN-13: 978-0615724263 (Custom Universal)
ISBN-10: 0615724264

Library of Congress Cataloging-in-Publication Data
Kircher, Marjorie A., The India Traveler: Overland 1973; Returns and Reflections 1983, 1997 / by Marjorie A. Kircher.—1st ed.
p. cm.
1. India—Travel and description—social customs—Hippie Trail.
2. Hippie Trail—Overland to India and Afghanistan—20th century.
LCCN: 2012923361 2013

Printed in the United States of America

Gottlieb Press
Portland, Oregon

For all my friends along this journey

And other intrepid world travelers

# Contents

# Author's Note



All the people of these stories are real, but I've changed most of their names and some of their towns to protect their privacy. Any resemblance of their fictional names to other people of similar name is coincidental. The events and conversations are told from my own recollections and perspective. My friends and fellow travelers would have their own angles on events and cultural observations. Dialogues are reconstructed from memory.

I am grateful to many people for helping me as I wrote this book:

For thoughtful editorial advice and encouragement at all the right times, I am indebted to Edith Mirante. I greatly appreciate Tena Hoke, Alexandra Jones and Rebecca Meredith for inspiring words and editorial commentary. Ali McCart of Indigo Editing helped me immensely with her professional polish and advice on the details.

For early reading and suggesting this was a worthwhile project, I thank Judy Cameron, Susan Katz, Loren and Becky Schmidt.

Thank you to Kamlesh Bansal, Miten Bhatia and Rita Gupta for advice and insights into aspects of Indian Culture.

For technical assistance, wisdom and reassurance, appreciation is extended especially to Mitch Gilbert; also to Miten Bhatia, Jim Binkley, Julian Fifer, Mike Meredith, and Karen Steingart, who saw me to the finish line; finally to Jerrol Eshleman for helping me get bearings in the webbed world.

Thanks to all my friends in India who hosted me in their homes and shared their lives with me through the years.

I am forever grateful to my husband, Mitch Gilbert, for his kind encouragement throughout the meandering soul-searching process it took me to write this book.

I came upon a child of God,
He was walking along the road,
And I asked him, where are you going?
And this he told me,
I'm going on down to Yasgur's farm,
I'm going to join in a rock 'n roll band,
I'm going to camp out on the land,
I'm gonna try an' get my soul free.

We are stardust,
We are golden,
And we've got to get ourselves
Back to the garden.

Then, can I walk beside you?
I have come here to lose the smog,
And I feel to be a cog in something turning.
Well maybe it is just the time of year,
Or maybe it's the time of Man,
I don't know who I am,
But you know, life is for learning.

We are stardust,
We are golden,
And we've got to get ourselves
Back to the garden.

By the time time we got to Woodstock,
We were half a million strong,
And everywhere there was song and celebration,
And I dreamed I saw the bombers
Riding shotgun in the sky,
And they were turning into butterflies
Above our nation.

We are stardust, billion year-old carbon,
We are golden,
Caught in the devil's bargain,
And we've got to get ourselves
Back to the garden.

"Woodstock"
Joni Mitchell
1969

In 1854, my great-grandfather Heinrich left Germany on a sailing ship to the United States. He was fourteen years old and traveled alone, making his way washing dishes, peeling potatoes, and other odd jobs on the boat. The family handed down his stories: he was looking for a new life and opportunities, maybe things he'd heard about America—freedom and money. I know he went looking for adventure. He was not content; wanted to get out and have a look around. He found new pathways and rechanneled his story, eventually marrying my great-grandmother Louise and raising wheat and ten children on their land in southern Kansas. He and his hired cowboys, we heard tell, herded cattle up from Texas on the Chisholm Trail, sleeping on the ground at night, digging holes to settle their hipbones. His youngest daughter, my maternal grandmother, Maude, decided the city was for her. She shed the language of the old country and put on airs in Wichita, where Heinrich had by then founded a bank and bought a hotel with his new riches.

Eventually I came along and moved with my parents back to southern Kansas near our ancestor's lands. There, my father found his opportunity in the Ford dealership of a small town. I got a taste for adventure there, in 1950s America. I got to ride with my dad in a first model Thunderbird, a two-seater with round windows in the back. Another time he acquired a Model A from an old farmer who traded it in for a new Ford. We rode the Model A down Main Street in frequent parades. In those times, our small Kansas town had no crime to speak of and the adults didn't fear for us children wandering the streets. My best friend Kathy and I rode our bicycles all day and went anywhere and as far as we wanted, even leaving town if we felt like it—my first travels, the sweet taste of freedom. The floors of our house were covered in Maude's collection of Persian carpets, bought decades ago in Wichita from Lebanese immigrant friends. I would play for hours on the colorful patterns, imagining faraway places and times.

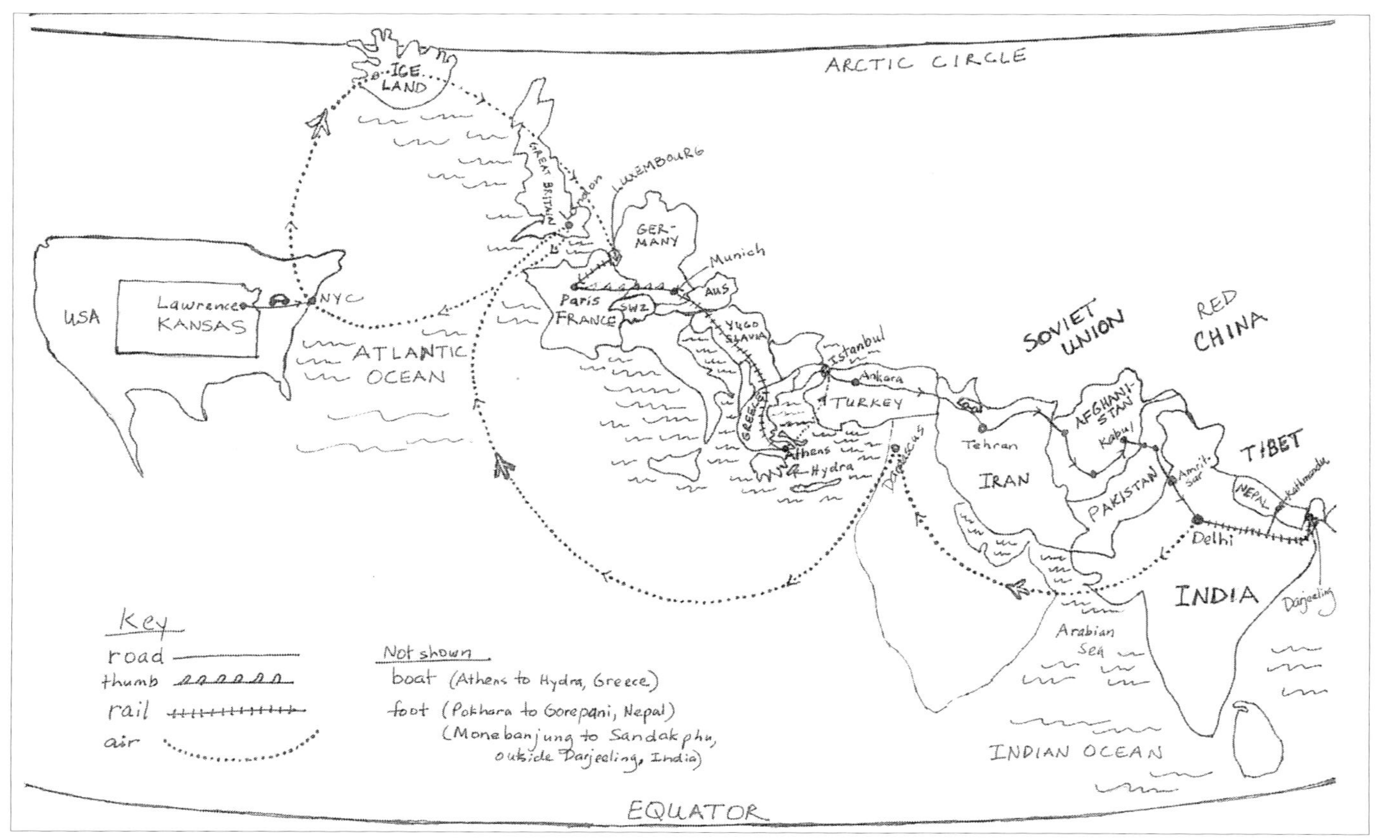
ARCTIC CIRCLE
ICE LAND
GREAT BRITAIN
London
LUXEMBOURG
GER-MANY
Munich
AUS
Paris
FRANCE
SWZ
YUGO SLAVIA
GREECE
Istanbul
Ankara
TURKEY
Athens
Hydra
Damascus
USA
Lawrence
KANSAS
NYC
ATLANTIC OCEAN
SOVIET UNION
RED CHINA
AFGHANI-STAN
Kabul
Tehran
IRAN
PAKISTAN
Amrit-sar
Delhi
TIBET
NEPAL
Kathmandu
INDIA
Darjeeling
Arabian Sea
INDIAN OCEAN
Key
road
thumb
rail
air
Not shown
boat (Athens to Hydra, Greece)
foot (Pokhara to Gorepani, Nepal)
(Monebanjung to Sandakphu, outside Darjeeling, India)
EQUATOR

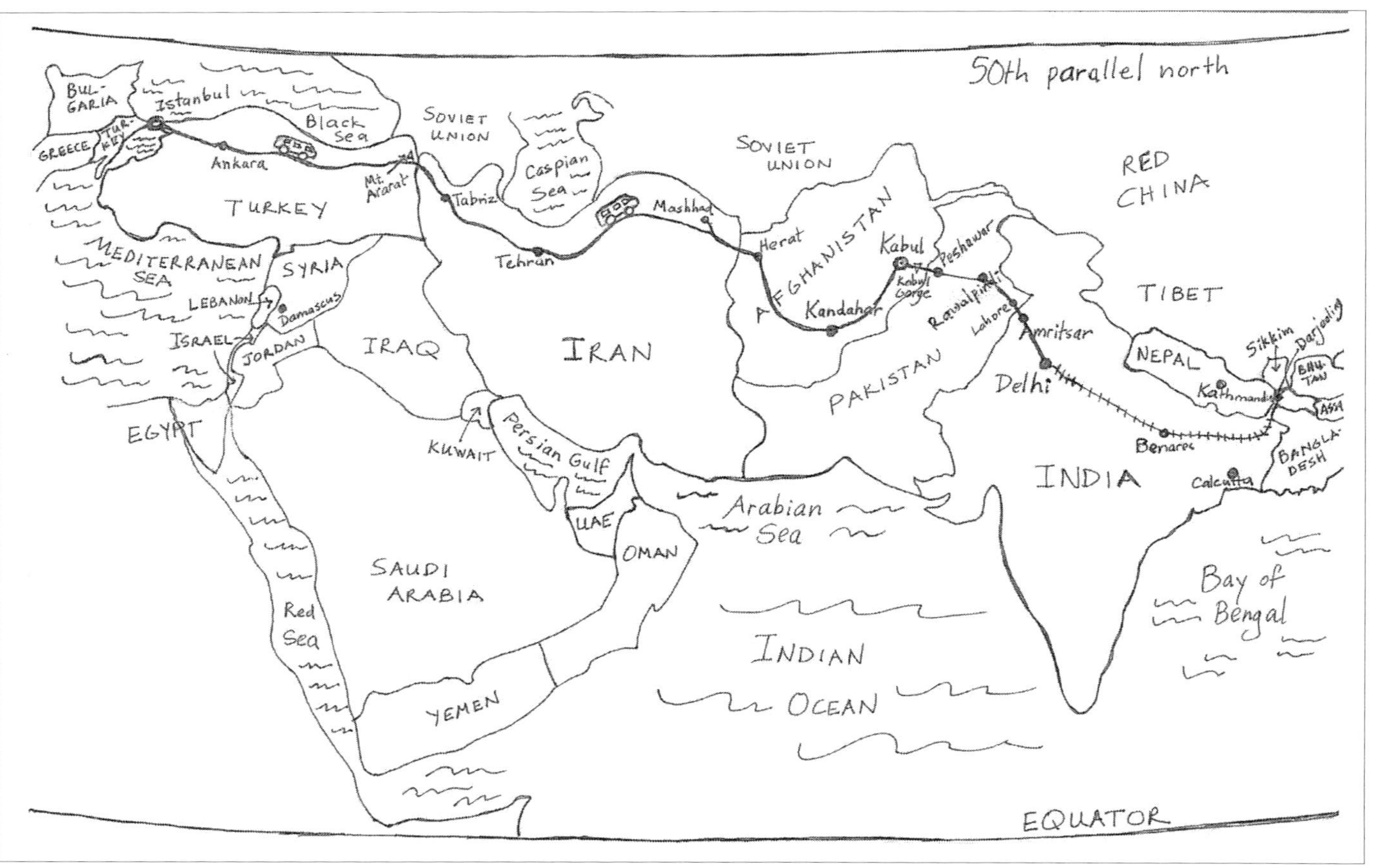
50th parallel north
BULGARIA
GREECE
TURKEY
Istanbul
Black Sea
Ankara
TURKEY
Mt. Ararat
SOVIET UNION
Caspian Sea
Tabriz
Tehran
Mashhad
SOVIET UNION
Herat
AFGHANISTAN
Kandahar
Kabul
Kabul Gorge
Peshawar
Rawalpindi
Lahore
Amritsar
Delhi
RED CHINA
TIBET
NEPAL
Kathmandu
Sikkim
Darjeeling
BHUTAN
Benares
Calcutta
BANGLADESH
INDIA
PAKISTAN
IRAN
MEDITERRANEAN SEA
SYRIA
LEBANON
Damascus
ISRAEL
JORDAN
IRAQ
EGYPT
KUWAIT
Persian Gulf
UAE
OMAN
Arabian Sea
SAUDI ARABIA
Red Sea
YEMEN
INDIAN OCEAN
Bay of Bengal
EQUATOR

CHINA

JAMMU
AND
KASHMIR
Srinegar
Ladakh region
Rohtang Pass
Manali
Dharam-sala
HIMACHAL
PRADESH
PAKISTAN
TIBET
Amritsar
Chandigarh
PUNJAB
UTTAR
PRADESH
Jindh
HAR-
YANA
Delhi
Agra
NEPAL
Annapurna
Range
Mt. Everest
Pokhara
Kathmandu
SIK
KIM
BHU-
TAN
ARUNACHAL
PRADESH
ASSAM
WB
Raxaul
Darjeeling
RAJASTHAN
Jaipur
Ajmer
Lucknow
Benares
(Varanasi)
Patna
BIHAR
Bodh Gaya
BANGLA-
DESH
WEST
BENGAL
Calcutta
BURMA
Bhopal

INDIA

Arabian
Sea
Bombay
(Mumbai)
Hyderabad
GOA
Bay of Bengal
Madras
(Chennai)
Bangalore
Mahabalipuram
(Mamallapuram)
Pondicherry
TAMIL
NADU
KERALA
Madurai
Cochin
(Kochi)
INDIAN
OCEAN
SRI
LANKA

Marjorie Kircher

Passport Photo, 1973

# Part I

## Overland to India, 1973

It was winter in the Catskill Mountains, 1974, freezing cold, snow on the ground. Bare grey tree branches were framed in each window of our house on a quiet street. I'd moved to New York State a few months earlier with old friends Pam and Dan and a bunch of cats. Less than one year before, at age twenty-two, I'd left Kansas. I went to Paris where I met up with a friend, intending to travel with him to India. It didn't turn out that way—instead I found the adventure of my young life, making my own way through Europe to Istanbul, onward through Turkey, Iran, Afghanistan, and Pakistan before unbelievably finding myself crossing the border into India.

On that winter's day in the Catskills, a Sunday afternoon with nothing to do, I was thinking a lot about my trip. I started writing some things that happened, longhand with pencil in a spiral notebook. I kept that notebook with me through many decades and many moves, though I never read it again, until one recent summer day when I found the old journal, its penciled cursive fading and rust crusting on the binding wire. I turned the pages to read, easily slipping back into the 1973 journey.

I realized this trip had been my destiny. I found new pathways, new places to go in life. It was in Paris that I met Allen, who opened the door to Oregon, where I've now lived over half my life. And on this trip I got a good view of the economic circumstance in which many people of the world live. I came face-to-face with historic places and works of art and architecture, and I returned home with a lot to think about. The images and vivid emotional memories of this trip continue to influence my life and work, my thoughts and what I like to read, even what I like to eat. For years I've been telling parts of this tale to friends and family when memory is triggered. Now I am putting the oral stories all together into this written piece. I type-copied these stories exactly as I wrote them in 1974, incorrect or awkward language preserved intact. The entries are set apart and noted under the heading *Journal 1974.* I've written a great deal more of my recollections and musings, noting the retrospective entries under the heading *Memoir*, or comments designated *Note*, between parentheses. At points this resembles a dialogue between my younger and older selves.

In my first passport are the actual dates of my trip:
Entered Luxembourg January 11, 1973
Entered India April 5, 1973
Left India June 11, 1973

***Journal 1974***

*Dancing Eastward: Travel Essays*

I smile with memories: Fading images of lands far away. Great moments of wonder by creations of nature and man, sustained only by my recollections, now by my pen. I try to assimilate these miscellaneous experiences, from subtle appreciation of great works of art in Paris to adrenalinated experiences with armed Afghanis in the middle of the Kabul Gorge, or, drawing a breath, trying to hold for an instant an image of eternal snow peaks in Nepal. Some experiences are affected by previous knowledge and conceptions—I had ideas about the Himalayas, though I knew very little about Nepal. I had known Manet's *Luncheon on the Grass* for many years. I knew almost nothing about Afghanistan, except what I had been briefed along the way from other travelers, mostly fearful things.

*Paris*

I started my journeys in Europe. At first, things were difficult. It seemed to me that Parisians didn't like foreigners, especially Americans, and particularly if they didn't speak

French. Well, somehow I survived my first day in Paris, including my first encounter with famed Parisian rats, scratching in the walls of my hotel room. It was horrible (and at the same time very funny)—squeals and scratches and squeaks all night across the ceiling, up and down the walls. When I did sleep, I had dreams of 3-foot, 40-pound rats swinging by their toes from the windowsills onto my head.

### *Memoir*

I was much engaged in my studies of English literature at the University of Kansas in Lawrence. I found truth in William Blake, Samuel Coleridge, and William Butler Yeats. Chaucer made me laugh in *The Canterbury Tales*. I marched in the streets in protest of the war in Vietnam. In 1972, I lived in a big, sunny old house on Tennessee Avenue, down the hill from the university. Four of us paid the rent, and two others spent a lot of time there. One of my friends in the house was Jeff, a young man of dramatic personality studying theatre arts and imitating the rest of us in satirical vignettes. When he enacted me, I was always searching for the meaning of life. Another was Gary, an art major who displayed live chickens in his art installation in the basement of the student union building and kept a black widow spider as a pet in a bell jar. While driving his pickup truck, he'd pretend he was riding a horse in a canter. Jeff and Gary were hanging out late one evening in Jeff's room and I joined them after my studies.

As I seated myself on the floor, Jeff asked, "Hey, Margie, you wanna go to India with us next year?"

"Sure," I said nonchalantly.

"Actually, we're serious, we're going *overland* to India and Nepal. We've heard it's really great there."

One must consider the sociocultural context here. I cannot imagine my friends getting this idea without George Harrison first discovering Ravi Shankar, and the Beatles having gone to India some five years earlier to meet with the Maharishi Mahesh Yogi Transcendental Meditation (T.M.) guru. They led us, the restless youth of the world, into the spiritual ways and musical sounds of the East. Jeff and I had been initiated in T.M. when the instructors came through Lawrence the year before. I had studied three courses in Buddhist thought offered by the philosophy department at the university. Mr. Streiff, a favorite high school English teacher of mine (who I was to discover much later rubbed shoulders with some of the Beat poets), when asked by the editor of the student newspaper, "Happiness is…?" had given an answer that made me curious: "an archaeological dig in Turkey." One of our other housemates had a boyfriend, sometimes a guest in the house, who had "been there," through the Middle East to India. He told an impressive story of survival when his backpack was stolen by bandits in Afghanistan. He had learned in those remote countries to relieve himself by squatting with his bare feet on the toilet seat—pretty weird, but an indication that daily life was really different somewhere else. Jeff and Gary had talked to him at length.

The idea of going to India gradually took root for me, and I checked out a book from the university library. I can't remember the title or the author, but it was very old and musty, bound in flaking, dark-brown leather with gold embossing. It was an account of a man's travels in British India around the turn of the twentieth century. The book itself was a fascination. I would open it late at night after my studies, breathe in its old-book scent and, carefully turning its fragile pages, read a chapter describing an exotic India, faraway and long past. I kept the book for months, repeatedly renewing its loan. No one else was requesting the old tome. My fascination with India and Nepal was growing, along with the notion that I could actually go there. It became my post-graduation plan. I talked about it with all my friends. I think I enjoyed their reactions when I said I was "going overland to India." It raised my status a bit. My mother, meanwhile, thought the idea was a humorous fantasy and never took me seriously.

Jeff and Gary left for Europe months before I could go. The plan was that I would finish my studies and then join them "at Christmas in the Pyrenees mountains, between France and Spain," Jeff wrote in early autumn from Europe. But things started changing before I got there. Gary found Jesus in Europe (a shocking turn, knowing him) and wanted to return to the United States to worship, giving up the India part of his trip, but Jeff's letters waxed enthusiastic for eastward travel. Our meeting place was modified to Paris. By Christmas 1972, I'd finished all my coursework for graduation. Upon completion of the last final exam, I walked dreamily down Mt. Oread Avenue through the University of Kansas campus for the last time, ready to begin my post-baccalaureate plan "to complete my education in the real world," as I told my friends and family.

I'd saved money during college by habitual scrimping. The economy in the United States in the 1960s and 1970s was more robust than nowadays. The cost of everything was relatively low, and it was possible to live well in Lawrence with very little money. I was used to the student life and applied a philosophy of non-materialism, appropriate to the times. When I left Kansas in January, I took about $500 in American Express traveler's checks. I also took along four bank promissory note cards that, if a local bank abroad would agree, would each entitle me to buy $250 more in traveler's checks. I left $1,000 in my mother's bank account in Wichita to cover these cards, plus an extra $500 for her to wire me upon request. It was hard-earned money I'd saved from my summer waitress jobs during college. That's $2,000 for six months abroad; three in Europe, three, Asia. It was 1973, and the American dollar was an esteemed and valuable currency that held its value throughout the world.

I'd gotten the vaccinations for India (at that time, cholera, polio, smallpox, typhoid, and yellow fever; also a gamma globulin shot to boost my immune system) and held a cheap one-way air ticket ($125) from New York to Luxembourg via Icelandic Airlines. I had a good down sleeping bag and a fancy Swiss Army knife, a gift from a friend. I acquired a sturdy aluminum-frame backpack and packed it with stylish jeans and a sweater. I made a long red skirt and a headscarf, as someone told me I might need to cover my head and legs in the Middle East. I sewed a deep inner pocket into the skirt for hiding money and my passport, and I made a small cloth bag that could hang inside my clothing, suspended from a belt. A lot of the preparation was guesswork, as I didn't know what to expect on these travels. My friends Pam and Dan were driving to the East Coast after Christmas, so they gave me a ride to New York City. Off I went into the world, filled with fanciful imaginings of foreign lands.

**Paris**

The long plane ride to Europe was unnerving, flying high over the inky waves of the Atlantic Ocean. I'd taken only two air trips before that; usually I traveled by Trailways bus. We changed planes in Iceland. An eerie sun perched on the horizon within a dramatically colored sky, vivid purples and golds in swirling bands. I was very nervous and boarded the wrong plane, before finding the right jet and settling in for the final flight to Luxembourg. I drifted through the arrival and immigration procedures at the Luxembourg airport, exhausted and queasy from having sampled free cognac offered on the plane. When I opened my bag to find my passport, I noticed my address book was not where I thought I'd put it. I wasn't worried. My backpack had a lot of pockets and I figured I'd go through them later. I got coffee and sat down to wait for the evening train to Paris. When it arrived, I got on and sank into a comfortable seat, relaxing with the smooth ride. An hour later I remembered the address book and searched my luggage. A jolt of adrenalin coursed through my veins as I realized I really had lost it. I had most of my friends' and family's addresses committed to memory, but the book had the information for the hotel in Paris where I was supposed to meet Jeff.

I arrived in Paris at night, not too happy, even more exhausted. I went to the information booth for help, not sure what kind of help anyone could give me. The purply-red haired French information lady was worse than no help at all. She began insulting me in English, using a harsh voice, emitting little puffs of air from her lips for emphasis, as the French do: "What have you? You have nothing! You have no address, no place to go, no ability to speak the language and no Francs! It's hopeless!" My introduction to Paris. I immediately formed a negative opinion, though I was just as soon rescued by a pair of really nice Parisians—a father and son who had witnessed the scene and kindly scooped me and my big-frame backpack into their tiny Citroen car, saying they would help me find a hotel. I'd met the son, a student, on the train from Luxembourg. They took me to a little hotel in an area "where students lived." That hotel was where I endured the squealing rat noises and the huge rat dreams.

A disturbed night was followed by a hopeful morning. I awoke to sun filtering through filmy white curtains. I lay in bed, dreamily, with an uncanny awareness, a memory of numbers in my head. I sat up suddenly, exclaiming, "46 Rue Vaugirard!" the address I'd lost the day before. I will never forget it. But I had already thought of a way to find Jeff, to go to the American Express Post office and check if he'd left me a message. I went, and he had, with the news that he'd moved to a friend's place nearby at 21 Rue Cujas. I ended up boarding at 46 Rue Vaugirard, then a student hotel in the Latin Quarter between the Metro stops of St. Germain and St. Michel. I bought a small, blue alpha-indexed notebook with the French word *Repertoire* printed on the front cover, and wrote in all the addresses I could remember of my friends and family at home. I easily recall those once important addresses after all these years. The blue notebook had extra pages if I wished to write other things. I would soon be filling it with the names of new friends.

Jeff was staying with three Americans: Allen (whom he'd met in Rome on the street a few weeks before) and two roommates, Susan and Allison. I arrived breathless and sweating at their garret apartment after climbing seven flights of stairs (no elevator). Just as I was taking off my backpack in the kitchen, Jeff broke the news that he didn't have the money to go to India, but he had ideas for how to get some. I stopped breathing. I felt dizzy. Doubts filled my head. Should I have stayed in Lawrence? India had been a dream for a year. How could I abandon this? Allen was sympathetic, kindly offering me a breakfast of oranges and yogurt, a combination I relish to this day.

I lived in Paris for a month. I felt out of place in the beginning. It was the first major city in which I'd spent much time, and a foreign capital at that. I decided right away that I didn't like Paris—too big, grimy, and not friendly. A week later, Allen, Jeff, and I went to Switzerland for a week's vacation. On the drive from Paris, we stopped in Geneva, which was lovely with a spreading blue lake reflecting the dark silhouetted hills at dusk. We stayed in Sass Fee, an alpine mountain village like one I could have imagined from old storybook illustrations. No cars were allowed, and they brought visitors into the town in a horse-drawn sleigh, complete with woolen lap blankets and jingle bells. I bought some big, heavy Swiss hiking boots and slogged on trails through wet snow, taking in the crisp clean air and lovely views of the snow-covered Alps, with the Matterhorn prominent. In Switzerland, I started feeling better about being in Europe.

Upon returning to Paris, I resolved to give the old, famous city I'd found myself in a second chance. I learned how to travel on the Metro underground system. Allen suggested I visit art museums. I had not realized how many famous works of art lived in Paris. It was thrilling to stand before the actual paintings I had recently studied in my art history classes at school. My favorite museum was the little Jeu de Paume. The Louvre was, well, magnificent, beyond comparison, intoxicating. And I was getting to know Allen, Allison, and Susan. Paris was getting better. We went to the Bird Market on Sunday. We bought *moules* (mussels) in another open-air market to bring home to cook, as an alternative to our habit of eating out in cheap restaurants every night. I experimented with odd French dishes, ordering things like tripe and inky indigo squid. Neither of these appealed to me, though the preparation in those budget restaurants was probably not the best. We would sit for long hours talking over coffee and pastries beneath mirrored walls, emulating the Parisian café life (as I imagined from novels) and watching French theatre people. Allen introduced me to French crepes, which we ate for lunch from small stalls on the street. You ordered savory or sweet ingredients. The delicate crepes rolled with sauced mushrooms or sugar and butter were such a treat. I also loved to stop for a little bag of hot smoky chestnuts, roasted in charcoal braziers on the street.

It was a time of new ideas and social upheaval around the world. Much of note was happening in 1973, an unusual convergence of portentous events. Nine days after I arrived in Paris, on January 20, 1973, Richard Nixon was inaugurated into the second term of his ill-fated presidency. Two days after that, the US Supreme Court overturned state bans on abortion in Roe v. Wade, following oral argument presented by a twenty-six-year-old Texas woman attorney. The Paris Peace Accord was signed on January 27, 1973, in my new city of residence, formally ending direct US involvement in the Vietnam War. In the next month, Red China and the United States would agree to establish liaison offices, the beginning of another avenue into Asia. In April, the World Trade Center would open in New York City and the British House of Commons would vote against restoring capital punishment by a wide margin. In May, Skylab would be launched, the

United State's first space station. In October, the Bosporus Bridge would be completed in Istanbul, Turkey, connecting the continents of Europe and Asia for the first time. In India, Indira Gandhi was prime minister, widely popular and revered as Mother India.

Paris was a center for radical thought. Allen and I went to see Gloria Steinem talk in a bookstore near the Sorbonne university. The small, hot room was crowded to the max. People were talking and milling, so we couldn't hear well, but I got a pretty good view. Steinem was seated in the center of the room between two large black women who were smoking cigarillos and looked like twins—Americans I think, and her bodyguards, so I fancied. It was thrilling just to see her, a strong female spokesperson of our time.

Jeff was running out of money, and his schemes for getting more were not working. Despite his flagging travel plans, I proceeded with my own preparations, finding out from other travelers that I would need visas for India and Nepal as well as several of the other countries on the way. My quest for these visas brought me into the elegant embassy quarters of Paris, an interesting area I may not have had occasion to venture into otherwise. It was quite a task and took a long time getting all the visas, as I needed to leave my passport in each embassy for several days.

An old passport affords a great souvenir and record of travels, especially in those days when the dates were carefully handwritten into large complicated, multicolored inked stamps and, in the case of India, even some official paper stamps pasted in. Looking at the visas in my passport reminds me of border officials in little outpost buildings across the Middle East stamping our passports with a great staccato pomp and flourish. Four of my visas for Central Asian travel (India, Nepal, Iran, and Afghanistan) were issued from Paris embassies. The Pakistan visa was applied for in Kabul, Afghanistan. Perhaps I had not realized that I would cross Pakistan. There was no requirement for Americans to have a visa for travel in Turkey at that time.

Allen was a student at the Sorbonne studying French historical thought, a program that had some connection to the University of Oregon in Eugene. We would argue about which was the best town— Lawrence or Eugene—pointless as neither of us had been to the other one. He was to win that argument a year and a half later when I moved to Eugene, sight unseen on his description of Oregon in a letter: "…a beautiful rainforest with whales rising from the Pacific Ocean." He had an eye for spotting and collecting antiques and other curios, and I was lucky to tag along with him when he practiced his craft in raucous open flea markets around Paris.

Allison, from Minnesota, with long blond hair, had a penchant for men from Northern Africa, which seldom went well for her. One night, one of her Tunisian boyfriends ran up the seven flights of stairs in heated pursuit of Allison, who managed to get inside the door just ahead of him. "Quick," she screamed. "Help me close the door!" We all sprang to our feet and bolted for the door, almost too late, as his foot was already inside. He tried to force entry against three or four of us trying to push the door shut. Suddenly we realized he was gone, and we'd been pushing the door against his abandoned shoe.

Returning to the flat another night, Allen, Susan and I were locked out and sat in the hallway waiting for Allison to come home with a key. We heard huffing and puffing as someone was making his way up. A red-faced older man emerged breathless at the top of the stairs. As he walked in our direction, a door to a broom closet opened across the hall from us; an older woman in a housedress pulled him in and promptly closed the door. We looked at each other with puzzled amusement. "That is *so* Paris," said Allen. We waited for Allison in the hall for more than an hour but no one came out of the closet.

**Allen's Frank Talk about Travel**

One afternoon I went for a visit to the garret apartment. Allen was there, Allison too. Jeff wasn't. Allen and I had become friends during the weeks I was in Paris, and he gave me his frank opinion about my traveling to India with Jeff. "I know he was your roommate and friend at school, but I don't think he'd be a reliable travel companion. Maybe you could go to India without him." Allison agreed. Though I can't recall the reasons or flaws we discussed (and I give Jeff credit for the overland to India idea and inspiring me to leave home), I remember agreeing with them and feeling appreciative that they cared enough about me, a new friend, to give me this advice. Soon after, I told Jeff I would go to India on my own. I think he was relieved. I suspect he didn't really want to go and didn't know how to tell me.

With this obligation ended, another opportunity immediately surfaced on the streets of Paris. I was waiting at a street corner to cross and fell into an easy conversation with a tall, curly-haired young man in a fringed buckskin jacket. His name was Donald, from Canada. Many young people were traveling East in those times, and lo and behold, so was Donald, but he had a bolder idea than I: to hitchhike to Afghanistan. And, like that, I was invited. We exchanged Paris phone numbers to meet later. I was pleased to tell Allen that I'd found a new plan for India. Allen, protective toward his friends, wanted to meet Donald. We met for a café au lait. Donald seemed to both of us like a nice guy—clean cut, confident, and courteous. The idea of hitchhiking scared me a bit, but it was the time for adventure, and "hitchhiking to Afghanistan" had a nice sound. Hitting the road with your thumb out was not uncommon among college students in those days, evoking a kind of Kerouac fantasy. Donald was only going to Kabul, so I figured I'd take a train or bus from Afghanistan to India. Those countries seemed close together from my viewpoint in Western Europe.

I said my goodbyes to Jeff, promising to send him postcards from India. We had a long conversation on the phone many years later, recalling old times, but I was never to see my Kansas friend again. I went to say goodbye to my new friends in the garret apartment on Rue Cujas, assuming ours was a brief alliance, that would end on a pleasant note with my departure. By an uncanny coincidence in November of the next year, I would run into Allison in San Francisco at a special exhibit featuring Rodin sculptures. I was literally enroute on a move to Oregon, where I would see Allen for the first time since Paris. And four years after Paris, I was to move from Oregon to Boston to go to graduate school, where I resumed a friendship with Susan, who, again by coincidence, happened to be living in the area.

Donald and I left Paris. I brought along some French cheese and bread, fruit, and nuts for the hitchhiking journey, since one can't count on mealtimes in that situation. He was appreciative of the provisions and told me so. The day went smoothly. A number of nice people stopped to give us rides. Even the French and German truck drivers were polite and considerate, without the tension I'd felt on my one previous hitchhiking adventure, two years before, between the Northern Mexican border and Wichita, Kansas. I was hitchhiking with an American woman I'd met on a Mexican train. One middle-aged guy with black stitches holding together wounds across his face picked us up in Oklahoma City. He wasn't driving well, and when he told us, "I've been drunk for four days," I feigned a stomach ailment and demanded that we be let out of the car. It worked; we were freed of him, without mishap. After that, I figured I could protect myself anywhere.

Donald and I made it as far as Munich. We put our luggage into a locker in the train station and found a cheap youth hostel, where we booked dormitory beds for the night. The hostel warned us they locked the front door promptly at 11:00 pm; you had to be in on time if you wanted to sleep there.

Donald said, "And now, I want a *real* meal with meat. I am tired of eating your nuts and berries. After that, I want to go to the Hofbrau House."

I was surprised by the change in his tone, but we went to dinner. The evening in the Hofbrau House started out fun, and I was thrilled to be having what I imagined to be a real German experience. Many hours went by, as my hitchhiking companion drank more and more beer, laughing and singing with others around him. I thought about the hostel rule and reminded him, but he became angry and refused to leave: "Don't spoil my fun."

When we finally left, hours past the curfew hour, Donald said, "I'm gonna fin' that youth hostel and scale the wall." He growled on, "You can do whatever you want. And I'll tell you another thing, I only brought you along because I thought having a female would make it easier to get a ride, but I don't think it would have mattered." And he disappeared into the night.

Now what was I going to do? I'd heard one could sleep in the train station nearby and found my way to it. I was cold and lonely and scared, with only the clothes on my back for the night. Donald had the only key to the locker with our luggage. A social scene was happening in the railway station, lively for that late hour. I found a group of youthful travelers who spoke English; some were Americans. I explained my dilemma, that I had nowhere to sleep. One of them said, "You can crash in my van." He led me to his VW van and slid open the door. Other sleepers were in there, but I figured that was OK, better than being alone in a vehicle parked on the street. Munich didn't seem all that safe to me. The owner went to sleep in his hotel room. I had found a place to sleep, but the rest of my trip was now uncertain. I had taken Donald's rude words and departure to be a dismissal, a travel alliance come to an end after less than a day. Looking back on it, it's clear he had emotional issues, especially recalling what unfolded the next day.

I awoke with the light of day and greeted the other waking strangers yawning in the van. The grim night was over. The owner and others came to join us, asking me, "Hey man, wanna go to Dachau with us?"

"Sure," I said, thinking, What is Dachau? We drove out there in the van.

I can still see the ovens, and am haunted by the feeling of standing in the "shower room" (gas chamber) and staring at the evil spigots. I'd been schooled about the Holocaust and read the diary of Anne Frank as a child, but nothing could prepare one for being in that place. The concentration camp had been cleaned up but left largely as it was, preserved as a kind of museum. It was hugely effective. It left the correct impression: horrifying, hideous, shocking; unthinkable! There were large pictures on the museum walls, blown-up photographs of skin-over-skeleton people clad in striped prisoner suits and bodies thrown together in heaping piles. Outside, rows of concrete slabs marked the foundations where the rat- and disease-ridden sleeping barracks had stood. How could humans do this to humans?

I was fortunate to meet Yaman at Dachau (of all places). I had noticed him as we went through the building exhibits, a shy, dark-haired man who'd joined the loosely knit group I had gone with to the camp. The museum was set up so you ended the tour in a small chapel-like room. Yaman and I lingered in it, the only two there, both clearly shaken by the horrific displays and trying to seek comfort in the religious words and relics. The others in our group had gone through more quickly and disappeared.

He invited me to lunch. I learned Yaman was from Istanbul, Turkey. He asked about my travels, and I poured out the whole Donald story, embarrassed because I didn't know what had caused his anger and abrupt abandonment on the midnight streets. The new feelings of uncertainty left me thinking things could go wrong. I confessed I didn't really want to hitchhike all the way to Afghanistan. Yaman asked where we had been headed next after Munich. I answered, "Greece."

To which he exclaimed, "That is where I am going too! Why don't you come with me on the train? I am leaving tonight." Marvelous, a new plan and a nicer travel companion. But there was a big problem. My backpack was locked in the train station and I didn't know where to find Donald for the key. Yaman suggested we go there and ask the stationmaster to open the lock. When we arrived at the train station, unbelievably we found Donald, standing before the opened locker. Great; luck had returned to me. I introduced him to Yaman, explaining that I had found someone else to travel with and he didn't have to worry about me tagging along anymore, thinking that he would be relieved and free to pursue his own plans at his own pace. We hardly knew each other, and it didn't seem to me we got along very well.

Immediately, Donald grew red-faced angry and, shaking his fist in my face, spoke with a snarl. "If I ever see you again, I swear I will square this with you!"

I was speechless. My mouth dropped open, and I looked over at Yaman, who had wisely faded into the shadows with eyes averted, waiting. Donald didn't take a swing but instead shouldered his pack and left in a huff.

Yaman came forward and said to me, "He is not a man!"

Travel alliances among "world travelers" were easily made in that cultural time known as the Sixties, which actually includes the early 1970s and the time of this journey. We were all experimenting with our own ideas of freedom. For me, that included the liberty to make quick friendships and trust others. You had to go by your instincts and take a few chances. The friendship with Donald was a disappointment, but I was to learn how right I was to trust Yaman. In retrospect, I already knew more about him from his responses at Dachau. And if I hadn't hitchhiked to Munich with Donald and been locked out of the youth hostel, I most certainly would never have met Yaman.

Yaman and I left on the train to Athens that night, what was to be a very long trip through the southern tip of Germany, Austria, the former

Yugoslavia, and the northern Greek peninsula. We traveled inside a comfortable rail compartment with six people, three seated on each side, facing each other. At one point as we were passing through Yugoslavia, the occupants included a man from Austria and two Yugoslavians, husband and wife—big people with big parcels, a jug of wine, and bread, which they shared with us. The sixth passenger was a Russian man traveling alone. We were able to understand each other different ways. The Austrian man and the Yugoslavian man had fought in the war on opposite sides and were delighted to converse. Though they didn't share the same language, I noticed each would speak in his own language, and the other seemed to understand. Yaman would fill in the details, translating for all of us, mostly using German and English. He could speak several languages. I remember thinking in that train compartment, I'm the only American here, almost the only Westerner, but I feel very comfortable and happy, as if I am among old friends.

I remember the moment Yaman introduced me to David, later that day in the train. He'd said he needed to walk and disappeared. I was puzzled. About an hour later he returned, excited about a new friend he'd just met. He told me about David the American and that we should look after him, as he was recovering from a surgery (appendectomy) he'd had several days before in Italy. I followed Yaman back through the train. I had not known you could walk a train by pressing a button to open the doors, which allowed you to walk across the metal platform between the cars. After passing through ten cars like that, Yugoslavian farm fields visible through the windows on the left and right, Yaman found the car he was looking for, and I followed him into the compartment. There sat David, occupying half the seat next to the window. He smiled sweetly with the introduction, looking pale in his convalescence. He wore a black leather jacket. I learned he was from Brooklyn and had been studying English literature. He demonstrated a switchblade he'd just acquired in Italy, "like the gangs in New York." He was traveling with a complete volume of Shakespeare, a hardbound English dictionary, and for a change of clothing, a black velvet tuxedo and a bow tie. I liked him immediately.

**Greece**

At last the long train ride ended. Two of us had boarded in Munich; three stepped off after we pulled into Athens. Greece was sunny and magical. I loved the people, who engaged you immediately with their warmth, smiling eyes, and easy conversation. Music was everywhere. We walked through the streets dressed in our finest clothes, I in the middle with David (in tuxedo) and Yaman on each arm, laughing and fielding comments from Greek men as we passed. We decided on a restaurant for dinner. You made your selection from brightly colored roasted vegetables and meats swimming in olive oil in large pans near the front window (exotic cuisine to me at the time). As soon as dinner was over, the dancing and gaiety began. Musicians played loud and exciting songs on old classical Greek instruments. Everyone was drinking ouzo or retsina and throwing colored paper streamers. You threw the long, thin paper coil across the room while holding on to one end. Soon everyone was connected in a web of colored paper ribbons. A local woman with her family and friends at a table across the room made eye contact with me, and then told the waiter to send me a drink. I'd never seen anything like that. People got up and began dancing a lively Greek dance: several held onto a single embroidered handkerchief held above their heads, twisting the cloth as they moved, rotating in a circle. Laughter, smiles, and twinkling eyes everywhere you looked. I thought, This is what I've been missing all my life! The Greeks know best how to share their simple pleasures with a whole restaurant of strangers tied together in a pulsing hypnotic happiness.

**Don't Tell Her I'm Turkish!**

One evening we went to an Athens discotheque. Yaman met a young Greek woman and seated her at our table. He leaned over to me and whispered, "Don't tell her I'm Turkish!"

I looked at him, puzzled. "Why not?"

"Please, don't say anything, OK? I'll explain everything later." I was expecting some kind of personal story about the young woman, but instead, I was to learn about the long-seated conflict and animosity between the Greeks and the Turks (reconfirmed in a visceral display by a Greek sea captain on another trip to the Dodecanese Islands of the far-eastern reaches of Greece, 1989, when he answered my innocent question, "Is that Turkey there, on that distant shore?" with a bellowing "Noooo!!" even though it could not have been anyplace else). I hadn't realized history could percolate into daily life like that, a lesson I remembered decades later with the 1990s conflicts in the Balkans.

We were in Athens several days. The Acropolis was stunning and of utter fascination to me. You could explore it without restrictions and there weren't many tourists back then. I have a clear memory of climbing up to the Acropolis one starry night with David. We sat cross-legged on the floor of the Parthenon, leaning against one of its huge fluted marble columns. We had a great discussion about history and literature. I remember thinking it was so cool because we were actually discussing these subjects in the Parthenon, like I imagined the ancient Greeks might have done. I kept having these wonderful pinch-me feelings, I can't believe I am sitting here inside the Parthenon, in Greece; if my friends from home could only see me now!

Travel plans just evolved day to day in those times of our younger, carefree selves. It was Yaman's idea to go to the island of Hydra, agreeable to David and me. We left on a boat. Hydra was a good choice because it was just an hour from Athens, yet it was a small island with no roads. The majority of tourists came on cruise boats in those days, spending only a couple of hours in the port before going away. In a little restaurant upon arrival, Yaman negotiated in Greek with someone who led us away to a house we could rent for a month. It was owned by a grandmother who, when we rented it, moved in with her family across the narrow cobblestone path. The house had two rooms, one large with kitchen equipment at one end and narrow beds beneath the windows, and a small bedroom David occupied, surrounded by his books. The Greek grandmother, dressed in black, would come into the house in the morning, saying, "*Endroxi, endroxi*" (It's OK, it's OK) to get her black glasses and other things, and probably to observe that we were all sleeping separately. David used the two-burner portable stove, supplied by cooking gas in a bottle, to make odd things I had never heard of: Turkish coffee, very sweet with the grounds at the bottom of the cup, and a dish of rice cooked with orzo pasta. He was nearly my age but seemed very worldly, which I attributed to his growing up in Brooklyn.

The house had no bathroom. There was an old porcelain toilet in a tall crawlspace underneath the house, open on one side. You flushed it by throwing a bucket of water into it quickly (a new skill I found useful on occasion later in life). We sponge-bathed from a sink attached to an outside wall.

A donkey was tied with a rope outside our door. He stood on straw beneath a metal awning. It seemed like every hour, he made these loud and startling braying noises, "Hyah-eeehh!, Hyah-eeehh!, Hyah-eeehh!," really disturbing the peace. And he wasn't the only donkey around, several would go off like that all day.

Yaman taught me another important skill in Hydra: when you need to come down a steep hillside, use a wide stance, bend your knees, and take many small steps while you are rapidly descending. This worked on a flower-covered hillside where the three of us had wandered on an excursion. I use this step method frequently in Oregon, where I live on a sloping hillside and often hike around trails and mountain valleys. I always think of Yaman when I descend a hill.

Also on that hill, Yaman took David aside to talk man-to-man. "David, my friend, I have questions for you." He often questioned David on the ways of Western women. Yaman seemed to be troubled by girlfriends around the world, whom he called long distance (before cell phones) to try to resolve things with them. I often wondered why he didn't just ask me, a Western woman, about women, and further, why he later took David to meet his parents in Istanbul but not me. I didn't know much then, but looking back, it's understandable. Yaman, like Istanbul, had one foot in the West and his other in the East. He respected his parents, who were, I am guessing, traditional Muslims. Back then, I didn't fully appreciate the wider boundary between men and women in the East, though I am sure Yaman was atypical for his culture and made every effort to expand. He was refreshing to be around, as he was polite, respectful, and considerate, in contrast to some of the Western youth I often ran into, who could be rude in their rejection of social niceties. He eventually married an American woman and immigrated to the US, but I am getting ahead of my story.

Reading Orhan Pamuk's book *Istanbul*, I am thinking about Yaman again. According to Pamuk, people of Istanbul are caught between East and West, with the desire to modernize and be Western, the cultural history to be Eastern, and the geographical position to be both. I am reminded of the debate about including Turkey in the European Union.

Yaman and I laughed when comparing our travel plans back then: he was interested only in traveling in the West and frequently did so, and I was hell-bent on getting to India, fascinated with the Middle East in between. He dressed properly in tailored trousers and jackets, I in the colorful gypsy fashion of the day.

We were very cold in Greece. My passport stamps reveal we entered Greece "16 February 1973" and left "14 March 1973." Our little house in Hydra was not heated, with thin walls and no insulation. I sometimes spent hours reading inside my down sleeping bag. I held the book in my hands, wearing thin wool flannel mittens that had a hole through which I could reach one finger to turn the pages. I was reading *The Hobbit* and *The Lord of the Rings* trilogy (J. R. R. Tolkien). These books figured greatly in my travels. I had made my way to the eastern edge of Europe, and every day in Hydra, I was aware of a looming decision: would I go to India by myself, crossing the mysterious and dangerous Middle East, or give up my dream and return home, meandering alone through Europe? I talked to many other travelers, heard lots of tales, some scary. At the same time, the hobbits were making their journey into the land of Mordor, encountering many obstacles and often, great dangers. One could be robbed or worse in the Middle East. One could go in there and never return. Yet, all in all, things were turning out well for the Hobbits. We met a group of three guys who were living in Hydra for a few months, flamboyant and creative men from San Francisco who dressed in colorful clothes with flowing scarves and wore Calandre (Paco Raban) French perfume. When I returned home, I bought this scent and wore it for years. Their house was furnished whimsically with bright colors and draped voile. The men were dedicated world travelers, so I spoke to them of my dilemma. They listened, and one laughingly exclaimed, "What kind of a choice is that? Definitely go to India!" That was just what I needed to hear, and I returned to ideas of myself in India. And maybe I *could* cross the mysterious and exotic Middle East.

Hydra was beautiful, but we had to fill the days, finding varied ways to escape boredom, the cold, and the rain. David often went to a little café in town with a large stone fireplace, where the local men gathered, and sometimes I joined him. No buildings were heated. If I sat on the large hearth near the fire, I could feel warmth on one side of my body as I read my books. Yaman, often restless, would hike in the hills surrounding the village. Huge packs of feral cats offered some amusement, gathering around the port just before the appointed arrival times of the ferry and freight boats. Some days I walked alone on donkey paths away from the village to the silvery olive orchards on the other side of the small island. There were no sandy beaches, yet I enjoyed views of the deep cobalt-blue Mediterranean Sea from rocky promontories.

We'd befriended a small group of people living on the island, mostly from other countries in Europe and at least one urban Greek and a few US ex-pats, whom we'd meet in the evenings for dinner or drinks in their houses. I recall these people as intellectual and artistic, a little aloof. One afternoon several of us were caught in a driving, cold rainstorm while walking atop a sea wall outside the village. We found a little café with a chained lock on the door. When we peered through the window and saw a man inside, we made pleading gestures until he opened the door to give us shelter. Words were exchanged in Greek, and the man brought out a little brazier he'd crafted from an empty biscuit tin. He set it on the concrete floor and made a fire to grill sardines. We sat on small wooden stools around the brazier, warming our hands over the glowing coals and snacking on those delicious freshly caught silver sardines. Outside, high waves crashed on the sea wall, spraying the windows of the café, but we felt happy and satisfied inside.

We'd rented the house in Hydra for a month, but Yaman became restless after about two or three weeks. He told us he wanted to return to Istanbul, that he missed his family and his work, dealing carpets at his shop in the bazaar. He regretted leaving David and me, and he made us promise we'd fly to Istanbul to join him after Hydra. I had to figure out how India would fit into this, and decided what I would do: find a cheap student discount flight from Istanbul to Delhi and fly to India, avoiding the specter of crossing the Middle East alone.

David and I left our house in Hydra, and looked back as the black-clad grandmother was busily whitewashing the steps up to our former cottage, wasting no time in putting her house back in order.

**Turkey**

It was raining when our plane landed in Istanbul. Yaman was there to greet us and we were happy to see him, now in his own element. Istanbul was fascinating to me. I'd look out the windows of a streetcar and see a 1940s Buick in beautiful condition motoring next to a man sitting in an ox-drawn wooden cart; the exquisitely slender minarets of a large old mosque visible in the background through the grey fog. My memories of Istanbul are in sepia tones. I felt the melancholy of the city in the old men's faces and the sad music in the cafés. It was cold.

The next morning, Yaman took David and me to his carpet shop in the Grand Bazaar. I had never seen anything like it: shiny copper pots and beautiful objects everywhere. I was mesmerized by gem stones and jewelry, and bought a pair of gold earrings inscribed with the word *Allah* in Arabic, with tiny glass eyes set in the centers to ward off the "sign of the evil eye," which is envy. I still wear them. Yaman said, "Look around the bazaar and then come into my shop. I am going to sell you a carpet!" I knew I couldn't buy one, having barely enough cash to get to India. David and I seated ourselves atop a pile of rugs, and Yaman sent for tea. A boy from the market came back with orange blossom tea served in tiny glasses balanced on painted porcelain saucers. I took a sip of the steaming fragrant tea and closed my eyes. This was another moment when I thought, incredibly, Here I am in Istanbul. Yaman snapped out rug after rug, piling one on top of the other. Nice, but no, I don't have a lot of money and I want to get to India. Then, snap! He unrolled a beautiful rug on top of the stack, delicious colors of muted greens, blues, and mauves with a detailed geometric pattern. I sat up and leaned in for a better look, coveting. I knew good rugs—my grandmother had been a collector, and I'd grown up with them. He read my interest. I'll give you a good price!

"How much?" I asked.

Yaman replied, "Two hundred fifty dollars."

It was a lot of money for me, but I knew the price was too good to be true. He had a similar one with more mauves and dark blues for David, same price. Yaman was serious about each of us owning one of his carpets.

He said, "Just one thing, you have to promise that when I come to visit you in America, the rug will be in your home."

The good price was confirmed by Yaman's heated argument in Turkish with his partner just outside the door. David and I didn't understand the language, but we understood our friend was practically giving us his carpets. How will I get this home, I worried. No problem, he could mail it. I had been such a frugal student with a reputation among my friends for having and spending very little money. I had about $450 dollars worth in varied currencies in my hidden pocket. I figured I needed around $150 dollars for a cheap flight to India. If I bought the carpet, that would leave me $50, and there might be a problem getting cash for my one remaining promissory card once I got to India. I could do it, but it would be risky, not my style. I bought the carpet, departing from my old self.

(The rug was waiting for me when I finally returned to my family's home in the US, and I am still enjoying its beauty. I kept my word to Yaman; the rug has always been in a prominent place in my numerous homes, though now a little faded and worn.)

I noticed that the amount of Turkish lire one could get for a dollar was always the same. Yaman explained their currency was set to the US dollar without fluctuation. "Turkey has special relations with America, good friends." So that's why I didn't need a visa for Turkey when I got the others in Paris.

Yaman thought we needed some relaxation and wanted to show us one of his favorite places. The three of us boarded an old wooden ferry boat in the Bosphorus on an ink-black night. The Bosphorus is a strait of water dividing the Asian and European halves of Istanbul, joining the Black Sea and the Sea of Marmara, the site of thousands of years of historic events and a treasured vista for residents of Istanbul. Other passengers, long-faced older men, would stare at me or out into the night, smoking. Ship horns made a haunting, fading trace of sound across the dark waters. We disembarked in a small port and took a taxi to Yalova, an old town on the eastern coast of the Sea of Marmara, on the edge of Asia Minor. I felt that I was in a living map of a geography lesson.—How far am I from Kansas?

We soaked in an ancient indoor marble pool fed by hot springs. It may have been an old Roman bath, but I wrote in postcards home that it was a Turkish bath, with real Turkish towels and white Turkish terry robes and white slippers. From curved windows in the arched ceiling high above, long shafts of light pierced down through billowing steam and dim shadows. Voices were muted and echoing. Only men were in there, staring at me. I felt more and more that I was in a different culture. Next morning in a Louis XIV–style decorated room, we ate an exotic breakfast (not bacon and eggs) that included olives and oranges. It seemed weird to me, but David just took it in stride, as if he always ate olives for breakfast. Maybe in Brooklyn. To this day I relish eating olives at breakfast and always think of Yalova, Yaman, and David.

We were there maybe two days. Yaman made an international phone call from there, not so easy in 1973. He had to wait hours for the call to go through and had to be notified when it did. I have a visual memory of watching him cross a brick-paved street to take the call. He continued to be troubled by these international girlfriends, and the mysteries grew more puzzling. David seemed to know what was going on, but I wasn't included in the men talk. We left Yalova.

I had not seen much in Istanbul yet. A note hand-copied into my blue Repertoire notebook under "T," for "Turkey," suggested, …"A good place to meet people and eat: The Pudding Shop."…Yaman said that wasn't such a good place. I dropped by the Pudding Shop and had to agree with him. The walls and floors were unwashed, and blue smoke hung in the air. Bored old men hid behind newspapers. A couple of Western men with long hair leaned back in their chairs, stretching their pajama-clad legs under their table. Even worse, the puddings were tasteless. (Later I learned it was an infamous hippie hangout and contraband exchange place.) I heard so much about the Blue Mosque and had a list of monuments and places to see, but I spent my days visiting travel agencies instead. I was troubled again, having learned there were no cheap flights from Istanbul to Delhi. I had already decided I was not crossing the Middle East alone. Another handwritten entry in the notebook, on travel tips through Turkey: "Istanbul—

Erzurum…train is much easier and safer, but incredibly crowded. You'll probably sleep in the aisles….Cheapest fare is 64 lire, leave from Asiatic Railway Station." I felt glum.

Yaman appeared at my hotel the next morning, a little out of breath. He had been trying to help me find a way to India, looking in travel agencies and tea shops where travelers gathered. "I found a private bus that is leaving for India. They have a few seats left. Unfortunately, it leaves tomorrow morning."

I realized this was my last chance. I signed up for the ride and posted a letter to my mother, telling her I was leaving for India and asking her to "wire $500 to the bank in Delhi that was affiliated with Wichita's First National Bank." On the following morning, after tossing and turning through the night, I appeared in the appointed place for the bus to depart and bought a ticket to Delhi from the driver for $50. Yaman and David met me there to say goodbye. Quickly, the three of us walked across the street to see—my last opportunity—the Blue Mosque. There was only a little time before the bus would leave. I slipped off my shoes and opened the heavy door. Inside, incredible beauty. Light shone down in long rays from stained glass windows in the blue-tiled dome high above. Men knelt prostrate in prayer on an array of colorful carpets covering the vast floor. I listened to the hushed echoes resounding from marble surfaces. Then I closed the door and hurried back to the bus. We hugged good-bye and I boldly stepped aboard the old, beat-up, purple and orange Mercedes bus and sat on one of its rigid, low-backed bench seats. The vehicle was probably built to be a school bus and had known its better days.

The David and Yaman story doesn't end there. David and I had an active letter correspondence for a few years afterward. We even met about once a year, in San Francisco or New York, when one or both of us were moving across the country. We seemed to repeatedly land on opposite coasts, then switch places. Then one day in 1980, I received a postcard addressed to my home in Oregon, from Istanbul: "Wish you were here," signed David and Yaman. They told me they had become business partners, and had come to Istanbul to export carpets to the United States. I eventually learned that David married his longtime girlfriend and settled in upstate New York, opening a Turkish import carpet shop. They had a child, a son, whose fate, two decades later, would be to learn the carpet business in Istanbul, from Yaman's brother in the bazaar. From David, I know that Yaman immigrated to the US and married an American woman after ending a family-arranged engagement to a Turkish woman in Istanbul, thereby making a settled choice between the East and the West. He set up a carpet shop in the American southeast. He has two children, a boy and a girl.

In a phone conversation with Yaman in January 2007, he told me, "David is my best friend; we talk five times a day. I have to get off the phone so I can call and tell him I talked to you."

When I think of their long, close friendship, I consider a certain element: David is a Jewish man, Yaman, from a Muslim tradition. Though I am guessing neither is religious or political, I think this lifelong important friendship is remarkable and reflects the depth of these two men.

There is one more thing. American friends of mine who've recently traveled to Istanbul told me most of the carpet shop proprietors in the bazaar are Sephardic Jews of old Arabic heritage, taken in centuries ago by an Ottoman emperor. Could empathy for colleagues explain why Yaman was visiting Dachau that morning in Munich when we met? Religious and cultural origins were not part of conversations among the three of us in 1973. Or perhaps I don't recall; I knew so little about it then.

***From an email correspondence with Yaman***

*Jan. 7, 2007*

Dear Yaman,

It was so great to talk with you last week, and I was very happy to make contact!

Well, where to start, after 34 years? I think I may have mentioned on the phone, last summer I found an old journal with some jotted memories from the 1973 trip and was reading them, and started writing more. I remember you and David and those times. I am thinking how life is really just a billiards game, motion redirected, chance encounters that really change our lives. I remember the moment I met you. We two were standing in the chapel in Dachau, aghast. I noticed that you, too, had been deeply moved by the horrors we'd just seen there. The others had disappeared. (Who were those other people we were with? I don't remember them very well, an assorted group of Americans and Europeans, rag tag group I'd met the day before.)

Then, you invited me to lunch, then to Athens, and then you found David on the long train ride through the former Yugoslavia. Looking back on Munich, I think you may have saved me from a possible disaster, remembering that Canadian guy I'd hitch-hiked with from Paris. I was at a point of despair about the rest of the trip and my long dream of going to India. Your kindness and invitation to Athens gave me hope, to continue the journey in good company.... My one regret was in cutting short my stay in Istanbul. I figured I'd be back, but I've never returned. I still want to see more. I remember, just before the bus left, running across the street to see The Blue Mosque, opening the door, and being enchanted by the beauty and stillness. I remember light through blue glass in a high dome, with hundreds of carpets on the floor, a few worshipers in prayer.

...That is interesting that David got you reading English literature. Looking back on it, I think David was my first friend who was a fellow English major. As I mentioned, David was a big influence and became an intellectual standard for me for reading modern literature. I doubt if he knows that. He was reading the *Alexandria Quartet* (by Lawrence Durrell) while we were in Hydra. Now I've read it twice, such a pleasure.

Yaman, you and David have remained my good friends all these years, even if you didn't know that and we haven't conversed. The Yaman and David story has been retold so many times to my husband Mitch and my friends, it's become a fable. Mitch said you should come to Portland to visit us.

Well, this letter is maybe a little too long and boring, but I've thought of another memory—Yalova, where you took us for relaxation and Turkish baths, where I learned to eat olives for breakfast. I loved that.

Do you remember things as I do? And what else? I have more fond memories of Hydra, but I'll save that for later.
Margie

*Jan. 8, 2007*
Dear Margie,
What a wonderful e-mail!!!
Such a great welcome home present.
Your memory is awesome. Your letter brought tears to my eyes.
Will keep in touch, can't write right now.
Please give my kind regards to your husband, hope to see both of you one day.
Love,
Yaman

***From a holiday card sent by David***
*Jan. 27, 2009*
Dear Margie,
Happy Holidays to both of you;
Happy Decades;
Happy Millennium

…The almost unimaginable time that's passed since we were all in Hydra, frozen in the winter nights, down at the docks and the bar café in the day, and then made the most unexpected trip of my life—to Istanbul. How fateful! I've had a rug shop in … for 27 years now and our son, who's 26, has been involved in it for 8 years, been to Istanbul three times and lived there in a hotel for 5 months, visiting Yaman's brother daily to learn about rugs. Everything is mysterious!

I'm glad you're well, and that you wrote to me, instead of writing me off (I've intended to answer you before, and then too much time seemed to pass.)

However, memory is like its own being, a living, swelling, vital being, and we are all flowing through each other's memories because of that trip long ago. What a wonder!
Love,
David

***Memoir***

The bus left Istanbul one cold, sunny morning in March 1973, slowly making its way out of the city and onto the narrow dirt road that would take us eastward through rural Turkey, connecting to other dirt roads that would traverse mountains and deserts en route through many countries and border crossings to our destination, Delhi. Late in the afternoon of the first day out, we on the bus looked around observing each other and gazing out the windows at the remote landscape. You could read it in each one's face, the questions: What have I done? What is going to happen? I had this raging headache, unlike any I'd had before. A British guy with long curling locks in the seat across the aisle from me started complaining about not having his tea and crumpets, and he wasn't kidding. The guy on the next seat chided him with, "Ah, stop yer whinging!" (meaning "complaining" in British slang).

Nowadays, I marvel at my young self and willingness to step on that bus for the ride into the great unknown, despite a few misgivings and that tension headache. I didn't have as many ideas of what could go wrong. I had no thoughts that boarding that bus could change everything in my life.

The two drivers who owned the bus were adventurous characters, allegedly on the run from something, but I never found out what. The one who did most of the driving was an ex-truck driver from England, and the other, an ex-mechanic from Australia, making them both well qualified for the trip, along with what I would come to respect as their uncanny street savvy. They were making their living by driving ragtag Western flower children, mostly young men, on that old bus back and forth across the Middle East and Central Asia, from Istanbul to Delhi, so I thought. Most of the passengers were European, with a minority of Americans. The drivers followed the usual route, along parts of the old Silk Road through Turkey,

Iran, Afghanistan and Pakistan, entering India near Amritsar. We called ourselves world travelers, or WTs and saw ourselves distinguished as that, compared to those at home who never ventured out into the world. In the run down hotels where we spent each night, we all teamed up and slept several of us to a room, on the floor too, young men and women. We did this without much discussion, and probably not to save money, as the hotels were cheap. I think we all felt an unspoken apprehension and desire to band together in these lands, wildly unfamiliar to us. It was easy to be friendly with most everyone on the bus. Stopped in a village for tea or a meal, we all walked in a big group through the streets. I don't remember exactly how many were on the bus, about fifteen to twenty. Some would get off and others come on as we made our way through the capitals, but I was on for the whole trip. I was one of the few women on the bus, the only one traveling alone.

**Hunger**

We had been traveling along primitive roads and through very small villages in eastern Turkey all day and had not found anywhere to buy food. I was very hungry; others were too, and there was a lot of talk about it. Finally the drivers parked the bus in one of the tiny villages. We got out and walked along a dirt street, looking for food. The wonderful smell of something baking was in the air, and we followed our noses. A glass storefront revealed men inside, dressed similarly to others we'd seen in nearby villages, wearing long shirts over baggy pajama pants and embroidered cloth skull caps in subtle blues and tans, colors repeated in the landscape. The men watched us through their window. As we approached the building, they started gesturing wildly with their arms. They seemed to be shooing us away, sweeping their arms from their heads outward. Disappointed, with gnawing hunger, we turned away from the bakery where we had hoped to find food at last.

A few of us looked back over our shoulders in retreat, and noticed their movements becoming more exaggerated. We finally realized their gesturing language was opposite ours; that they really wanted us to come inside. Delighted, we retraced our steps and crowded into the store, greeted by welcoming smiles and nods. The smell of baking bread was heavenly in our ravenous condition. A baker tossed a large disk of brown dough (resembling pizza crust), aiming deftly with an elliptical rotation of his hand. The circle flew into the big wood-burning oven, adhering to the inside wall of the hot earthen cone. They removed the flat bread with long wooden paddles when it was ready. We ate with great pleasure. I remember this hot bread as the most delicious thing I have ever, ever eaten. Thanks in part to hunger.

***Journal 1974***

*Turkey*

Throughout the progression of the journey, I had frequent dreams in which I would find myself suddenly at home in Kansas, terribly frustrated because I knew I was supposed to be on the other side (of the world) and was figuring out ways to hurry back before I missed the bus to Delhi. I remember waking up in the middle of the night in a dingy Turkish hotel and feeling relieved to be there and not at dull home where I wasn't supposed to be.

***Memoir***

My new bus friends and I discussed Ataturk, past president and father of the modern Turkey, famous for his efforts to Westernize the country. I liked to say his name. Some said, "Time stopped when Ataturk died," hence the appearance (in 1973) of a 1940s–1950s era West, with all the great old American cars and men in baggy tweed pants with woolen billed caps.

Conversations among world travelers on the road to India inevitably came around to two questions. The first, "How long are you 'out' for?" usually made me feel outdone to admit I was out for only six months when many travelers I met were on the road (or planned to be) for a year or two. That was less common for Americans, whose mind-set and work obligations usually afforded less time. Central Asia and India were farther away for Americans than for Europeans. With less time, I think Americans were less likely to get the idea to stray far from home. Lots of travelers from Australia and New Zealand had long stays in India, but they didn't travel East from Turkey unless they'd been living in Europe.

I found the second question, "Are you traveling to India for meditation or for drugs?" to be annoying, and my usual response was "Neither, I've come out to see filth and squalor," which often drew silence, ceasing the inquiry. There were drugs offered along the route, but that didn't have more than an occasional appeal to me. Frankly, I was there to see the world, and living on the ground cheaply within cultures so greatly different from my own was disorienting enough. I remember thinking, Why complicate the experience and compromise my observations?

In the back of my French address book, I copied passages I liked from someone else's book on the bus as we headed eastward. As I read these quotes now, a man's face comes to mind, a fellow rider who shared his books with me. His name was Alan, and I always thought of him, with affection, as Alan "Watts Ginsberg." He wore thick glasses with black frames, a real intellectual hippie with big rosewood love beads hanging around his neck. He said he taught philosophy at Berkeley. I smile in remembering those times and the words that inspired my youthful self. There is a little A+ penned on the cover of my notebook. Professor Alan put it there, showing his approval of the quotes I had chosen from his book, *Love's Body* by Norman O. Brown, a collection of other works.

My handwriting was shaky—the road was bumpy:

"Meaning is not in things but in between; in the iridescence, the interplay; in the interconnections; at the intersections, at the crossroads. Meaning is transitional as it is transitory; in the puns or bridges, the correspondence."
Cf Richard, J.P., *L'univers imaginaire de Mallarme*, 1962.
Hartman, G.H., *The Unmediated Vision, 1954.*

"A play of light, an iridescence, in the empty air. Against gravity; against the gravity of literalism, which keeps our feet on the ground. Against weighty words, the baggage of traditional meaning and the burden of the law; travel light. Gravity is from the fall, and is to be defied; deliver us from the pull of the fundamental. Practice levity, and levitation. Oh for

the wings of a dove, the spirit, the winged words that soar, the hyperbole or ascension."
Cf Lubac, H., *Histoire et esprit, 1950*. Richard, J.P., *L'univers imaginaire de Mallarme*, 1962.

"Feet off the ground. Freedom is instability. The destruction of attachments; the ropes, the fixtures; fixations, that tie us down."

"Wisdom is in wit; in fooling, most excellent fooling; in play, and not in heavy puritanical seriousness. In levity, not gravity. My yoke is easy, my burden light."
Cf. Matthew XI, 30.

"Enigmatic form is living form; like life, an iridescence; an invitation to the dance; a temptation or irritation. No satisfying solutions; nothing to rest in; nothing to weigh us down."

Under the copied passages, I wrote these words of my own:

"Truth in Turkey—Alive, free, dancing Eastward."

***Journal 1974***

*Eastern Turkey: Stuck in the Turkish Mountains!*
What to do when a drunk Bulgarian has gotten his transport truck stuck in a snow bank, jack-knifed along the edge of a very skinny (mountainous) road that you need to pass your big bus through at 2:00 in the morning, when the wind is strong and it is 30 degrees below zero! How could we be so lucky as to be under the light of the full, risen moon! The scene: cold, mysterious, glamorous, and *very dangerous*! Deep, deep snow and biting winds. Such dark, crystal clarity, not a cloud in the sky. And at the moment when we were most decidedly stuck but good in the snow, someone cried "wolf!" I couldn't feel two of my fingers. Wow, a pack of wolves, about ten, silver

> long-haired Russian wolves, in ghostly silhouette, stole silently up a nearby slope in the moonlight. Their distance was about fifty yards. They were intimidated by our number, but I would not have minded if they had been a bit closer, just that I might have gotten a better look and a bit more thrill from imminent danger.

***Memoir***

I remember clearly feeling completely alive and in the moment during this incident. In my thoughts, I realized there was nothing I could do; it was in others' hands. Word spread among the drivers stuck in the snow that the Turkish authorities were sending a tow truck to rescue the Bulgarian transport truck. It finally arrived, but their methods made us fear. If they'd succeeded in pulling the truck out of the snowdrift, it would have landed on our bus, which was wedged in next to the truck but headed in the opposite direction. Luckily, a few guys from our bus including Ronnie (an American from Brooklyn who I was to get to know more, later) managed to dig the snow out from under our tires and place flattened cardboard boxes under them for traction, so the bus could disentangle and we could go on our way. The Turkish mountains were geologically old, softly rounded, unforested hills beyond hills. You could see quite a distance in the moonlight.

We didn't usually drive after dark, instead lodging in cheap, drab hotels in villages, but on this night, we drove straight through to get to the Iranian border during the limited hours they would be open for passage.

***Journal 1974***

> Later that night I did get a better look (at a wolf): I was riding in the front of the bus wide awake all night, not wanting to miss anything this cold moon-mountain land had to behold. Suddenly, one of those huge, beautiful creatures ran in front of the bus. He had a large turkey in his jaws, which he dropped in fright (as he was running to get off the road. We missed him thank god, but) the turkey was a mess on the road, bloody gore.
>
> Next morning, the sunrise over the snows was lovely. It came up from behind the mountain where allegedly a piece

of Noah's ark was found. The piercing white, rosy rays of the sun shining forth from the summit of this snow-mountain were nearly convincing that there must be something holy about it. It was fun to think of it that way. (Note: We know it as Mt. Ararat; in Turkish, Agri Dagi, in one of the mountain ranges of Eastern Turkey. Not far from here, the bus driver pointed over his left shoulder saying, "That's the Soviet Union over that hill." I was really thrilled, to think I could be that close to the feared and forbidden USSR. For a child growing up in 1950s America, the Soviets were Number One Enemy and, thus, remote and unapproachable. I couldn't wait to tell my friends back home.)

*Iran*

We arrived at the Iranian border later that morning. I was in rather ill humor, being very tired from no sleep and not having had a chance to brush my teeth that morning. The one place we stopped in Easternmost Turkey was a real frozen shit-hole (not even a village) and an ugly old man had tried to kiss me and besides, the water wasn't at all appealing, even to brush ones teeth in. Kind of a drag after such an incredible night; anyway, that's how I arrived at the Iranian border. Not at all in a mood for the misplacing of the American passports, which they found after the drivers gave them *baksheesh*, bribery money. That was followed by the "accidental" omission of arrival stamps in the seven American passports, including mine. Without proof of arrival in your passport, you'll have a hard time getting out of Iran. Luckily, our drivers thought to have everyone check this before leaving the border station. When a group arrives at a border en mass, it is the responsibility of the drivers to collect all the passports and turn them in for arrival stamps With so many in hand, it is easy for the border guards to "overlook" some of the passports. Peculiarly, all those "overlooked" happened to be American passports. Iran had just thrown several American oil speculators out of Teheran about two weeks previous to this. Subtle, eh. (Note: Things were heating up politically for the Shah at that time, a friend of the Americans. Border guards were expressing their own politics in the handling of passports. Regarding the intruding attempt at kissing, from the grisly old man in Eastern Turkey, Turkish men were known to rudely grab young Western women's privates in public places. This happened once to me, and I heard several stories from other young women. It was humiliating. With the optimism of youth, I carried on, undaunted, though it remained an unappealing memory.)

In Iran, on a dusty back road
The children roll rusty hoops with wooden sticks
In front of mud houses.
The mothers sit cross-legged
Blowing on the cooking fires
While the fathers scratch in the dust beyond,
With bullock-drawn wooden plows.

***Memoir***

**Iran**

We had been traveling through arid, sparsely populated country, day after day, through small villages with minimal electricity, since we'd left Istanbul a week before. Then the bus pulled into Teheran and it was a shock. This was a modern, Western-style city, and we weren't used to that anymore. We'd just driven out of the desert. The people were city folk—sophisticated, attractive, walking with a hurried pace. I marveled at the wide paved avenues and modern traffic lights. It surprised me that people spoke English comfortably. They were well mannered and friendly. I vividly recall many things with pleasure about Teheran. The ladies' dress was fascinating and beautiful. Their fashionable Western designer clothes were barely concealed beneath full-length transparent veils (*chadors)* they held closed in front with their hands, just beneath the eyes. I thought of Scheherazade's veil. When they needed to use their hands, the chador would fall open, showing their faces and clothing. Another delight was the small juice bar stands on every corner selling freshly squeezed pomegranate juice. I'd never had such an exotic drink before. I liked it a lot, and stopped frequently for the refreshment.

We were leaving after three days in Teheran, boarded and seated on our benches, except for two Italian passengers. At last the hennaed and tie-dyed couple appeared and strutted down the aisle to their seats, trailing the scent of patchouli oil. The driver stood up and confronted them, "Off the bus!" Puzzled, they refused to get up. They protested and pleaded. He persisted, "I watched you come out of the house of a well-known drug dealer. Leave, immediately. You are endangering all of our lives." They sat there, silent. After a few tense moments they jumped up and left the bus. The driver addressed the rest of us, explaining that possession of drugs in Iran was punishable with death, and he knew from a friend's unfortunate experience that the Iranian authorities would include all foreign bus passengers in the sentence. I admired the man for his street savvy and caution, and I was glad to be on his bus and not another. He knew a lot, even who the local drug dealers were.

***Journal 1974***

*Afghanistan*

It is difficult to describe the thoughts one experiences while beholding something so inconceivable as the Afghani extraterrestrial moon crater desert, or the eternal snow peaks of Nepal. My simple reaction was a desire to somehow "imprism" this in my memory. I wanted to sustain this pleasure: that moment of sublime experience—the created desert itself not apart from my own awe and disbelief. What could I do? I stood there, quietly enjoying my presence. No journal, no camera can ever express it quite the same afterward.

These un-reflected moments of pure experience will never be repeated. Recollection is a different thing. Memory of experience is in itself another experience.

(Note: crossed out, rejected paragraph: I laughed inside, out there in the middle of that desert. Such a shame I could never “bring along home” these things. I would have put this desert in a jar to show, for others to experience.)

*Memoir*

**Afghanistan**

I have many vivid recollections of my short stay in Afghanistan. I often think of these experiences, especially in light of recent history with Osama bin Laden, the Taliban and the US Bush–Cheney and Obama Administrations. Afghanistan is on our cognitive world map of concerns now, but at the time I was there, it was a remote place few of my friends at home could locate on a map.

Of all the countries I traveled through on this youthful expedition, Afghanistan really stands out in my mind, for the wild terrain as well as the people. I found the Afghani people I encountered to be open-minded and welcoming to us foreigners. I noticed respect for me as a person. The men not did not try to touch me inappropriately or make low comments under their breath, like some men in the countries we’d crossed previously. Many of the tribal people were confident and independent, perhaps similar to an American persona in some ways. My good memories of the Afghani people I met prompted me—seven years later in Portland, after reading an article in the local newspaper about two Afghani families who’d immigrated here after escaping the rough situation in Kabul following the Soviet invasion—to call one of the families and invite them to dinner. I had a feeling they would trustingly accept, and I was right. To this day, Aisha and her family are among my most treasured and long-term friends in Portland. My enduring friendship with Aisha has enriched my life.

Back to the bus trip: We arrived in Herat, shortly after crossing the border from Iran. The date we entered Afghanistan is written in my passport in Farsi or Pashto, which I cannot read. It was sometime in late March 1973. I recall our first evening there. The memory is a haunting fragrance in the night air of a soft spring evening. We walked among attractive houses and genteel people. It was dark, without electric lights. I felt comfortable, and at the same time, a pleasant excitement. I liked Herat. Thirty years later I made a discovery, an unmistakable connection in reading an old book *The Road to Oxiana*, the account of Robert Byron’s historic journey through Herat and other parts in 1933–34, in which he described the mysterious scent: "...That same elusive smell...which now, in its overwhelming sweetness, brought the minarets of Herat before my eyes again. It emanated from clusters of small, yellow-green flowers (footnote in the book: the oleaster),...which, if ever I smell them again, will remind me of Afghanistan...."

Next we stopped in Kandahar, which didn't leave much impression. It was bigger and not as pleasant as Herat.

The women we saw in the villages along our road through Afghanistan in 1973 wore tent-like, pleated, blue-grey burqas, covering their bodies from head to toe. Their eyes peered through a crocheted screen mesh. You see the same burqas in photographs today. When I was traveling through Afghanistan, I often wished I was wearing the veil too, to be incognito and view the world from a private place. The men we saw wore long shirts loosely draped over pajama-type pants of many folds and tucks, fitted tightly across the calves. They wore huge turbans of colored cloth wound tightly round and round in a glorious head-extending crown. I have not seen turbans of that enormous size in recent photographs of Afghan men. Styles change, everywhere.

I fell asleep one afternoon on the bus. Time and kilometers passed as I dozed, head bobbing. Upon awakening, I looked out the windows. My first thought was, We are traveling across the surface of the moon. I scanned across a greyish-brown desert without any vegetation. Small wavy ripples of dark sand extended across the surface. It looked like the surface of water on a windy day and extended to the horizon. I watched a man in the distance behind an animal pulling a plow, trying to farm the barren landscape. I couldn't decide if it was out of desperation or optimism.

Later on we stopped at a checkpoint. A few trucks and a VW van were parked on the hard sand. I watched a few men milling around the vehicles, through the dusty window of the bus. My eyes fixed on a man in Western dress standing near his van. I gasped, recognizing the fringed buckskin jacket and curly hair. Donald had made it to Afghanistan. His parting words in Munich still rang in my ears as I sank low into my seat under the window, but I wasn't fast enough. He'd spotted me and came up tapping on the window.

Someone on the bus nudged me. "That guy knows you." I looked up, smiled, and waved at Donald, but I wasn't about to get off the bus. Shortly after, our engine started up, and the driver put it in gear. I was relieved as we pulled away and steered back onto the road.

Ancient abandoned cityscapes appeared ghostly on top of high mesa-like hills. Different ones came into view as we rounded curves along our dusty road. From the book *West of Kabul, East of New York* by Tamim Ansary, I've learned one of the abandoned cities may have been the winter capital of the Ghaznavids (Persian Muslim dynasty), abandoned nine hundred years before. Lulled by the monotony of the barren desert landscape, I fell asleep again. When I awoke we were pulling into a parking lot of what looked like a Howard Johnson's restaurant, enormously confusing. I'd gotten used to passing through villages in the desert belonging to another century. The building turned out to be a Soviet outpost. In a daze, we went into the restaurant and ate hamburgers and fries with an odd-tasting catsup. I had no knowledge of Soviet troops in Afghanistan in 1973, but I accepted the reality quickly. I had wandered outside the restaurant and strolled up a barren hillside when a soldier came over the horizon and pointed a Kalashnikov at me, yelling and motioning until I stopped and retreated, a quick modern history lesson.

On we rolled to Kabul. We spent five or six days there, resting and walking around the streets. Several of us needed visas for Pakistan. Kabul was the capital, center of government and commerce, though many streets were unpaved. We dodged mud puddles. Bats swooped past single electric lightbulbs hanging from long wires at stalls in the night bazaar. Without the nightglow of a fully electric city, many stars were visible above the clear chilly Kabul nights. I enjoyed shopping in the bazaar on the famed Chicken Street and bought a long tribal dress with embroidered mirrors on the bodice. Many stalls displayed sheepskin maxi coats, badly cured and stinking of sheep. Young Western travelers coveted these hippie coats, whose length, when worn, brushed the top of their boots. I marveled at the pink and green embroidery stitched on the outside of the garment and the long, oily woolen tangles hanging around the open front edge. I was tempted, but I didn't buy one. It would have been a burden when I got to India.

Kabul lies in a high basin, about 6,000 feet in elevation, flanked on two sides by rugged old mountains, the Southern slopes of the Hindu Kush range. Those jagged, dark, blue-grey mountains, snow veined with elevation up to 16,000 feet, were in constant view as we walked through the streets, a reminder of wild mysteries and the road trip ahead. I felt exhilarated. Kabul is an ancient town of almost 3,000 years, on the crossroads of the old Silk Road trade route. Many ethnic groups from the far reaches of Europe and Asia traveled this road throughout its history. The many Afghan tribes bear evidence of varied ancestry, and it is common to see people on the streets of Kabul with light brown hair and blue eyes. The Afghanis I met on the street or the staff in our small hotel always smiled brightly with their entire face, exuding a generous spirit and readiness to engage in conversation. Most spoke at least a little English and were eager to communicate using words, gestures, and facial expression. Several of us Westerners, both men and women, shared a large dormitory room at the hotel. The Afghanis observed this, quite a difference from their own custom (most are Muslim), and were tolerant of us, making no openly critical remarks or attempts to shame us or change our habits.

It was turning to spring. We enjoyed sunny, warm afternoons after chilly mornings in Kabul. I thought of the drive south in a few days, anticipating the legendary heat of India. I took inventory of my warm winter clothes and offered my purple wool coat, a pair of jeans, and my thermal long johns to one of our hotel men. He was happy to receive these clothes and thanked me many times. If he didn't need them for himself, he would know where to get a good price in the market, so it was a worthy gift. I kept my warm socks and Swiss hiking boots, figuring I'd need them for Nepal, also my long skirt and headscarf, for the rest of the trip through Afghanistan and Pakistan.

The bus drivers appeared at our hotel one morning and spoke with their loyal passengers. They planned to depart for India the next day. Other young people joined the bus in Kabul for the final leg of the journey. That's where Louie from Toronto got on. He was to figure more, later in my story.

The day we left Kabul will always be with me. We headed out early on a bright morning, rested and eager for an imagined magnificent ride through the Khyber Pass we expected to reach before day's end. I enjoyed the sweeping views of the barren, erosion-carved landscape as the old bus rounded hairpin curves, advancing in a slow, winding spiral down the narrow road of the steep Kabul Gorge, where the Kabul River flowed far below. I marveled at several large local transport trucks on the road, every square inch magnificently cartooned and colorfully painted, bearing the careful English lettering, "Afghani Airlines."

I was surprised when our driver laid on the horn, tailgating the beautiful truck ahead, and even more amazed when he moved to the left side to pass within the small breadth of the mountain road. I looked ahead for reassurance of no approaching vehicles. I felt a little hot and dizzy. Our bus was too close to the truck. We drove ahead of the truck and stopped on the road. Something was wrong.

I watched the Afghani transport truck pull in front of us at a diagonal and stop, clearly meaning to block our passage. I felt a drowsy detachment, despite the unfolding excitement. Several men in huge turbans, clad in long shirts and wide pajama trousers, leaped from their truck brandishing long bayonet-tipped rifles, shouting and arguing. One man pointed his rifle at our driver's head; another pointed his gun at one of our tires. A moment of tense confusion and apprehension, yet I felt less and less connected to the progressing events, as though I were watching from a distance. I felt even hotter and more dizzy. I saw our drivers run to the back of the bus.

The Afghani men shouted and argued with each other in their language. They yelled at our drivers and demanded "40,000 Afghanis!" in English. The drivers growled back, "No, too much!" Harsh words and argument flew back and forth. I could see the tension in the drivers' faces and bodies as they jumped back onto the bus. One of the Afghani men jumped aboard our bus after them and stood up front by the door, holding his big rifle pointed toward the roof, his head encased in a gigantic flat turban, like the rings of Saturn. Other men moved the truck out of our way, and the driver started our bus. The tribal man rode standing on the bus as we proceeded down the Gorge, followed closely by the Afghani Airlines truck.

Gradually we travelers learned the story: When we had attempted to pass the Afghani truck, our bus nicked the truck's side mirror, cracking the glass. When we stopped, the truck owners demanded an immediate payment for this damage, "40,000 Afghanis!" (the name of their currency, worth about $40 at the time). The owners of our bus refused to pay it, insisting it was an unfair price. They went to the back to get a pistol (odd they hadn't carried it closer at hand in tribal country, but just as well). The truck owners agreed to the bus drivers' terms, that we would continue driving en caravan to the next "police stop" outpost to settle the price.

I felt the full heat of the fever as we bumped along the road, then I was cold and shivering. I glanced at the strange man in the big turban with the gun standing in the front, but I felt detached from this tense episode unfolding. I no longer cared what was going on; I only wanted to lie down and sleep, anywhere.

We drove on to a police stop, where everyone got off the bus. We were in a remote place, no town or village, but there was a building at the outpost with a couple of policemen seated around a desk on an outside veranda. The Afghani truck men and our drivers approached the officials to tell their sides of the story.

The rest of us entered the low building. Inside we found a pleasant sitting room. Woolen Afghani carpets in black and red patterns covered the floor. Rays of the late afternoon sun passed through paned windows as people settled themselves into wicker chairs. I left through the back door and wandered off down a foot trail, looking for a place to sleep away from everyone. I found a little "nest" of dry pine needles under some low tree branches, where I lay down and fell asleep. I had no fear, wanting only to sleep, half expecting to die. I had no idea what was wrong with me, unconcerned that the bus might leave without me or that no one knew where I was.

I don't know how long I slept, but I awoke to sounds of singing and unusual musical instruments with drumming. I sat up, feeling better, and went to look for the sound. I gazed over an embankment to a fascinating sight: a camp of nomads, colorfully dressed in long flowing garments, were singing and playing instruments and skin drums. The people sat on the ground amidst large black leather tents, tautly drawn and staked low to the ground. The sun was lingering on the late afternoon horizon, washing the nomads in golden light. I watched in pure delight for quite a while, from my perch above the camp.

As dusk approached, I found my way back to the other bus riders in the nice room. They were waiting for tea. One of the British women I knew was a nurse, and I told her of my fever. She gave me aspirin, and after another hour, I seemed just fine. I never figured out what was wrong with me, but was relieved it was over. A boy entered the room with a tea service. He was an odd kid. He had a difficult time serving tea, confusing the order of the cups, saucers, teapots, strainers, teaspoons, biscuits, and sugar bowls, placing the objects randomly about the low tables. We helped him rearrange everything and pour the tea. He left grinning. I wondered if he was a slow younger brother or son of one of the officials and considered that perhaps everyone had a place in their society.

Meanwhile, trouble was brewing with the police, our drivers, and the Afghani truckers. Hours passed while we waited and waited as darkness fell. Everyone knew we'd missed our chance to view the Khyber Pass in daylight, but no one complained. We were all a bit tense, not knowing how all this was going to play out. Eventually the story sifted back to us, from one of the drivers, "…And when I said, 'Then they pulled their guns on us,' the policemen immediately jumped up and arrested two of the men, saying, 'They'll get ten years in prison for this!' " Apparently this was a reaction to an alleged incident that had occurred a few weeks before when other local tribesmen had shot and killed some foreign backpack travelers. The drivers spent the rest of the time negotiating permission for us to leave and continue our journey, as the police insisted we stay for the men's trial. It could be many weeks before the trial would occur. Finally the drivers won permission to leave by agreeing to return to Afghanistan in a month's time for the trial. They told us later in private they had no intention of this and were planning their return bus journey to Europe along a southern route, by way of Iraq.

We were really upset by the idea of the tribesmen spending ten years in prison over the day's incident; several tried to complain to the police. Alan "Watts Ginsberg," my name for the philosophy professor, came up with a Berkeley-style solution. He wrote up a petition requesting that the men be released. We all signed it, hoping it might help. Alan presented our petition to the Afghani police, who regarded it and us with puzzled amusement. We left shortly after, motoring through the dark Khyber Pass en route to Pakistan. We never heard the outcome of the men's detainment. The drivers told us we were lucky, as the rule of law in the Afghani backcountry is usually the rule of the gun. Years later I was to learn from Louie that our bus was loaded with concealed hashish, even as the outlaw drivers negotiated with the police over a cracked side-view mirror and justice for the tribal men. Those guys really had gall.

I still wonder about the fate of those tribal men, who may have been punished in the extreme after trusting our drivers and the implied potential for a fair settlement by the local police. On a map I see that this occurred in the geographic area formerly inhabited by the Mujahideen guerrilla fighters, funded covertly by the US against the Soviets in the 1979–1989 war, now controlled at times by the resurgent Taliban. I think about the historic and cumulative anger toward the West.

. . .

I am sure I did not notice what was occurring in the ordinary moments of the bus trip during the heat and cold, the unwashed dust, the fears and discomforts. I had no idea the lifelong connection I was making to the Middle East and Afghanistan in that brief time, even to other cultures in the region I would never visit. My trip across four countries opened a world to me that I still can enter, decades later, with a little rose or cardamom in my tea, a dried apricot and a cracked walnut in a late afternoon. I listen with pleasure to recordings of old music from tribesmen in Turkey, Afghanistan, Azerbaijan. Those cultures are so old and have influenced each other for untold centuries.

Traveling rapidly eastward through those countries gave me a unique perspective of the region. I viewed one culture blending gradually into the next. Borders are arbitrary, especially in the ancient societies. The bread, yogurt, and tea in Turkey were very different from the same foods in India, yet I observed the differences between adjoining countries' foods, dress, and mannerisms as gradual shifts. This must also be similar for the languages spoken in the region, though I, as a monolingual English speaker, was oblivious to that.

My memory is a festival of colors in the street, combined in startling ways I had not seen—bright tangerine with clear Persian turquoise or garnet red with darkest night blue in the women's dress or the carpets in the bazaar. I can close my eyes and see gemstone colors—muted reds, blues of a clear sunny sky, rich greens of the early spring and the forest, warm amber and sand tones of the earth, golds. I recall scents: unusual flowers (oleaster, orange, jasmine) and oil essences I cannot name, delicious cooking smells wafting as I passed an open kitchen door.

The music offered melancholic lament in the voices and instruments. The use of quarter tones, warbling, wailing, unusual harmonics, and tonal qualities seemed the perfect voices of the cold land of severe barren landscapes, recalling the sight of that farmer with the plow in the desert.

In February 2010, in southern California, I went with my Lebanese friends Carrie and Fawaz to a party in their Iraqi friends' home. Everyone was dancing in the living room to loud music supplied by a DJ friend with a laptop. Just as I realized the music sounded hauntingly familiar, the host came to tell me, "That is the *old* music, from the 1970s." It was the same musical phrasing I'd heard in restaurants or coming from loud speakers outside shops, from the days in Teheran or in tea shops in small villages along the way in Turkey, Iran, and Afghanistan, even though I was never in Iraq. And I had that same feeling of comfort and acceptance among strangers I'd felt on my travels in Middle Eastern countries long ago.

Other memories of sound: animals braying or snorting, horns blaring, carts rumbling over stone streets, amplified popular music and shouting voices in the street, scooter horns—*ennnh ennnh ennnh*—and scooter engines—*puh-puh-puh, n-n-n-n-n-n-nhh!*

The taste is bittersweet pomegranate, fresh warm flat bread, fragrant orange petal essence, lemons, dried fruits, and spices.

But of all that binds me to the Middle East and Central Asia, it is mostly the people. Home from the travels, I may meet someone from Iran or elsewhere, and immediately recognize the unique kindness and genteel graciousness. Talking is unhurried. In conversation, one is listened to with genuine interest and thoughtful responses. I have written how Aisha, my Afghani friend, and her family have enriched my life, and I've been fortunate to have made other friends from the region who have also broadened my life. Carrie is a treasured friend I've known for over twenty years. She and her sister Mishka, who is also my friend, were born in Alexandria, Egypt, eventually settling in Beirut after a journey in search of home with their Alexandrian parents (their mother is of Greek lineage and their father of Lebanese and Syrian blood). I met Carrie through a friend when her husband Fawaz (born in Syria) was doing an advanced medical fellowship in a hospital in my town, before they moved to southern California for the Lebanese-type climate and to be near childhood friends who had also immigrated. Mishka, a writer, lives in Beirut. I enjoyed her wonderful book *Balconies, a Mediterranean Memoir,* in which she expresses a love of place and why one might cling to it inside the trauma and uncertainties of long wars. In long-time correspondence and visits, I relate to Carrie on many topics of mutual interest beyond the Middle East connection. We can converse for hours exploring ideas. I do not know if this friendship transcends culture or if it is because of a cultural familiarity, but I know that in the presence of Carrie, I feel relaxed and at home. I've noticed with Americans and Europeans, there is often an evaluation, measuring and competition, however subtle the undertones may be.

If the marvelous cordiality and personal warmth of Middle Eastern peoples should disappear in a younger generation's impatience and eagerness to further Westernize, it would be a profound human loss.

**Pakistan**

I have only a little recollection of Pakistan. We were there over one night, and the next day we drove straight across the northern part of the narrow country. Entry stamps from my passport said "Entered Pakistan, Via Torblam Khyber, April 4, 1973." The first town on the Western border was Peshawar. (In later years, Peshawar was to become a hub of Taliban skirmishes with the Pakistani army in the nearby Tribal Territories.) We continued on the road through Rawalpindi, all the way to Lahore, the eastern town bordering India. I remember the city we spent the night in was densely crowded, a crush of people who gathered around the bus in curiosity, preventing the vehicle from moving. It was steamy hot, paralyzing heat. The voices were harsh and loud. Housing was made up of dense, large apartment buildings with old and ornate wooden facades. I wrote nothing in my journal about Pakistan, but there was plenty we didn't see there. The Pakistan chapter of David Tomory's *A Season in Heaven* was one of my favorites, especially the part about the no-Purdah dancing women of Kafiristan shaking mulberries from the trees. Eric Newby saw a similar thing in the same region in 1956, described in his account *A Short Walk in the Hindu Kush.*

**India**

I know we entered India on April 5, 1973, from the stamp in my passport, "Entered on Attari Road." Even now, I can easily recall the moment we crossed the border into India from Pakistan.

Within, I felt a quiet excitement, Ah, I have reached my goal: I am in India!

The bus was stopped at the border post. The bare branches of a dead tree outside held fifty roosting vultures, necks craned downward, watching. My bus friend Louie commented irreverently, "What kind of country can support this vulture population?" Nervous giggles followed a huge buzzing insect flying into the bus. Several border guards jumped aboard in proper khaki dress—stiffly pressed shorts and white belts; red tassels swung from the tops of their khaki-colored knee socks when they clicked their heels, nearly thirty years after British India. Steaming heat, very hot, hard to breathe.

We spent the first night in Amritsar. I recall the splendor of the Golden Temple at night, reflected in the many dark pools below the raised walkways. We stayed in an *ashram*, on the hard marble floor of a huge open space where we spread our sleeping bags on thin carpets. We were awakened in what seemed to be the dead of night to ashram dwellers singing to the accompaniment of the harmonium. If I had ever been tempted by a 1970s idea to live in an ashram someday, that settled it for good. It just seemed so austere and unkind: cold and harsh. I was glad to leave and head for Delhi. The long bus ride across the Middle East and Central Asia was about to end.

Before we reached Delhi, Louie invited Ronnie and me to travel with him across India to Darjeeling, where he was expected by an uncle who lived in a mission as a Jesuit priest.

April in northern India: the hot, hot season. Delhi was searing in mid-afternoon—sticky black asphalt, shimmering radiant waves over the empty streets. I realized that most people were in their homes, observing the afternoon pause. We learned to stay in too, taking showers with our clothes on. There was no hot water faucet and the water that came out of the tap was lukewarm. Afterward, we'd lie under the ceiling fan for a bit of relief until our clothes dried a few minutes later. When the sun set, I would go out with friends from the hotel to explore the streets or take in an Indian movie in our favorite air-conditioned theatre, entering under a huge garishly painted marquis.

In Delhi, I stayed at the Ringo Guest House, a cheap hotel near Connaught Circus, with several people I'd known on the bus. Louie and I stayed in a dormitory room. Two others in the room included young Betsy. She had not been on the bus and, at only seventeen years old, was traveling completely on her own. Betsy was American, from Connecticut, and a very cheerful person, frequently smiling. Louie observed that she was prepared for everything, having whatever might be needed in her backpack—she generously shared safety pins, Band-Aids, clothes pins, etc. I recently tried to contact her with her parents' decades-old address. I received a kind reply from someone now living in their house who had never heard of her. Too bad. It would be interesting to know what Betsy is doing these days, one who traveled across Asia by herself with such cheerful confidence, just out of high school.

The Ringo was a few meters down a narrow side street from the Air India office, where a large billboard (and my landmark to find the hotel) read, "We love you, Mr. Patrick Moynihan!" depicting a cartoon-drawn Raj character in a turban kissing a sketch of Mr. Monahan (then US ambassador to India) on his bald head.

Ronnie stayed at an even cheaper traveler's hotel a few blocks away, where the guests' *charpoy* (string) beds were lined side-by-side on the pavement outside. He came to visit at our hotel one morning, shaken, as he'd awoken to find a young traveler dead on the charpoy next to his. Apparently he'd died in the night. Ronnie didn't know the details, but we speculated on all types of dreaded traveler's maladies and diseases. Hepatitis was a common fear. We were spooked.

I did errands in the mornings before the heat rose. I went to the American Express office to get my mail, but the only letter there was from my grandmother, written on an aerogramme. It was unusual to have no mail from my mother. I went to look for the bank where I figured my mom would have wired my money, those with a "First" or "National" as part of their names. First Bank of New Delhi sounded close, but they had no money for me. After inquiring in several different Indian banks, I still hadn't found the wired money, but I was eventually able to get $250 in traveler's checks and rupees for my fourth (and last) promissory card. That, plus a little cash I had left in my wallet, was enough to travel around the country for a while. Living in India was really cheap in those days, for a Westerner. I wrote my mom a letter wondering why she hadn't sent my money.

Louie, Ronnie and I made a brief side trip to Agra to see the Taj Mahal. We decided we could afford to live like kings since our dollars were worth a lot of rupees, so we booked the train trip in "Air-Con" class. We boarded on a hot day, expecting cool air in our car, and were amused to discover their way of making air conditioning: fifty fans were mounted on the ceiling. When the train started up, all the fan blades whirled into motion, whipping up the hot, dry air. We arrived in Agra and found an icky hotel. I don't remember much about the Taj from that trip because I was ill with a stomach bug, the only time on the trip I was laid up with this ailment. My memory of this Agra trip is lying on the bed ill and reading Kurt Vonnegut's *Slaughterhouse Five*, which did not help my bad mood. I felt discouraged, one of the few times on the journey. The guys were sympathetic. I felt well enough to view the Taj briefly the next evening before we returned to Delhi.

Our decided day to start our travels through India was nearing. I re-packed my stuff. By now my backpack was pretty organized: I rolled the clothes into neat bundles and stacked them in the large compartment. Toiletries and books went into the many zipped pockets. Ronnie came over, and we said our good-byes to the people we'd befriended at the Ringo, some from the overland bus. We boarded a long, coal-powered train and were off to Darjeeling. We moved eastward for many days and nights across the hot, parched Northern Indian plain. No air-con, not even a fan, though at least we had reservations and a padded bench in an uncrowded compartment. Coal dust particles drifted in through the open windows. The train made a lot of stops, each announced by the brakes' deafening screeches. The heat gathered around us while we sat motionless in the many stations.

**Thirst**

We had boarded naïve about thirst. Before long, we came to know the desperate feeling, trapped on that moving train in the huge Indian heat. No dining car, no bottled water in portable plastic bottles for sale back then. We hadn't carried water. After what seemed like hours, the train pulled into a large station where drink vendors stood on the platform outside the horizontal iron window bars of our train car. Without knowing how long the train would stay in the station, we burst out of the car and onto the concrete, bought two or three Coca-Colas each and chugged as fast as we could swallow, driven not only by the thirst but also the awareness that the drink man needed his glass bottles back before we left. We had begun to understand enough about India to know that to lose those could impoverish him. I can still taste the rescuing quench of that warm Coca-Cola, the best drink I've ever had in my life. Thirst, like the hunger in Turkey, drove the pleasure.

Later I figured out a way to carry clean water: For a few paise I'd get a *chai walla* (tea stall man) to boil his big kettle for ten minutes, the time I'd heard it took to kill serious disease organisms like hepatitis. Then I'd fill my canteen with the hot water and wait for it to cool.

After slaking our thirst, Louie and I reboarded and settled into our compartment. The train started to move, but Ronnie wasn't there. It was a weird feeling, wondering what we should do. The three of us didn't know each other well, not like we would if we were committed traveling companions who had left home together. I was feeling like we should get off or we'd have to find his mother in Brooklyn and say we lost him.

Louie said, "No, he can take care of himself."

And then the compartment door slid open and Ronnie walked in. We were overjoyed to see him, to which he responded, "What's the big deal? I got on in another car."

Our destination was Darjeeling, a hill station in the Indian North, up near the borders of Nepal, Sikkim, Bhutan, and the state of Assam, then a politically sensitive area. To visit Darjeeling, we needed special permits, which we had gotten in Delhi. The train passed through Benares, the holy city on the Ganges, where we disembarked. We spent a few days there, visiting the Ghats every day, the ancient stone steps leading down into the river. Indian life is highly visible there. Funeral pyres were going day and night, families gathered in mourning. Hindu pilgrims had come there from all over India, often coming to die so their cremated ashes could immediately join the Holy Ganges. There was a feeling of tranquility near the river. I imagined half-burned body parts floating in the water, though I didn't actually see any.

Louie got the idea we should swim in the Ganges, taboo among most world travelers ("You don't know what's in there") but commonplace among all Indians present. Ronnie wouldn't have anything to do with it. Louie and I hired a small boat to row us out away from the bank. He stepped out of the boat and immersed himself in the Ganges. With trepidation, I followed. The Indians always immersed themselves in the water fully clothed, and we copied—I in my long purple-batik cotton *lungi* skirt, Louie in his white cotton loose pants and white sleeveless top he wore every day. We dog paddled a few minutes and got back into the boat. To this day, I am proud to say I have swum in the Ganges! And nothing bad happened to us.

We had to leave the big train in Siliguri (eastern Indian town), and transfer to the "toy train" that would pull us up along a narrow-gauge rail track into the hill stations and Darjeeling. While waiting for the transfer, we sat in a dirty little restaurant. It was hot, and we weren't very hungry so we picked at our rice and dal. (A typical daily meal in the Indian sub-continent includes a huge mound of white rice and a small cup of *dal,* different kinds of beans or lentils cooked to a thin liquid with many fragrant spices.)

Louie pushed his food away, looked over at me and said, "Remember when your mother told you to clean your plate, because of all the starving kids in India? Well, they can have it." We laughed but knew it was no joke; as we spoke, children were gathering outside the back door of the restaurant, begging for leftovers. This was a typical occurrence around eating places in the Indian towns we visited.

The train was delightful, old, wood-paneled interiors, and they served a lunch—huge mounds of steaming white rice on round brass plates with bright yellow dal, with a little mango pickle on the side. On the train we sat on long wooden benches, placed lengthwise beneath the windows, so you looked straight across at other passengers. Fascinated, I watched a large-bellied Indian man dressed in pure white clothes sitting in the half-lotus position on the bench, the sole of his top bare foot turned upward. He was eating his lunch with great skill, using only his right hand. When I tried to copy eating with my hand, the food dropped down my front. Years later, I learned how to eat with my right hand, from a waiter in an Indian restaurant in Portland: after scooping a small amount of food into all your fingers and raising your hand (don't tilt your face), you push the food with your thumb toward your mouth, from the tips of your fingers. I am now pretty good at it. The food tastes better from your hand.

We arrived and stepped off the train into fresh cool air! Darjeeling was beautiful, built into the side of a very steep hill. I was unfamiliar with streets cut into a mountain so that the next street over was actually up above the one I was standing in. We were warmly received by Louie's uncle, Father M. Unfortunately, he had devastating news waiting for Louie.

The Jesuit first pulled Ronnie and me aside and told us, before he told Louie, that his mother had died unexpectedly in Canada months before our arrival. His family had had no other way to contact him, and sent word to Father M. We did our best to comfort Louie, but it was tough, and there was nothing he could do at that point but stay in his sadness among the Jesuits and us his new friends. It wasn't practical for him to return immediately to Canada, and the rest of his family was beyond the funeral.

The good Father M. worked as a Jesuit among the poor. He showed us around the school and agricultural center, explaining the projects. I was interested in the chickens in coops on the roof. The eggs would roll down a chute to be collected.

Indians were interested in us and never shy about striking up a conversation on the spot. I was often approached with an introduction along this order: "Hello, madam. Where are you coming from? What is your purpose in coming to India?" In Darjeeling, a woman spotted me walking and crossed the street to talk to me, saying she had so many things to ask me, beginning with "How much money do you make in America?" At first I found this irritating and didn't like it. After I'd been in India for a while, I gradually came to realize how warm and accepting Indians were. Their ease in asking intimate questions indicated they were treating us strangers with the familiarity of family members. Now, I never fail to ask a foreign traveler I meet on the streets of Portland, "Where are you from?" in my acquired Indian persona.

Eventually, we said good-bye to Ronnie when he left for Nepal, intending to climb to the base camp of Mount Everest. Louie would stay on at his uncle's for a while.

I made plans to go on a trek outside Darjeeling for a few days. Louie's uncle arranged an excursion for me through a local travel agent he knew. His associate paired me with Mrs. Elliot, an English woman of mid-fifties age who also wanted to trek in the nearby Himalayas. She had lived in India as a child and was on a nostalgic journey. We were accompanied by two local young men, one a guide and the other a porter who carried Mrs. Elliot's luggage. I carried my own. The mountain peaks of Kanchenjunga and Everest were visible in that Northeastern area. We were trekking inside India, but very close to the Nepali and Sikkim borders.

***Journal 1974***

*First Glimpse of the Himalayas*

Experiences that touch the heart. Oh! Nepal. I long to see those soft brown faces again. So simple and so kind. Love. Tibetans and Nepalese. The strong, weather-worn faces of the Sherpas; kindly. They gave Mrs. Elliot and me popcorn and curd, grinning and nodding. We sat around their fire gratefully. We were tired and the mists were outside again, cold and a little wet.

*Samdakphu (or Sandakphu) Walk—Ascent—First Full Day*

(Note: Samdakphu was our destination, a small hill station on the trek.)

That day, it was so misty we couldn't see each other. It was such fun. The mist concealed a good deal, but things would appear unexpectedly; a few extra steps might bring one suddenly to behold a gorgeous rhododendron tree in full bloom. I felt that day as if I were on the edge of reality; the mists made all visual images vague. When something appeared, it was generally of such a nature to cause me joyous astonishment, be it a rhododendron tree, long thick mosses hanging from gnarled black branches, a sudden drop into a vast sweeping valley—that I could fall into if I took two steps to the right—or a brown-faced, bare-footed porter bearing fifty pounds (at least!) of salt in a straw basket on his back. At one point, the four of us rested after a very steep ascent. After gaining my breath, I looked around and noticed our situation: we were seated on a tiny knoll of earth which rose above the rest of the world; the "rest of the world" being totally obscured by mist, nothing was certain but this tiny bit of grass, ourselves, and a skinny thorn bush.

In the afternoon of the same day, I was feeling a bit weary when from an unseen spot below our path came a sweet melody; a girl was singing. The mists were so thick I could not see her, but I remember the vague color of rhododendron blossoms and the pattern of the dark gnarled branches—she was somewhere amidst the trees and her voice was clear. Our porter answered her with the next bars of her tune, one similar to one he had been singing in the afternoon. Another unseen voice joined with the same melody from a path above ours. Those hill people sing to find each other in the mists.

I remember it well now, but memory is a different thing. During the experience, Mrs. Elliot and I would have to pause, just to collect these things, sort of let it all sink into the memory bank: a painful awareness during the experience of how soon it would only be a memory.

(Note: I will add another memory to this story: On the last day of our trek, our guide was in a big hurry to get home to his village, where he wanted to attend a party. He was trying to get us to move faster and not pause to look so much. One time when Mrs. Elliot and I were gazing into a vast and beautiful valley, he came up to us, looked at the view, looked at us, and said, "What are you looking at?" We laughed, to his annoyance. I realized later that he had probably never traveled more than a few miles from this area. I try to remember that when I'm in a beautiful but very familiar home place.)

***Notes Handwritten in 1973 on a Tattered Indian Aerogramme***

The aerogramme folded up into a 4 x 5 inch rectangle, with an artist's illustration of a propeller plane in one corner, a rhino in another. These notes were hastily jotted, probably recorded in an already nostalgic effort to remember my experiences in the Himalayas upon returning to the Indian plain. The following are a few memories of the villages in the order Mrs. Elliot and I passed through on our trek to Sandakphu:

Darjeeling, India—Sandakphu
Monebanjung—priest-doctor
Chitrie—Monestary, met a (Tibetan Buddhist) Rinpoche who smiled and laughed looking at me, then said, "tell your friends in America, Tibet is ours, and we will get it back!"
Megma—temple statues and giant prayer wheel
(Note: a monk in this place showed me a room with a large glass case. Inside were statues representing the "100 incarnations of the Buddha," including a fierce angry one stomping on a baby. I asked to see the last incarnation. It was a very small standing Buddha, in meditative repose with eyes closed and one hand raised.)
Tonglu—rhodo(dendron) wine
Jaihari—Tibetan family restaurant
Kalapokrie—Tibetan family first night up
Sandakphu—12,000 ft.
Trekking, mist, singing, moss forest, rhododendrons, vast valleys, Tibetan and Nepalese families, our porter always singing

***Memoir***

A wild thunderstorm raged while we tried to sleep in a hut at Sandakphu, the summit of our trek. All through the night, chain lightning flashed the windows white in a strobe effect. Thunderbolts crashed all around us. We were snugly bedded in an old stone hut, feeling protected from the elements. The next morning when we went outside, Kanchenjunga was clearly visible in a stunning display. It was a mountain peak within a bright white range of peaks, a horizontal light bolt stretching across the bottom of the sky. Before the storm, there had been no visible hint of these nearby mountains.

After the trek with Mrs. Elliot, I moved to a little hotel in Darjeeling where I met Madeline, a nurse from Paris, also traveling on her own. The hotel staff placed us together as roommates in a small tidy room, and we got along well. There was no heat or hot running water there, and in the morning I was surprised when the staff brought in a large bucket of steaming hot water and a ladle, "for bucket wash." It didn't take long to figure out how to make a lovely bath and wash my hair with this system. I bathe with a bucket wash to this day when the electricity goes out in Portland, feeling worldly with my skill acquired as a youth in India.

Late one afternoon I walked out of Darjeeling with directions to a Buddhist monastery farther up, on nearby Tiger Hill. Upon my arrival, a welcoming monk invited me to sit on the wooden floor and join the others in chanting. I became mesmerized by the rhythmical resonating tones and lost track of time. Hours later I emerged into the shadows of the moonlit night. Trees were visible as tall black silhouettes. An eerie fine mist covered forms near the ground, and the sparse electric lights of Darjeeling twinkled below on a lower hillside. It was a stunning sight to behold, and I felt very happy and at peace as I walked back to Darjeeling through the dark, sparkling night along the steep hillside. Looking back, I realize with interest that I've dabbled in Buddhism in this way all these years since my youth, always circling the periphery. I prefer the observation.

Another day I rode a jeep up to the Tibetan Refugee Self Help Centre, a project of the Dalai Lama and his family to employ new refugees in their native handicrafts. Their projects also intended to raise awareness of the Tibetans' plight. Contact with Tibetan people in all hill stations of India and

Nepal was a highlight of my whole trip. These people had a presence and were well-respected by the Westerners I knew because of their modest beauty, religion, and visible pleasure in life despite their sad circumstances—they'd lost so much, yet radiated happiness and amusement in daily interactions. You wanted in on their secret.

Madeline and I decided to travel together and head to Nepal. She walked with me up to the Jesuit center to visit Louie and bid adieu. Looking back on those days, I recall the quickly formed social networks of young people traveling abroad. It is probably easier in general for younger people to make new friends and alliances, but I also think there was a different social ethic in that era, an openness and frankness with each other, which led to quicker friendship. We were more willing to trust strangers. It seemed amplified among young Westerners traveling in Asia; probably the cultural contrasts also drew us closer together. Many of us were traveling alone, at least not with friends from home. There weren't many women traveling alone. Most of us welcomed companions.

You may have noticed that my travel friends were often men, often a trio of two guys and me. This may have made you curious. Though I didn't seek that arrangement, it seemed to occur often and was comfortable to me. We were not lovers, but companionable friends. This kind of co-ed friendship was more common in those days, part of the social experimentation of the Sixties, with intentional equality between the sexes. In those times, it was common in the cheap hotels along the trail through the Middle East and India for young men and women to bunk together in large rooms with many beds. We had to undress in the presence of the opposite sex, people we didn't know well. Attitudes were respectful, a sort of unspoken code of the road, without open stares or guffaws. And the lack of privacy was not conducive to intimacy.

Louie and I met up again by chance months later in Delhi at the Ringo Guest House. Ronnie and I spent an afternoon together in Brooklyn the following year. We rode the Cyclone wooden roller coaster on Coney Island. At his parents' apartment, he showed me the part of his journal where he had written of his trek to the Everest base camp: "The air was so thin, every step was a terrible effort." Funny how certain words and images from another's account of his experiences can stay with you for decades! I made an attempt at the start of writing this story to contact both Ronnie and Louie. I knew Ronnie had a twin brother who was a dentist; I found his website and wrote to him. The reply was postmarked "Queens, NY, August 26, 2006" and read, "You found Ron's twin brother. Now if you could find him. He was living with me and then just left. That was December, 1981. There were rumors of Ron 'sightings' after but no contact. I'm doubtful that he is still on the planet." Disappointing and sad.

I knew Father M. was still working in the Darjeeling area, from a recent story I saw on US Public Television about his continued projects with poor youth in the area. Father M. responded to my inquiry about Louie by placing me on his newsletter mailing list. In one issue, I noticed the name of a woman from Ontario (Jean), whom I had also met at the Jesuit community in 1973 and, according to the newsletter, continues to journey to India to assist Father M. in his work with the poor. I sent a letter to her on the off chance that she may have also known Louie.

**Louie Rejoins the Story, April 2008**

Jean answered my letter promptly with an email giving me an address for Louie in a town in British Columbia, Canada, within the same Pacific Northwest region that I am living—remarkable. I wrote to him and sent him this story in process. We connected after thirty-five years and spent an hour on the phone discussing our past travels and lives to date. I'd forgotten that Louie was also an English major and the same age as me. He said, "We opened up the world!"—referring to those such as us, adventurous youth in the 1960s and '70s boldly traveling the far reaches of the world on a shoestring budget, showing it could be done without the previously assumed trappings of luxury and wealth. Louie commented on my story, making some astonishing additions. One was the part I hadn't known about our bus drivers; apparently, from confidences he was let into and kept at the time, the drivers had some other business on the side, smuggling contraband from Afghanistan into India. I was shocked, but it made sense, given how little profits they were making from their vagabond bus passengers. Louie told me the drivers had a part of the luggage compartment specially outfitted in Istanbul with a hidden storage bin. As he understood the story, our bus carried no drugs through Turkey or Iran, where punishment for possession was merciless, but in Kabul, where laws at the time were less strict, the drivers acquired hashish to sell in India. I remembered how they'd thrown the Italians off the bus in Teheran. No wonder they were so savvy; they were professional dealers themselves.

Louie made a good observation (I always enjoyed his commentary throughout the journey and even now): "We may have viewed India in 1973 at the end of an era, when things were still much the same as just after Independence in 1947."

We went on to discuss the remnants of a 1940s era India we had seen, such as the toy train to Darjeeling that was built to carry British and Indian Raja families out of the plains heat up into the cool hill stations; the British Victorian influence in old Empire buildings; the Rolls-Royce-reminiscent but practical design of the Indian-built Hindustani and Ambassador autos, for example. After that, India began to change as Asia was changing, joining the relentless hustle-bustle drive and grind of the Westernized-modern twentieth century, when more machines would bring choking pollution we didn't endure back then. And just before the turn of the twenty-first century, India passed one billion in population count; more than twice as many people now live in India as did in 1973.

. . .

Madeline was an unusual young woman. Louie thought she was reserved. Looking back, I would describe her as introverted and serious minded. While packing to leave Darjeeling, she decided that she would pare down her belongings to the bare necessities. I was impressed with this decision and a bit envious, knowing I could not take that plunge and be without all my material possessions (mostly clothes and various souvenirs I had acquired). I noted that her newly culled belongings, tied up neatly in a little cloth bundle, contained all her cosmetics and toiletries but no change of clothing. She wore plain blue cotton pants and secured her longish blond hair with a rubber band at the nape of her neck. Though she wore a paisley shirt, I would not describe Madeline as a hippie. And what did I look like then? I wore wire-rimmed octagonal glasses with long hair to my waist, which I also pulled back in a rubber band. I often wore long, brightly-colored cotton skirts and rubber flip-flop sandals.

On the way to Nepal, Madeline and I boarded an Indian train without a reservation. In the no-reservation train cars people could just keep boarding, crowding into compartments usually occupied by six. We were among the first to board and had seats, but people kept pushing in, finding small spaces on the seats and floor around us. It was amazing how they could maneuver their bodies to fit. At one point I counted about thirty people in our compartment.

We were in for an authentic Indian experience. Babies were not diapered but went bare bottomed, with a leather thong tied around their little bellies, usually with a decorative glass bead. I thought it a practical solution until I found myself sitting near babies in the crowded train. When a baby starts to pee (or worse), the mother picks him up and holds him over the floor (your feet) until he's done. People blow their noses without a handkerchief in a similar way, onto your feet. It was very hot that day and even hotter with the body heat. I couldn't move, and my body was squished from every angle. The train pulled onto a bridge over a wide river forty feet below. There was a reverent hush, then murmuring as people offered prayers and tossed coins out the window. It was not difficult to figure out we were crossing the Holy River Ganges. I noticed a lack of body odors in this large group, packed closely together in the heat, perhaps because a daily bath is one of the most important Hindu rituals, and most people follow a vegetarian diet. This trip lasted about six hours. Though uncomfortable, I considered it worthwhile for experiencing Mother India up close and crowded.

The train trip was followed by the usual unpleasant border crossing—confusion, delays, and hassles. Next, we boarded a bus for another long ride into Kathmandu. Madeline and I were young and took this all in stride. Local people were traveling in the same way and didn't seem bothered, so we accepted the discomforts. We'd both been in Asia for a while, so our ideas of physical comfort were tempered. Fortunately, that has stayed with me over the years and continues to make my travels easier.

**Nepal**

**Kathmandu**

It was the first week of May. Madeline and I found a cheap hotel near the area of Freak Street and Pig Alley, a favorite haunt of world travelers and wandering pigs rooting for garbage scraps. The room was small and seemed OK. That night, however, someone nearby experienced a living nightmare. We were awakened by blood-curdling screams and cries from the building across the street. It seemed to go on forever. We peeked through the shutters and saw people leaping onto the balcony from every direction, lots of people active in the middle of the night. The next morning, our hotel proprietor told us that a family had been attacked and badly knifed by a thief. The people we saw climbing onto the balcony were neighbors who caught the murderer and turned him over to the police. This still remains a mystery, why a person would attempt such an act when neighbors and friends are so willing to get involved and come to the defense of a victim. I never saw or heard any other violent acts in Nepal after this one on our first day. Most Nepalese people gave an impression of kindness, friendliness, and acceptance. I never feared to walk down streets after dark.

Mornings started at dawn for the Nepalis. We would awaken to smells of smoke from the morning cooking fires and the staccato rhythms of women slapping dough between the palms of their hands to flatten it into thin *chapati* disks, followed by a sizzle as they threw them onto a hot metal griddle.

In a tiny restaurant, an eight-year-old waiter, probably the proprietor's son, welcomed us with an easy and professional confidence and a handwritten menu in phonetically spelled English. When he came back to take our order, I inquired about the buff steak, pointing to the menu.

"Don't you mean beef steak?"

"No," he replied. "It is *buff*—water buffalo meat, madam."

We went to a small government office to obtain trekking permits in our passports. After waiting for two or three other foreigners ahead of us, we obtained the prize: an ornate purple stamp complete with an Aladdin's lamp-type insignia and elaborate Nepali lettering handwritten in blue ink with a fountain pen, similar to Hindi with the running bar across the top of the letters. On May 5, the day after we obtained the trekking permits,

Shambu Tamang, a Sherpa, became the youngest person to climb Mount Everest. He was a teenager, estimated to be sixteen or eighteen years old. After some days in Kathmandu, Madeline and I left together on a bus headed for Pokhara, the town where one could start walking into the Himalayan hills and through the villages along the wide foot path that led to Jomsom, toward Mustang and the Tibetan border.

**Jomsom Trek**

There were no roads for vehicles in the mountains at that time, and all traffic between the villages in the mountains—all movements of goods and supplies such as salt and coal—were carried by humans on footpaths or by pack pony trains, which consisted of a group of small sturdy horses suitable for the steep rocky trails, roped together and led by a few men. Each animal carried two loaded baskets hanging on either side of its belly. The ponies wore melodic bells of different pitches around their necks, so when a pony train passed us on the path, the trek was enhanced by a trailing series of harmonious musical tones. The horses were very small—I collected some of their discarded metal shoes from rocky streambeds for a souvenir. They measure about three and a half inches long by two and a quarter inches at the widest point. Individual men or women carried loads of goods in long open baskets woven to fit against their backs. The loaded baskets were counter-balanced by wide leather straps worn across the top of the head, near the hairline (see photo). After observing an elderly Tibetan woman carrying a large load of coal on her back up a steep stone staircase, my burden felt much lighter. I had prepared for the trek, inspired by Madeline, carrying only a woven cotton satchel with bare necessities and my sleeping bag. I usually carried the Nepali satchel on my back the way it was intended, suspended from a wide band worn across the head. I'd left most of my belongings and newly acquired treasures, such as a bronze Buddha bought in Darjeeling, in storage in our Kathmandu hotel. I remember that after the trek, carrying my heavy backpack (probably thirty pounds) felt substantially lighter. If I ever felt tired and weary shouldering that pack, I would just think of that grandmother with the load of coal and feel a burst of energy. That memory still lightens my load on a hike to this day.

***More Notes from the Tattered Indian Aerogramme, 1973***

Nepal
From Pokhara to Gorpani and Poon Hill
Walking so intensely the first three days, talking with Madeline—of a sudden, pausing, in awe—Anapurna coming and going; Matchapuchar, Pony train bells tinkling, waterfalls in the rainforest

*Village Names along the Jomsom Trek:*
Suiket—little girls braided my hair
Noh Danda—little trouble getting there
Birtchanti—waterfall, rapids; Buddhist lama wearing a brass hat with sun reflecting on it (village at base of staircase)
Ulari—met couple from Japan (top of staircase)
Gorpani (Note: *Ghorpani* means "cold water." This was a very small village from where we ascended to Poon Hill for a view the next morning.)
Poon Hill—10,500 Ft. Anapurna Range, Matchapuchar, rhododendron petal strewn path, above clouds

***Memoir***

The beautiful rainforest and vast, sweeping valleys of the Himalayan foothills were magical, especially as I was accustomed only to the subtle beauty of Kansas landscapes at that time. The high, jagged, pure-white glistening snow peaks of the Himalayas were an astonishing sight. We ate all our meals and slept in small villages we passed through along the foot road. It was the Nepali custom then to knock on the door of a house and ask for food or lodging for the night in exchange for a few rupees. In 1973, there weren't a lot of foreign trekkers through this area, maybe two or three others in each village where we stopped, and the local custom of lodging in random homes could accommodate the few extra Westerners. This was wonderful because you could engage with the families in simple conversation or laughter. Beds were sparse, and we often slept in our sleeping bags on the dirt floors. The following are the villages we went through on foot along the Jomsom Trek, also written on the old aerogramme.

I can clearly remember the Buddhist lama in the round brass hat, saffron robed, who rode with ease on horseback with his attendants along a narrow path high above us as we bathed in the waterfall pool. The morning sun reflecting from his brass hat gave him a holy air.

The ancient footpaths of Nepal were constructed straight up and straight down, sometimes in stairs made of stones, not made in switchbacks the way we do it in the American West that I am accustomed to hiking now. One day we trekked up a stone staircase, which took the entire daylight hours. We stopped for the evening in the village at the top and looked down at the village far below, where we had stayed the night before at the base of the staircase. Names of villages in Nepal are written phonetically in English and in Nepal, are sometimes spelled many ways. Birtchanti, the village at the bottom of the staircase, is also spelled "Birethanti;" Ulleri (or Ulari) was the village at the top. Noh Danda is also spelled Naudanda.

In one of these villages, we spent the night in a really nice local house, made like the others of smoothly sculpted packed mud and straw, with a painted door. The man who owned it had a hurricane lamp and pumped up the pressure to give us light after dinner for a longer conversation. Other trekkers were staying in his house too. We sat at a long plank table with bench seats and drank homemade *chung* rice beer offered by our host.

One of the other trekkers pulled a news magazine from his pack and put it on the table. I winced as I looked at the featured story, "Watergate," implicating top-level US officials in an unprecedented election scandal. For a moment I wished to be home while this crisis unfolded. My thoughts were interrupted when a young fellow with long blond hair suddenly crashed to the floor, passed out cold in mid-sentence of a story he had been telling. Chung beer creeps up on you, someone explained.

**Trekking with Anne**

At some point along the trek, I parted with Madeline. I met a new hiking companion, Anne from New South Wales, Australia, probably in Gorpani, as that is a point at which many trekkers turn around and only the very committed with lots of time continue on. The next village, Tatapani (meaning hot water, for its hot springs), is a long descent downward from Gorpani. Those who turned around there had a steep climb back up afterward. In my notes on the aerogramme, I did not record Madeline among the group on Poon Hill that morning, but Anne was there. It is possible Madeline turned around sooner and returned to Kathmandu.

***Journal 1974***

*Poon Hill – Jomsom Trek (Out of Pokhara, Nepal)*

We started for Poon Hill while the mists were still obscuring whatever was supposed to be there. Anne and I were complaining a good deal on the way up. The sun had begun to climb and was very hot on our backs; the air was sultry. The incline was very steep and the altitude around 10,000 feet; climbing was strenuous.

We were less than halfway up when we had to stop for breath. Hesitating, I lifted my gaze from my heavy feet, straightened my back, and turned around to see how far up we'd come. I was astonished at what I saw! Behind us, the clouds had been moving rapidly. And now before us stood jagged white-silver, shimmering in the morning sun. These glorious peaks were there; soundless, stolid: eternal. Yet ten minutes ago we were completely unaware of their presence, they being thoroughly camouflaged by transient cloud. How delightful! Having glimpsed what awaited us at the top, we continued up our steep mountain with considerably more spring. What we had seen was only one mountain in the Anapurna range, and we had been told that at the top of Poon Hill, one could sit and participate in an alleged 180 degree panoramic view of the entire Anapurna Range and Matchapuchar Mountain. Upward, ho! The mists were uncertain and it was apparent that haste was in order if we were to reach the top before the clouds shrouded the mountains again.

We reached the top of the hill, which was inhabited only by several grazing cows and a large swarm of low-flying bees, a rare species that thrives on rare views. We seated ourselves amidst the bees and cows, who really didn't seem to mind sharing their little spot on top of the world with us. There were eight of us there, not counting the cows. We just sat, grinning and containing it all quietly. Conversation was simple. The emotion I felt was beyond expression, but it may be described as sublime joy. I was very honored to be there, in Nepal, sitting on the grass gazing at these towering Gothic forms: the jagged, icy peaks of the Himalayan eternal snows. Home of the abominable snowman, for all I knew maybe he had loped up that very mountain. I squinted my eyes, looking for tracks. A month ago, it had all been on the other side of the world somewhere, and now I was here, on that other side of the world. Kansas was then as geographically remote from me as the Himalayas had been all my life. It was hard to assimilate this. And at night there, the big dipper was completely inverted. This feeling I think was shared by all of us, whether from New Mexico or Australia, with wordless smiles and nodding of heads (as hippies often did). I remember one of the guys saying "Just think where we are..." No one even made pretense of being unimpressed or bored. (Note: I frequently observed an attitude of freaks in those times. They sometimes seemed bored and hard to impress, with an air of "I've-seen-it-already." But there on Poon Hill, in front of those incredible Himalayan peaks, we all shared blissful moments; time stopped; we were suspended in space, truly alive, content and happy, in a mutual state of awe and pleasure.)

As we sat there, the mists swirled in front of our beautiful mountains: they appeared to come and go as a vision, images that could almost have been created by our minds they now seemed so uncertain. Finally, they disappeared completely from sight and we walked down the hill through a rhododendron-strewn path, went into the hut and ate some stale

rice krispies for breakfast, with watered down water buffalo
milk.

***Memoir***

Trekking back toward Pokhara a couple of days after Poon Hill, Anne and I noticed we'd been walking by ourselves for hours. There were no other foreign trekkers and no local travelers with goods. We realized we must have taken a wrong turn. Though now unsure of ourselves, we kept walking down the small trail. At last we arrived in a very small village. We knocked on doors until finally a woman invited us into her house, but she did not offer us food. This was unusual. Trying to communicate with gestures that we wanted to eat did not get us anywhere. Though we had made it clear we would give her money, the woman shook her head and said, "No." We were very hungry and persisted, but the woman still shook her head. It dawned on us that she had little food to spare. Finally she gave in, serving us chapatis of a very dark color and dense, chewy consistency. We were pretty certain we were eating bread made from flour and mud!

I had the impression the people in this village had seen few if any other Westerners. Several children appeared after the meal and showed us their school books and practiced speaking English with us. We slept on the floor of the woman's hut that night, grateful for what she had shared and embarrassed that we had imposed. Off the next morning, we somehow found our way to the main footpath and continued our trek back to Kathmandu.

***From Indian Aerogramme Notes 1973***

Kathmandu—garish temples—full moon, Pig Street, Temple
by river at sunset
Swayambunath—man sitting in doorway, playing violin
sorrowfully at sunset,
the well with statues

***Memoir***

We heard of a hotel near the river, the Matchbox, recommended by other travelers because it was cheap and brand new. The name was catchy. The Matchbox was made from poured concrete; the rented rooms were grey cubicles, dark and bare. Water puddled on the floor of our room, maybe from a leaky roof. It was not even worth the cheap price, but we stayed, as we weren't going to be there long. One day as we walked along a lane in that river area, we observed about forty huge rats climbing up a building wall next to an empty field, their long tails hanging downward in repeated straight lines. It was a spectacle, a visual image I cannot forget.

Near the center of Kathmandu, on lanes leading away from the centuries-old Buddhist temples, stood conical mounds of garbage, each about three feet high, comprised mostly of rotting vegetable scraps. Mice darted about as children played near the piles. I know it sounds awful, but we became used to it, accepting it as part of the daily landscape. We just walked around the garbage.

Swayambhunath was a fascinating place on the outer ring of Kathmandu. One evening Anne and I walked up the long stairs of the old temple to see its gold-gilt, blue-eyed Buddhas facing in the four directions at the top of the well-known vista. We strolled down into the village below on a lane lined with wooden houses whose doors opened right onto the street. It had been a long day, not completely pleasant, as I hadn't felt well in the afternoon. We heard music ahead and came upon a thin grey-haired man sitting in his open doorway, playing his violin passionately in sweet, sorrowful musical strains. Unforgettable. We stood there, enchanted. When we finally continued our walk down the lane, we looked at each other with tears in our eyes, both exclaiming our good fortune to come upon that violin man and feeling so happy to be traveling—living, momentarily, in Kathmandu. Serendipity makes travel such a brilliant occupation.

Anne and I took a bicycle rickshaw ride across town in Kathmandu, headed to a museum. We agreed upon the price with the rickshaw driver before we climbed onto the small seat. It can be difficult, looking down as the man toils to pedal the bicycle and propel your weight. Probably rickshaw drivers are aware of that and huff and puff a little more, and sure enough at the end of the ride, the driver wanted more rupees than he'd agreed upon in the beginning. We'd been in India/Nepal awhile at that point and thought we knew the tricks, so we objected. He pulled up his shirt and showed us his prominent bare ribs, to display poverty. Slowly we realized our dispute with the driver was drawing a crowd of local spectators. A small round man, bespectacled, dressed in a *lungi* skirt and sandals made of worn tire treads, emerged from the group and inquired in perfect English about our problem. He considered the two prices, the one we claimed and the new one, about twice as much, that the rickshaw driver demanded. He conferred in Nepali with some of the others in the group and the driver. Then he proposed we settle by splitting the difference. Everyone nodded agreement—Anne and I, the driver, and the observing crowd—so we paid him and left the scene as the driver pedaled off and the crowd dispersed. Afterward I thought about Nepali justice, how we'd acquired a spontaneous judge and jury to settle our civil dispute on the spot, and the acute interest of passersby in perceived injustice.

We made ready to return to India, where a traveler's life was hotter and more difficult, but for me promised even more fascination than Nepal.

Our return journey was at least partly by luxury bus, meaning squishy upholstered seats and dusty drapes hanging in the windows. We passed through Lucknow, the sunny capital of Uttar Pradesh state, where we stayed one night. After dining in a restaurant, Anne admitted she was out of rupees. I felt annoyed and said, "Why didn't you say something sooner?"

She replied, "You kept spending money, so I did too." I lent her some rupees until the bank opened the next morning and she could cash some traveler's checks. I've recalled this small drama many times, seeing it repeated when people spend money just because their friends do, sometimes jeopardizing their own finances.

On road trips in India during those times, I often noticed ornate letters painted on the back bumper of a transport truck reading, "OK Tata." Apparently this was a display of support for Tata, a large Indian trucking company, though the reason is a mystery to me. It was so common that many travelers took to affirming agreement with the phrase, "OK, Tata," which always drew knowing smiles. It is interesting to reflect how things have changed. In 2009, Tata put in a bid to buy the Saturn car line from the US automaker General Motors.

Back in Delhi, we stayed at the Jain Guest House, a smaller place than the nearby Ringo and highly recommended by a woman I'd met earlier, in Paris. Few world travelers carried guidebooks and a lot of information was passed by word of mouth. The owner, Mr. Jain, was an advocate, the

Indian name for a lawyer. He was a kind man with eyes magnified by thick lenses set in heavy horn-rimmed frames. The tiny rooms in the guesthouse were quiet, set around a peaceful courtyard garden. The Jain family and their servants kept the place. A woman in a cotton sari swept the floors every morning with a short-handled broom made of tied sticks, moving forward with mincing steps from a squatting position. (Sweepers in India always assumed this tcchnique.) In the months before the monsoon, every surface in India was covered in a layer of gritty dirt. The servants attempted to remove this every day by wiping a cloth moistened with a strong solvent across tables and ledges, leaving a grimy film. It was the same at the Jain as everywhere else.

Once, I awoke in the middle of the night with stabbing pains in my legs. I looked over at Anne, who was also awake in the same agony. Both of us were in the same position, sitting up on our small charpoy cots, doubled over and grasping our legs in pain. What was going on? Earlier that day, we'd traveled to Agra on a bus in extreme heat. We had been drinking a lot of water, the only time I can remember consuming a whole gallon of water in one day. We were so hot, we didn't feel like eating anything. Later I learned that muscle cramps in the large leg muscles are caused by a loss of body electrolytes. After drinking a large quantity of water and not consuming salt and other nutrients, our muscles contracted painfully during rest following a long day of standing and walking.

We hung around the Guest House the next morning, visiting with friendly Mr. Jain and other travelers. Several people raved about a little milkshake bar nearby, so we set off with directions to find it on a side street. Suspending our fears of unpasteurized milk for the appeal of cool ice cream on a hot day, we chose tall glass bottles from lovely colors of pink, chocolate and pure white. It was really delicious, ice cold, from rare working refrigeration in Delhi. I can still recall the creamy, velvety-thick texture and wondrous tastes of strawberry and exotic Indian rose, very satisfying. We found out later the satisfying drink was made from water buffalo milk. We didn't get sick.

Anne and I frequented a particular restaurant near the Jain Guest House, specializing in south Indian food, where we both liked the *masala dosas*. We started talking to a small group of Indian men and women, friends who met daily, maybe a bit older than us. After we'd known them a few days, one of the men invited us to his home for lunch the next day. We were supposed to meet in the restaurant first. For some reason we didn't think the guy meant it. We didn't go. On the third day, we returned to the restaurant for a meal. The group of Indians was there, and the man who'd invited us was dismayed.

"We waited for you for hours yesterday! Why didn't you come?"

We were embarrassed and apologized, surprised they took us so seriously. He invited us again to lunch, set for the following day. We appeared on time the next morning and went to his home. He proudly served us beer on ice cubes as a hospitable gesture "because you are Westerners," though he was a Hindu and did not drink. His wife and mother had prepared a wonderful lunch, but they never joined us at the table. This would be my only visit to an Indian house for home-cooked Indian cuisine. We were lucky, though we didn't fully appreciate it at the time. I learned of the patience of the Indians.

In another restaurant, Anne and I met a sociology professor from a local university who made the usual inquiry: "And where are you coming from?" He nodded approval to Anne's Australia, but turning to me, he stated, "I think Americans as people are very nice, but as a nation, you are hooligans!" I agreed with him. Now, with decades more American history behind us, I must say he really hit the mark.

We joined an Indian bus tour for a day trip to the Taj Mahal and other tourist sights such as the Fatepur Sikri (abandoned fort town of Akbar the Great). Along the way, the tour guide had allowed such a short time at each sight that by the time we arrived at the Taj, Anne and I were so fed up we decided to take our sweet time. We spent as much time as we wanted viewing the Taj Mahal and its gardens. We figured if the tour bus left without us, we'd catch a train or another bus back to Delhi. But no, there they were, in the spot where they'd let us off—the driver, the guide and the whole group of Indian tourists had stayed there waiting for us for hours! They scolded us but unbelievably were happy to see us. I was reminded again of the patience and tolerance of the Indian people.

***Journal 1973, written on the trip***

(Note: I found the following entry in my blue French address book, indexed under "T," for "Taj." This is the only piece of writing that I actually put down in India, other than postcards I sent home that were lost through the ages):

> *Taj Mahal—In the making: 1631 to 1653*
>
> I saw the lady in all her splendor at sunset. Walking slowly down the long pathway, struck by the graceful beauty, like a queen preparing to sit upon a throne, gracefully lifting her many, heavily-jeweled skirts. A vibrant life-force, the building seemed to be breathing softly there in the sunset. Soft, pearly-white marble set against a soft, dusky pink sky, nearly the same colour. The four gates, the river behind it, and the beautiful gardens all complemented the exquisite architecture (more sculpture) so well. My friend Anne made a most apt observation: "a perfect harmony!" Everything was working together like one harmonious chord struck—at the time of our entrance through the main gate; ah, the first sight the eye beholds—and sustained throughout our stay. Oh, yes, the *sound* created by the human voices inside the building was unlike any other symphony I have heard before; deep hollow tones resounding against the beautiful inlaid marble. Coral, jade, lapis lazuli, onyx, mother of pearl, amber. The work inside the building surrounding the tombs was so beautiful—the work of many artisans from all over the world for 22 years. One lotus flower had 64 pieces of coral; each petal was made of two different colors of coral, separated by a thin line of mother-of-pearl; highlighted by other precious stones. (Note: We learned about this from a small, older Indian man with horn-rimmed glasses who attached himself to us and started lecturing with great information. As he spoke, he placed a flashlight directly onto the flower for illumination. I sketched this lotus flower in my book, labeled "actual size," measuring two inches wide by one and a quarter inch high.)

The symmetry of the domes and the minarets was so exquisitely perfect—from every angle, everything in perfect harmony; whether one was peeking through tall ferns and flowered trees to see it, or glancing at a minaret on the corner. One could also see dug-out canoes and straw tent-huts on the river immediately below. The sun was a perfect round helium ball; so much dust in the air, one could stare straight into it without blinking. The whole experience was so surreal. The Taj Mahal is so feminine. One is struck by such graceful femininity, it must be a conceptual image of the queen herself, the lovely lady that it was constructed in memory of. The king must have been very devoted. In the tomb downstairs, I could hardly breathe for lack of oxygen, the air was heavy with heat and the smell of sweat, incense and Indian hair oil. Such a sweet and heavy smell. The feel of the marble, so smooth, satin; everyone must be barefoot. (Note:The Taj Mahal was built by Moghul Emperor Shah Jehan as a tribute to his wife Arjuman Banu Begum, the Mumtaz Mahal (wonder of the palace), after her death in 1630 from childbirth.)

***Journal 1974***

I never was sure how I felt about the beggars; the poverty in India. Was it ever really pity, compassion? I think I suppressed the pity—or rather, just re-channeled? a reactionary tendency to feel guilt. I caused myself to be disgusted, irritated with those shiny-eyed scoundrels who tugged at me, and wouldn't stop it when I gave them money or food. The crippled ones or so many severely-deformed ones raised great personal emotion somewhere deep within. But these people, I think, were no less happy than millions of my own countrymen who pass away the lonely hours in front of a television set, or quietly drinking alone in bars. I could not commit myself to live in India, to adopt the lifestyle that most Indians lead. But the Indians love India. There is a widespread sense of nationalism there.

The consciousness is different. Life is so much slower. Haste meets only frustration, for nothing is organized well enough to happen efficiently. The rich are constantly among the poor in public; on streets, in buses—accepting it with indifferent yawns and well-fed belches. It is all defined by their religion, and very few consider alternate possibilities. Their minds are uncluttered with doubt. The poor accept the rich; the rich, the poor. Questioning would only lead to discontent and change of very revered traditions; it is better left alone. The heaps of garbage, the dying in the streets can be overlooked by most. (Note: Such things would not be commonly seen in India today; though a poor country, there are improvements from the kind of poverty I saw in 1973.)

The columnists of the *Times of India* loved to use shocking language: "Conditions are deplorable: the lower classes of South India have not even drinking water." The fat Indian (and myself) sit reading the newspapers, we shake our heads, and continue eating fatly while hungry faces peer into the window and push hands in front of us as we leave the restaurant—this is a favored trick, especially of the professionals—how could you refuse the hungry on a full stomach? It worked at first, but I became angry with them after a couple of weeks. They are rude. I am convinced they have pride, but of a nature I never really understood.

To experience full gamut of sensations. Sometimes I think I lack sufficient imagination for my own purposes. So I have to seek unimaginable experiences and gloat in the re-creation of images through memory and expression: effusion

Moments of recognition: having something to do with a lack of confidence in my creative imagination. A motivation for travel was to seek unimaginable experiences for purposes of the re-creation of images through memory and written expression. (Note: I am amused to read this, as I now understand that creative expression in writing or in painting is grounded in one's experiences, not entirely fabricated in the imagination, as I thought then.)

***Memoir***

It was late May, and I'd been in India nearly two months. I had purchased a cheap one-way plane ticket from Delhi to London when I had just arrived in the first week of April, overwhelmed by the heat and dirt and wanting a definite exit date. Then I got used to things in India and was not eager to leave. I had a problem, though: I had very little money left. I had been out in the world for nearly six months. I also thought of resuming my life at home, pursuing work and career. I decided to stick with my plan of leaving mid-June.

I wanted to do one more thing in the little time I had left. I bade adieu to Anne. It was understood that travel alliances with someone you met on the road were temporary. Each person made her own plan; if that was not what the other wanted to do, you'd separate. Anne and I corresponded for some time after the journey, but we lost touch. I found an old address of her parents in Australia and wrote to her a few years ago—no response. Internet searches don't work well when both first and last names are common. Anne wore long patterned skirts made of soft Indian cotton. Her silver ankle bracelet tinkled when she walked. She had a certain quiet flamboyance and was a nice, agreeable travel companion and friend.

I left Delhi, headed again into the Himalayas, this time north of Delhi into Himachal Pradesh state. I traveled with an American guy Denny from Hollywood, California, who worked in movies. We left on a bus headed for the Kulu Valley with the final destination of Manali, in the Siwalik Range of the Himalayas.

I have vivid visual memories of this trip. We stopped in Chandagarh, a town in the foothills where we saw an unusual housing project designed (I've since learned) by Le Corbusier, a renowned architect of the European 1920s Bauhaus movement. The large grey concrete apartment building was built with noble intentions to house the poor, en masse. We found the large hulk in dreary disrepair, stained with streaking black mildew and surrounded by tall weeds. Back on the road, we stopped for tea in Simla, the old summer capital of British India, and motored on to the small mountain hamlet of Manali, elevation some 6,000 feet. We stayed a night there.

The next day we hired a minivan that struggled up a steep winding dirt road that took us into the Rohtung Pass, elevation around 13,000 feet.

After rounding a bend on the narrow road, we were stunned. Before us, on the side of a steep cliff face, were several very tall, slender Buddhas, carved into the rock with magnificent detail.

We spent two nights in the Rohtung Pass, the first in a tent of thin cloth offering scarce shelter from the elements. I had a good down sleeping bag, but it wasn't warm enough. I was so cold that I slept lightly in a dreamy state, restless. I rose and went outside the tent several times. The night was beautiful at that altitude. Zillions of tiny stars from many galaxies peppered the huge sky; I felt exhilarated by the cold brilliant air. The next night, we slept inside a stone teahouse. I balanced precariously on a long narrow rock bench used as a seat during the day.

We rose early. People who lived in the pass gathered around the teahouse in the morning. Outside, a young Tibetan monk, clad in carmine red robes and wearing high top canvas shoes and sunglasses, laughed with a group of young, bare-legged sheep herders. One carried a baby lamb. We trekked a few kilometers into the pass on a rocky footpath. I stood in awe of the icy, jagged, majestic mountains. I sat for hours on a flat rock, gazing speechless into the sweeping glacial ravine. I felt as though I were in dimensionless space. I was on this spot in the Rohtung Pass when it first occurred to me that I could leave Kansas and live elsewhere, that perhaps I had already left. It was a moment of rotation, a clear thought, a motion-shifting contact of the billiard balls that started my life on a new vector.

I heard from a traveler in the teahouse that the Dalai Lama was at home in Dharamsala, a village not far from Manali. I gave serious thought to going there and made inquiries. Dharamsala was near, but it would still take sixteen hours or more to get there by bus, winding slowly through high mountain passes. My time was running out. I had just a few days until my flight left for London, and I couldn't change the ticket. If I went to Dharamsala, I'd have to leave almost immediately after arriving, taking another long day's bus ride back to Delhi. But it was such a rare opportunity. Even so, I could not imagine what I would have asked of the Dalai Lama. I let go of the idea and took a bus back to Delhi. Denny went to live on a houseboat in Kashmir.

Looking back, it's easy to regret not going there when I was so close. The forgotten discomfort of long hours of bus travel on narrow mountain roads seems easier from my living room chair. Fortunately, I saw the Dalai Lama when he came to Portland twenty-eight years later, in 2001.

Returning to Delhi, I was pleased to find Louie by chance at the Ringo Guest House, back from Darjeeling. Running into someone on the road again makes you feel like old friends. As he and I wandered around the streets of Delhi one day, we got separated in a crowd. I looked for him, moving through the crowds, but finally gave up and went back to the Ringo. Louie eventually returned. He offered advice that I still use: If you get lost in a crowd, don't wander around looking in a wide area, and don't leave. Stay close in your search and you'll find each other. Maybe he had this wisdom because he was from a city and I wasn't.

Both of us near the end of our travels, Louie and I were down to our last rupees. I was puzzled that I never heard from my mother or received the money I'd requested months before. Likewise, Louie awaited money wired from his dad. Each of us inquired at the banks every day, but we both came back to the Ringo disappointed. We made a deal, whoever got money first would lend to the other one.

Finally, I found a registered letter from my mother at the American Express postal office. She had received my letter from Istanbul two and a half months earlier, asking her to wire money to Delhi. But my request to send money to the Delhi branch of our Kansas bank, of course, had been a ridiculous assumption (or decades premature) of a well-connected international banking system. She was left with no place to wire the money and a lot of worry. She'd sent a letter immediately to India asking me to give her a specific name of a bank. That letter should have been waiting for me when I arrived to Delhi in April, remedying all confusion, but it never was delivered. (Later I learned she sent the important letter special delivery, which travels quickly but requires no signatures. It was likely the letter was stolen, as its tempting "special" postal stamps and markings from the US suggested money enclosed.)

When I arrived to Delhi in April and there was no letter or money from my mother, and not understanding the problem, I wrote her a flippant letter that said, "I even went to the First Bank of Delhi looking for the money but it wasn't there. I'm leaving to travel through India. See you in the uncertain future." Could you imagine getting a letter like this from your young daughter traveling alone in remote Asian countries? Thinking back, I can't believe I wrote that letter to my mom. But now she had a bank name! She quickly wired money to *that* bank and, with better advice from the US post office, sent a registered letter to me c/o American Express, Delhi, explaining where I could find my money. (Registered mail took much longer, but was less likely to be lost, as postal clerks had to sign for it at each point of its journey.) I was lucky the bank had kept the money long enough for me to return to Delhi and claim it. I made a loan to Louie, who was still waiting.

I had a couple of days left in Delhi. I wanted glass bangles, the souvenir whose little clink and tinkle I knew would most remind me of India. The bangle man calculated my bangle size by wrapping his hand snuggly around my hand at the base of the thumb. He was very good at estimating, because the rows of colorful bangles I selected were just the right size to pass over my hands with a squeeze and not entrap the thumbs when the glass circlets slid downward with arm movements. I carefully packed my India treasures in preparation for the trip home. I felt nostalgic in those last few hours, loving India as it was slipping away—even the heat and dust and the people always pressing close and asking personal questions. I vowed to return.

I left Delhi late at night headed for London on Syrian Arab Airways. The stewardesses were charming and kind and served delicious fresh food. I remember cherries. We set down briefly at daybreak in Damascus. I strained to see as much as I could through the tiny airplane windows. It looked sunny and dry, desert brown and golden tones, and had a look of *The Arabian Nights*, or so I fancied. I wanted to travel there one day.

In London I stayed a few days with Mr. and Mrs. Lamb, whose son I'd met at the Ringo just before I left India. He'd sketched a picture of himself in my notebook, and I used the portrait as my introduction. They were nice people and enjoyed comparisons between the British and Americans: "Is it true that in America you make tea with teabags?" and, "You should know we are working class people, the salt of the earth."

. . .

***Home Trip—Manali, India to Wichita, Kansas***
Log found in the blue notebook:

> Leave Manali, June 9, morning
> Arrive Delhi, June 10, morning, 24 hours
>
> Leave Delhi, June 11th, Monday night
> Arrive London, June 12, Tues. afternoon, 18 hours
>
> Leave London, June 15, Fri. night
> Arrive N.Y.C. June 16, Fri. night, 8 hours (Dan picked me up.)
> Arrive at Dan and Pamela's in Short Beach, Connecticut, June 17 morning.
>
> Leave June 21 night,
> Arrive June 23 morning, Lawrence, Kansas, then Wichita, 38 hours total (Note: longest leg of the journey home, by Greyhound bus.)

***Treasures***

I brought these home from my travels, packed in a cardboard box:

- Afghani woolen carpet saddlebag
- Afghani tribal dress, embroidered with mirrors, full length to the feet
- Afghani leather passport purse, decorated in pink and green embroidery
- Woolen shawl, thick and colorful, from the Tibetan Self-Help Centre in Darjeeling
- Tibetan cloth incense bag, double-pocketed and colorful
- Tibetan cotton bag, hand-woven yellow and blue with wide head strap, used for trekking in Nepal
- Tibetan red cotton string hair braid extension
- Prayer bell (*drilbu*), Tibetan, beautifully cast in five metals with a continuous pattern on the bell and a Buddha face cast into its handle—it has a lovely tone when rung, which can be sustained by running a wooden stick quickly around it's rim (purchased in Darjeeling)
- *Dorje* (purchased in Darjeeling)—both the *dorje* (thunderbolt scepter) and *drilbu* (hand bell) are used together in the Tibetan Buddhist prayer ritual, with the dorje held in the right hand, the drilbu in the left
- Bronze Tibetan Buddha, eight inches tall. This is really special to me. I took a long time choosing it from other Buddha statues in a little shop in Darjeeling, finally selecting for the serenity of Buddha's face and his open hand mudras. Its value is increased by a stamped metal panel soldered onto the bottom, signifying there is a Buddhist prayer sealed inside
- Tibetan prayer wheel, small, seven inches long with crude bevels surrounding glass-chip jewels
- Book: *Tibet, Its History, Religion and People*, by Thubten Jigme Norbu (24th incarnation of the 15$^{th}$ century Tibetan monk Tagtser and the older brother of the Dalai Lama)
- Green stone Buddha, four and one-half inches tall

- Boxes of Five Roses brand incense and assorted boxes of sandalwood incense
- Two heavy, raw silk shawls, one white, one orange, both with complicated embroidered patterns in blue thread (very beautiful)
- Cotton hip belt, embroidered with mirrors and edged in small bells
- Heavy glass beads, subtle blue and orange colors
- String of turquoise beads (rough stones) and mountain coral (purchased on trek in Nepal)
- Glass bangles, iridescent orange and green, with fake gold-plated aluminum bangles to border them (purchased in Delhi)
- Dangly rhinestone earrings, plated with flaking fake gold
- Brass bowl—heavy, old, six inches across, was used by a merchant to hold his change, and I convinced him to sell it to me
- Brass water glass
- Two brass water-carrying urns, six inches at the widest point (you would see people carrying these small water jugs by the top rim, for personal use)
- Greek woven woolen bag (the turquoise-blue color of the Mediterranean Sea, embroidered with bright multicolored thread on one side, bold black and gold stripes on the other)
- Old garishly painted calendars of Hanuman and Lakshmi
- Little red book, *Quotations from Chairman Mao Tsetung*, Foreign Languages Press, Peking, 1972 (purchased from street stall in Kathmandu)
- Chinese propaganda book about "the people's liberation struggle" (purchased in Kathmandu, from same stall)
- Moghul prints, miniatures of war and palace scenes
- Hindi prints, miniatures of Krishna mythological scenes
- Bodh Gaya boda tree leaves with fading Buddha images (gift from Madeline)
- Old worn rupee (paise) coins: one with Mahatma Gandhi, one with three lions, one with a tiger, and one with a lotus
- Discarded horseshoes from pack ponies, collected from streams I forded in Nepal (I look at these and hear the tinkle of their bells.)

- Colored woven-grass bowls
- Gold earrings with glass eye insets (to ward off the sign of the "evil eye") from Istanbul

. . .

When I returned to the States, my friend Dan taught me how to make Indian food, which he learned to make, literally, from Ravi Shankar (a whole other story, but it belongs to Pam and Dan, not me). Though I don't remember being especially fond of the Indian food I'd eaten in cheap restaurants and street stalls, I have since developed a love for the cuisine, beginning at first with nostalgia. I continue to cook and eat Indian food frequently. When I was traveling in India, I dreamed of hamburgers and milkshakes, but now I eat Indian food more often than burgers.

In November 1974, I moved to Oregon, where Allen from Paris was living and finishing his graduate program in French historical thought. Oregon has a rainforest climate with wild rhododendrons like Nepal. Many of his friends became and remain my friends. Allen eventually moved up north and lost contact with me, though we had more than two decades of close friendship after Paris.

I've left my footprints in many special places on the earth, and with these notes, I revisit them with fond remembrance.

A poem I wrote on a scrap of paper, tucked into my notebook:

I have witnessed
Sun rise over Mt. Ararat,
I have swum in the Ganges River,
I have heard my voice echo
in the Taj Mahal,
Who am I?

**Addendum—Correspondences**

***Letter to Louie***

*April 5, 1993*

Dear Louie,

It is exactly 20 years today that our bus crossed the Indian border. Remember?

If this letter reaches you, please write or call soon and I'll send you another detailed letter.

Hoping to hear from you,

Margie Kircher

A few weeks later, the letter was returned to me from Toronto, unopened, with a handwritten note in green ink on the envelope, "Unknown" with an arrow pointing to his name.

***Email correspondence with Jean, trying to find Louie's address:***

*Feb. 2, 2008*

Dear Jean,

I have your address from meeting you briefly through Father M. 35 years ago near Darjeeling, India. I am writing to inquire if you may have a current address or contact information for Louie, a friend I was traveling with at the time, and who is a nephew to Father M. I have started a project reflecting on and writing about that unusual trip in 1973 and its social context, and would like to contact Louie, though I've since lost touch with him.

Thanks very much.

Sincerely, Marjorie

*Feb. 12, 2008*

Dear Margie

Talk about a blast from the past!!! I'm now knocking 72 in the next month and my memory is not that great BUT remind me again—are you one of the CUSO workers who stayed with us or as I understand it, you were travelling with Louie? That is what you said in the letter.

...I do have a mailing list of Father M. supporters as I looked after his newsletter for 23 years. I hope this address for Louie finds him, as I remember he was a bit of a traveler in his younger days. Perhaps he has come to roost there.

The very best of luck to you. Jean

***Second Letter to Louie***

*Feb. 14, 2008*

Dear Louie,

I found your address from Jean, via Father M. in India. Hope this reaches you!

For a couple of years I've been writing the memoirs of my young travels in 1973 and you came to mind. I tried contacting Ronnie through his twin brother's website (reply letter enclosed.) Did you ever hear from him again? I tried contacting Betsy (Ringo Guest House) from Connecticut, but she is unknown to the current occupants of her house.

How amazing that you are living in BC. I've been through your town several times since I moved to Portland, Oregon many years ago, not knowing you were there (when I met you, I was from Kansas and you, Toronto.)

These memoirs (enclosed) are not finished—the more I write, the more I remember. You can see your name keeps appearing—an important actor and irreverent observer in the story! I'm not sure what I'll do with this, but I like having it, for posterity sake. What else do you remember? The Afghani adventure in the Kabul Gorge was my favorite. If it wasn't for you, I wouldn't have got the idea to swim in the Ganges!

Please drop a line if you get this.

Fondly,

Margie

Louie called a week later.

### *Newsletter from Darjeeling*

The Christmas 2012 newsletter from Father M.'s Jesuit society near Darjeeling contained the sad news that he had passed from life during the year. I learned he had died in late August and was buried in the Himalayan foothill community he had served most of his life. He was well into his 90s.

### *Letter to Madeline*

*April 14, 2008*

Dear Madeline,

I hope I have found you and that you will remember me. If you are the Madeline I am looking for, we met in Darjeeling, India in 1973 and traveled together to Nepal. I would love to talk to you by phone or email.

I am writing a memoir of that adventurous trip and decided to try and find some of the wonderful people that I met. You are in my story, and I remember you fondly. Do you remember my friend Louie whose uncle was a Jesuit priest in Darjeeling? I just found him after 35 years, living in BC, Canada. We had a great telephone conversation last week. We spoke of you.

I have worked as an occupational therapist for many years. I currently work with children, though I have worked in a hospital as well. I am married to Mitch. We live in Oregon, a beautiful state on the west coast of the US. Life in Oregon is good.

Please contact me.

Fondly,

Margie

I never received a reply to my letter. Both her given and surname are common in Paris, and I may have contacted the wrong person.

Tibetan shop and home in Darjeeling, 1973

Photograph by Nancy Bird

**Nepal 1973**
Center of Kathmandu

Photograph by Nancy Bird, who went to India and Nepal in 1973 and took a camera. I met her years later.

Westerner on the Jomsom
Trek, Annapurna in
background
1973

Nepalis in Annapurna region,
Nepal
(Note head strap load support)
Jomsom Trek, 1973

Photographs by Nancy Bird

# Part II

## Return to India, 1983

My trip to India in 1973 was a journey of youthful discovery, the enchantment of living within cultures vastly different from my own and being overseas for an extended period. I'd left home with a great deal of curiosity, hope, and idealism, within the context of the sixties era. One can return to the same places, but can never see them again for the first time. Having moved away from Kansas soon after that trip, I would not again view India and the Himalayas from eyes accustomed to uncrowded flatlands and spacious open prairie.

Culture shock is always a factor in travels to Asia (or from Asia to the West), but there is nothing as astonishing and fascinating as that first disorientating arrival. India is the opposite of America in many ways. In thinking of my journey, I came to value more and more the slower, undulating daily rhythms, traditions, the food with complex spice combinations; even the dirt that forced me to give up some pointless compulsions and beliefs, and the forthrightness of the Indian people with their intense interest in me.

. . .

For the next ten years, I moved back and forth across the United States in search of place, and preparing for a profession. I moved to Eugene, Oregon, after Allen (of Paris) wrote in letters to me of marvelous rain forests, snow-capped mountains with meadows carpeted in spring flowers, and whales breeching from the Pacific Ocean close to shore. Except for the whales, it sounded like Nepal. After I arrived, I enjoyed Eugene and backpacked in the Oregon wilderness. I worked and volunteered, eventually deciding to pursue graduate studies in occupational therapy at Boston University, leaving the West behind for a while.

As a respite from intense study in Boston, I enrolled in an Indian dance course in Cambridge. I cooked Indian feasts for my roommates and neuroanatomy teacher. My love of Indian food became more sophisticated, and I wanted hotter and hotter chilies in the curries.

I did not like Boston, so after completing my studies, I moved back to Oregon, this time to Portland, the Goldilocks place. It felt just right to me. I took my board exams and got my first O.T. job, practicing in a medical school hospital, working with people who were badly injured, first on the neurology ward and then in the orthopedic and plastic surgery clinics, with people who had hand injuries.

Some friends had moved to Alaska, and I went there to visit, camping on the deck of a public ferry making its way up the Inland Passage from Bellingham, Washington. I often thought about my experiences in India. I reflected on how I appreciated the frankness and honesty of the Indian people. I recounted the tales of my trip to many. Something would remind me of the trip, so I'd tell a story. I wanted to return and always thought I would. The memory of India beckons one back.

One day it came together. I was meeting another occupational therapist with the same hand specialty for dinner and I told her of my longing to visit India, even though I knew I could not leave my hand patient duties for more than a week.

"I'd love to take your job for a month," she said.

Within a week, I had a renewed passport and an air ticket in hand, and the trip had been extended to six weeks. This time I bought a round trip ticket, on Thai Airlines, again traveling solo. I would be traveling westward, over the Pacific Ocean through Bangkok to Calcutta. I bought my first camera.

I returned to India in October 1983. I planned the trip for fair weather, traveling just after the Monsoon season. I kept a journal on this trip, unlike the first, though much of the story I am now telling is again retrospective. As I write various episodes in this memoir, I recall connected experiences and ideas, going through branching portals into more remote memories, a pleasurable journey in itself. Travel is one of the best forms of education, and in reflection, writing gives one access to oneself.

. . .

**En Route, Portland to Calcutta**

I was restless during the long leg of the flight across the ocean and asked a flight attendant if I might go to the observation deck. He replied, "You want to go cockpit?" Of course I did. I followed him to the front of the aircraft to meet the pilots. The cockpit door was open; the captain looked up from the control panel and greeted me in Thai-accented English,

"Welcome! You want to see where Korean Airliner shot down?" Our Thai Airlines pilot pointed to the target area on a flight map and to the doomed airliner's planned route, from where it had drifted considerably. We also were supposed to be on that same commercial route but were flying south of it "because of tensions." The pilots just snickered when I asked how the Korean Airliner had gotten so far off its course.

That scandalous international event had occurred about one month prior to our flight, when the Soviets shot down an unfortunate Korean commercial plane, loaded with passengers, that had inexplicably gotten off its course and drifted into Soviet Union territory. I found an article I'd clipped from *The Telegraph*, dated 9/21/1983:

> *Korean Plane Helped Spy Satellite: Pravda*
> Moscow, Sept. 20 (PTI): Soviet Air Marshal, Pyotr Kirsanov said today the US sent the ill-fated South Korean airliner on September 1 synchronously with the flight of the American spy-satellite "Ferret" to obtain maximum information on the Soviet air defence system in the far east,...beyond any doubt the S. Korean Boeing was delayed in Anchorage for 40 minutes to strictly synchronize the plane's approach to the shores of Kamchatka and Sakhalin with the flight of "Ferret-

> D" satellite....The violation of the air space had, as the organizers of the provocative flight counted on, doubled the activity of the radio electronic devices (and) "Ferret" registered all this. (None of this was corroborated by US officials. In fact, many Soviet and American officials privately agreed this was a tragic mistake. Afterward, several Soviet military officials in charge of air defense in the Far East were allegedly demoted or removed from their jobs. It was never determined how the South Korean flight got two hundred miles off its course.)

I met a Dutch woman on the flight who was near my age. Both our itineraries stopped overnight in Bangkok, so we roomed together in a hotel. We had time to wander around and eat a relaxed dinner in a little thatched-roof restaurant perched on stilts over a pool of water lilies and lush tropical plants. I was glowing to be back in Asia! Soft fragrant warmth and an unhurried rhythm lulled me easily into travel mode. I bought two Thai bangles to mark my return to Asia. I enjoyed my day in Bangkok. The people were colorful with a quiet kindness. The next morning at the airport, a large group of Thais sat closely together on the gleaming marble floor awaiting a flight. Their luggage surrounded them, tied neatly in little bundles. I had an impression of modesty and tidiness.

The next day I left Bangkok on a small passenger plane headed for Calcutta. Just as we were preparing to land, I felt a tap on my shoulder and turned to see a blond-haired, fair-skinned young man. He asked me, "Do you realize that you, my wife, and I are the only white people on this flight?"

I hadn't noticed or thought about it. He asked, "Would you like to stick together when we land?"

Why not? He held a guidebook and some ideas for staying in a cheap hotel on Sutter Street. I learned the man, Joseph, was from Cairo, Egypt, and his wife, Ellen, from New York City. I didn't get a chance to know Joseph, though, because he had a problem with his passport (caught with a bad attempt at forging an expired tourist visa) and airport officials detained him. He decided to fly to Bangladesh to get the visa renewed properly before attempting another entry into India. There would have been trouble with his wife's visa had she stayed with him, so she and I went into the city together. We took the guidebook, a new *Lonely Planet*, and checked into a hotel on Sutter Street. The price was $4 a night.

**Calcutta, first days**

***Journal***

*Oct. 3, 1983*

I am awake because of jetlag and the oppressing heat. I'm watching three Japanese men sitting on a rooftop across from the window of my room. It is strange, they don't speak, just smoke for hours, all day and all night. (Note: I remember a young Caucasian-looking woman joining them on the roof. She had pale close-cropped hair and a flowing skirt.)

***Memoir***

Everything was pretty relaxed at our hotel. In the morning I went up to our roof where several other guests were gathered in the open air. I accepted a glass of milky tea offered by a hotel boy from a metal tote tray. Another hotel man in a lungi skirt shaved in the mirror above a sink attached to the wall, preparing himself before starting his day serving guests. Across the street on another rooftop below, a string of clothes dried on a line. I spoke with an older couple, probably in their 60s. They were Australian farmers who told me they came to India every year, staying in cheap hotels like this. He had a heart condition, and they wanted to be reminded of real struggles in life to keep their own troubles in perspective.

I took pleasure in thoughts of home—what would I be doing right now in Portland if I was not here on this rooftop in Calcutta? India was such a contrast to my life at home, it was hard to reconcile the two scenes, my life there two days ago and my life here, today in Calcutta. Long blue fluorescent light tubes buzzed and blinked in the lobby at night. Big lazy flies slowly circled and dive-buzzed my ears.

***Journal***

The fans are turned off until "hahf pahst" eight. In the betel-stained stairwell are life-size stand-up paper dolls of Thai airline flight attendants, faded and dusty. There is a sad Indian

> man in greasy rags who serves chai from dirty cups. I don't want to admit it, but why did I come here?

And, in an entry two days later:

> India, even Calcutta, is beginning to feel familiar, relaxed. I waited in line one hour for a train ticket without frustration. So I do remember how to handle India.

And two days after that:

> I just love being in India! The first day in Calcutta, I questioned my motives for coming here, but now I am quite sure this is what I wanted.

***Memoir***

I was so happy to be back—the colorful razzle dazzle circus of the senses, the incessant noise, the intense smells everywhere (rose and sandalwood incense, urine, dung, cooking smoke) the tastes (curry spice and chili mixtures)—everything combined into a vibrant intensity to behold and made me smile.

One day I set out on foot to visit Mother Teresa's Home for the Dying in a Calcutta slum. A few volunteers for the home were staying in my hotel and had given me the location, not far away. Walking through a slum street, I observed a shocking scene that I cannot forget. A dog lay dying miserably in the gutter, uttering desperate bellowing cries and barks. All passersby ignored it. I felt bad for the dog but powerless to help him. It represented the Calcutta slums for me. The people inside Mother Teresa's home, lying on rows of beds on the floor, at least had the dignity of not dying on the street, as had been the situation before she started the home in 1952.

Back at the hotel, Ellen waited for her husband. She was tense, as she had no idea what would happen or when he would be able to join her. As a diversion, she joined me on an outing. Just walking through the area around Sutter Street offered amusements. We saw huge red-lettered graffiti on a brick wall, “Commit no nuisance!” written in English. We laughed to ourselves as a couple of men stood before the wall, relieving themselves beneath the words. We visited the Indian museum at the end of our block. It was there I viewed my first real mummy. I leaned closely over the glass cover and stared into its shriveled brown face, as the relaxed guard snoozed nearby. Electrical wires stapled to the wall next to a large switch box hung alongside an ancient carved stone bas-relief sculpture of a Hindu goddess.

Most of the rickshaws in Calcutta were powered by men on foot. I called them human rickshaws. The driver stood within and pulled a rectangular wooden frame attached to a pair of large wheels; his passengers sat on a bench above the wheels. Humans powered many small two-wheeled trucks in the same way. If the load was heavy with many over-stuffed burlap bags, other men would help propel the load, straining as they pushed from the sides and back. Often the workers were barefoot or wore thin-soled sandals or flip-flops. In other towns I visited, nonmotorized transport vehicles were pulled by bullocks; rickshaws were driven by men on bicycles. Calcutta seemed closer to the bone. I passed by a small portable stove made of light, molded concrete on a wide sidewalk where men sold chai or toasted dried beans for snacks. The men looked comfortable in their sidewalk kitchen, sitting cross-legged on the pavement. An awning made of cloth and bamboo poles fixed to the building behind them protected them from the sun. Small, framed pictures of their personal gods hung from the building wall. They smiled warmly as we walked past, calling to us loudly to join them for tea.

I only stayed a few days in Calcutta, eager to pursue my plans for the rest of the trip. An important difference from the 1973 trip would be homestays I’d set up with Indian families through Servas, an organization with an uncomplicated goal of promoting global understanding through cross-cultural friendships. They make it possible for foreign travelers who wish to know local people (who in turn, wish to know foreigners) to connect in more than one hundred countries of the world. I had received invitations from two Indian families living in cities I wanted to visit. I also had an invitation from a family in a village unknown to me north of Delhi, in the state of Haryana. Servas recommends the guest traveler stay two days and two nights (longer if invited) and spend most of the time with the host family members, who are not to alter their routine, permitting the guest a chance to observe a typical day in their lives. Hosts provide all meals but are supposed to stay within their ordinary fare. Not all hosts could provide lodging but might invite the traveler to dinner or tea. This fostering of potentially real friendships is considered to be a simple and direct way to promote world peace. I purposefully contacted Indians who stated they were strict vegetarians, thinking this would give me more contact with authentic Hindu culture. My first Servas host contact was in Patna, an Indian town in Bihar state that was en route to Nepal, where I'd be headed afterward.

Ticket and reservation in hand, I headed to Calcutta's famed Howrah Terminal Station for boarding a train that would leave at dawn. Arriving there was unnerving. A vast sea of humans sat cross-legged, knee-to-knee on acres of dimly lit platforms, carrying on with life's activities—cooking, eating, singing, hair braiding, begging, sleeping. I navigated gingerly through the busy people as I searched for my reserved berth in a train car. The station was huge; it seemed there were endless tracks and waiting trains. When I finally found it, I was surprised to see a computer printout (in 1983, mind you) taped to the side of a 1940s-era train car listing the reserved occupants, including me, with my name spelled correctly.

I climbed the worn metal stairs of the car and entered the compartment. I greeted a woman seated on the opposite berth from mine, set my backpack on the floor between the berths, and sat down. Shyly, we started a conversation. Andrea was from Vienna, and I was sure we'd been placed by a thoughtful train reservation clerk who had paired two young Western women traveling alone. I recognized her as the young woman in the long skirt from the night rooftop scene across from my hotel. She had just taken leave of her Japanese boyfriend, also from the rooftop. We got along well and made a friendship on the long train trip. She was also headed to Nepal.

*Oct. 6*

I invited Andrea to spend a few days in Patna and accompany me while staying with the first Indian family. Admittedly, I was a little apprehensive of meeting the family, who would begin as strangers. Our host was Vibodh, a political science and history professor on a long holiday from a local university. We were both warmly greeted. Vibodh and his new wife, Nepa, invited us to join them in repose on their bed, resting from the afternoon heat. Though we'd just met them hours earlier, they treated us as family members, which was very comfortable. I was to learn in more visits to Indian homes that the master bed was a typical gathering place for families, an informal place to recline at ease.

Nepa painted the sides of our feet with a red tincture, "Just like Indian ladies," she said. She called downstairs to her seven-year-old servant boy, ordering him to bring her a sari from its hanging rack not two feet away from the bed where we all lay. The boy lived in the house and slept on a burlap bag on a stair landing. He did not go to school. I gave him a red balloon and he played gleefully, getting it airborne and chasing it in the stairwell, but Vibodh and Nepa did not like that. They explained that his job was to work and they didn't allow him to play. I was dumbstruck. They told me his father, an alcoholic, had abandoned him in the streets, and he was fortunate when Vibodh's family rescued him to live in their home as a servant. At least he now had food and lived inside, which seemed like a fine justice to them. I withheld further comment when I considered that I, as a Servas traveler, was there to observe and spread good will among nations.

After visiting two days, Andrea and I took a Tiger Transport night bus to Kathmandu. Vibodh and Nepa invited me to return to their home after Nepal, and I promised I would.

**Nepal**

My passport stamps record my stay in Nepal as: Oct. 7 to Oct. 27, 1983

***Journal***

> I am waiting at the border in transfer. This business with servants, especially children—new concept for me. I am thinking about human rights. Other people will and direct the actions, movements and prevent the thoughts by preventing education of others.
>
> Three days ago in Calcutta I sat on a rooftop and read Tolstoy's letter to Gandhi regarding love and world peace.

Now I am hot and dirty and just crossed the border into Nepal, waiting for bus to Kathmandu. We'll travel all night and arrive at 5 a.m.

***Memoir***

The "luxury bus" (as the Nepalis call it) had mushy reclining seats. Outside the night sky was brilliant with many stars. I watched shooting stars streaking across the indigo vault from the bus windows before dozing into sleep, half-sitting in the uncomfortable seat. I was awakened just before dawn, startled by blaring popular music cranked up on the driver's ghetto blaster at the front of the bus. It seemed outrageous to me, but I noticed the other waking Nepali passengers were uncomplaining. We descended in a wide spiral into the Kathmandu Valley, through a fluid twilight sky that hung, silent, in space just before the birdsong of daybreak. Small glowing lights of cooking fires dotted the silhouetted foothills and valleys, reminding me that people lived in those mountains. Andrea and I arrived in Kathmandu and found a little hotel room where we deposited our packs, then set off to see what we could find for breakfast in the cold foggy morning. Smoke from wood fires permeated the air in the central market amidst the old wooden temples. Sleepily, we bought milky chai poured into dirty glasses and searched for stalls selling boiled eggs, the closest thing to a Western style breakfast.

I hung around Kathmandu for a few days, taking pictures of wonderful old Buddha sculptures placed in small recessed shelves on outer building walls above doorways, and red and yellow cured goat and pig heads nailed on the doors of meat shops. I did not see any large garbage piles in central Kathmandu as I'd seen ten years earlier, nor did I see the big rats when I looked for them on the same building wall near the river.

I pondered the choices of Himalayan treks I could go on, weighing the options against my limited time, changing weather conditions, and conflicting advice from other travelers.

***Journal***

*Oct. 12*

Not having such a good time in Kathmandu today, I have to make a choice for trekking—Ghorepani: Machapuchare, Daliguri, Annapurna; jungle, rain forest—or I could go to Everest, but that is expensive, round trip flight plus guide and the real problem is could I get out if I got in—raining, pouring past two days and cloudy today—if it continues, could mean less flights out of Lukla with delays affecting the rest of my trip to India.

Sometimes other travelers tell you, one way is pointless and not good; "Go the way I went." Travelers tend to discredit others' journeys as not having been the ultimate experience. I remember this (from previous India trip)…Everest may be too grueling, an experience but not a pleasure? (remembering Ronnie's journal "every step was a terrible effort"). And what about Ladakh? Maybe I won't have time to go there either.

Conflicted feelings—am I fulfilling the purposes of my journey if I do not have experiences in the mountains? I'll still stay in India with families. I feel like I'm grappling for experiences. Yet, interesting things have been happening along the way, a walk to Swayambunath in the dark with Andrea, met Jugdish, a local artist who showed us his paintings—abstract and pretty good—his apartment was very small and bright—his whole family lived there. Then, on the same evening, we met Lobsang, a man who is half Nepali, half Tibetan, whose birthplace is Lhasa, Tibet; his background was interesting to us—his father had a trading company and ran yak trains from Tibet, India and Nepal. Now his family lives in Darjeeling where he studied English and economics; Lobsang works as a travel agent and a naturalist here in Kathmandu. He told us his grandfather is a master in tabla; he plays too. He claims to know all the birds in the wildlife preserve. He said he has never been to the high mountains, prefers nature in the reserve on outings…. The world traveler experience seems more aimless and self-indulgent to me than ever; the ultimate escape coupled with the ultimate experience: Kathmandu the playground.

And, later that afternoon…

Unexpected monsoon, endless rain. Today during a power outage, I made a hand splint out of adhesive tape, wire, a torn up magazine and a roll of gauze. It was for Lynora who had a hand condition (DeQuervain's Tenosynovitis) I knew would be helped by restricting motion at the wrist and thumb. It was a great fit, no pressure areas, maybe a better job than the ones I make at OHSU with all the best materials.

Places in Kathmandu: *Snow Man Fruit Drinks*—Good music, atmosphere, a lot of young Tibetans and Nepalis here.

*Lunch Box*—Place to stay away from. Self-important Californians seem to talk a lot and say nothing.

***Memoir***

Lynora was an interesting woman I've not forgotten. She was an American, probably mid-sixties in age, living in a hotel in Kathmandu. She arranged for her Social Security checks to be forwarded to Nepal from the US. As I made her splint, she told me the story of her ambition, to trek to the base camp of Mount Everest (18,000 feet altitude). She'd made at least three attempts and kept having to turn back, exhausted. She was a bit overweight with spindly legs and wore matronly print dresses on the streets of Kathmandu—not exactly an athletic appearance. She told me she walked with her porter in the mountains at a slow pace and spent a lot of nights in tea huts along the way. On the last attempt to Everest, walking very slowly, she recalled how she was passed on the trail by several fit young Western men, hiking quickly and impatient behind her. Days later, one by one, she then passed each of them as they were giving up and turning back, having not properly adjusted to the altitude in their haste. Lynora made it all the way to the base camp! That story (truth or fiction) has been a great inspiration to me when I'm a tired hiker.

Though it was October and monsoon season should have passed, Andrea and I were drenched in a huge downpour one evening in the street. A few days before, we'd met a group of three young Japanese travelers and accepted an invitation for dinner in their hotel room at the Stone House Lodge. Yosi, Ta (men), and Mari (woman) greeted us rain-soaked guests with warm traditional hospitality and genuine concern. Mari apologized profusely for offering us wrinkled skirts from her backpack to change into. Yosi was amusing, speaking in guttural sounds punctuated with many exclamatory "Ahh-so's." They fired up their camp stove to warm us and invited us to sleep the night in their tiny room to avoid getting wet in the streets again. They spoke limited English, and as neither Andrea nor I spoke Japanese, we sang together to pass the evening. Everyone knew Country Roads and Simon and Garfunkel songs. They were living like hippies in India (as we all did, in those days), an odd contrast to their traditional Japanese style and formal manners.

***Memoir***

I made a decision and readied to begin the Jomsom trek, the one I had gone on before, and for many of the same reasons: it was less than a day's bus ride from Kathmandu, there were plenty of villages to stay in, one trekked with frequent views of the high Annapurna peaks, and the weather was warmer and more predictable than the Everest base camp trek. While standing in a jam-packed crowd of Westerners for three hours at the small Trekking Permit Office, I remembered how there had only been a handful of travelers applying for permits in that office ten years before. I had a feeling things would be different in the mountains this time.

In the next days before the trek, I enjoyed Andrea's company in Kathmandu. In conversation, her observations were astute:

*"You are so careful with your clothes."* This was the first time I noticed that I tended to fold everything into neat little bundles in my backpack, while she just dropped her things into her bag and was done with it. It took me longer to pack.

*"Americans like to eat all kinds of food, more than anyone else. They'll usually try anything."* I've observed this to be true. I am like that, and I know lots of others who are too. I frequently eat from a variety of

world cuisines, as many choices are available in most US cities now. Restaurants and food markets owned by immigrants from many cultures are easy to find, offering a variety of authentic foods. Americans of many backgrounds frequent these establishments. When I travel in other countries, restaurants from outside the mainstream culture are much harder to find.

*"India accepts you, so you accept yourself."* That statement was poignant and has recurred to me often. I wish to discuss it. India is about slowing down; you have no choice, really, but to accept a slower pace. You feel layers of tension leaving you with every week you are there. And there is something else about India, something that goes to the heart. It is more than just a slower pace of life. Everyone comes home happy from a trip to India, resolved to live in a better way. The slower pace is a part of it, but I also think it is something about the interactions between people. I felt accepted there, even in a transaction in the market between strangers. There is a subtle honoring of the other person's soul in communication. I'm not quite sure how the Indians do that or how to discuss it, but you end up feeling respected and good about yourself. You feel complete. (That might sound trite and over-generalizing to one who hasn't been there.) At home in the West, I always feel a tension, a need to improve something—my work performance or my emotional life or my financial situation. There is an implication we seem to pass on to each other and internalize, however subtle, that we are incomplete and need improvement.

I propose a theory of emotional development, in comparing the two cultures. Growing the psyche from childhood within a given culture is like building a coral reef, where the ecosystem of personal emotions and actions can thrive. In the West, or perhaps I should say, in my own experiences growing up in the US, that coral reef might be built in part with notions like improving one's condition with constant growth and change. One feels impatience in this culture, with an implied expectation of more effectively succeeding, of acquiring more goods and riches or more and better knowledge, or of somehow becoming a better person. *I* want to be a better person. In India, the coral reef scaffolding of the psyche might be built with other notions, like acceptance of self and others, patience, and acceptance of things as they are, with an implied expectation of living a satisfied and contented life.

Both emotional systems have advantages and drawbacks. There is a background fear in the West of not succeeding and being outdone; this probably contributes to a lot of personal anxiety, worry and all the consequences, especially in our American culture. Too much patience in India may accommodate poor infrastructure and corruption, preventing motivation for change.

(Nowadays, the East and West are no longer isolated and influence each other's culture. Americans are widely studying Yoga and working on self-acceptance, in a self-improvement way. Many Indians have since become innovative engineers and entrepreneurs in techno-industry and are modernizing at a rapid rate. Indian cultural traits of self-acceptance and patience may foster the confidence needed to succeed in such endeavors, but persons are also likely to take on impatience and stress.)

Andrea and I parted a few days later when I took a bus to the Pokhara Valley to begin my trek. We kept in touch by writing occasional letters between Portland and Tokyo, where she had rejoined her boyfriend, and wrote a few times for a couple of years after she returned to Vienna.

***Journal***

*Oct. 13*

Left Kathmandu for Pokhara, first day traveling alone.
Pokhara—peace and quiet, at last! Gardens, flowers, animal
noises, near the lake. Noted great children's swing made from
tall bent bamboo poles outside my hotel. Trekking tomorrow.

***Memoir***

*Oct. 14*

On this trip, I had jotted a lot of notes almost daily in my journal. Some of these I've copied exactly and placed under the journal heading; other notes are best paraphrased, written with the perspective of memory. If the dates are important to me, I'll include them in the memoir heading. On this day, I started walking out of Pokhara headed to the Himalayas, on my own. I smiled with joy when I immediately encountered a pack train of maybe fifteen small ponies returning from the mountains for supplies, a mixture of nostalgic memory and thrilling anticipation of the trek ahead. A ray of morning sun backlit the little ponies' elaborately colored headdresses. Their melodic bells created a multi-tonal melody as they passed. The pony trains were larger and a bit wealthier after a decade of supplying increasing numbers of Western trekkers with Orange Fanta and biscuits in the mountain villages.

I trudged through the soft earth of the rice paddies. The sticky mud sucked down my boots, so I took them off, tied the laces together, and dangled them from my hand. I continued trekking barefoot, enjoying the warm squishy mud between my toes, though not having ankle support was challenging with a thirty-pound backpack. I had done the same trek in 1973 with just a satchel, but now I had all this acquired knowledge of how to be prepared and couldn't seem to leave the what-if objects behind. Skinny leeches, about one-inch long, arched up from the smooth, warm mud when I looked closely at the ground between my feet. I did not enjoy this day alone much. I was often approached by children begging for pens and candy. This was very different from what I'd encountered on the same path ten years prior when I'd been greeted warmly with frequent Namaste greetings, hands pressed together over the heart, and shy children. I thought of making an effort to find trekking companions when I stopped for the evening.

I stopped in Noh Danda (Naudanda) for the night and entered a hut with a "Hotel" sign, hand-lettered in English. Really tired, I made my way early to a sleeping room and stretched on the charpoy bed. On the bed across from mine was a young woman from Oregon, of all places. We spoke, propped on our elbows. She was nice enough, but I didn't feel a connection.

The biggest difference between the decades, trekking in Nepal, was the new accommodations. It is an old custom in Nepali villages for a foot traveler to knock on the door of a house and ask the family for lodging for the night. When Westerners discovered trekking in Nepal in the late 1960s (and when I was there in 1973), the villagers were able to accommodate the newcomers on these same terms. With lodging and price agreed, the occasional trekkers would join the family for the evening, sitting on the earthen floor around the cooking fire and conversing. By the time I returned in 1983, some of the more entrepreneurial local villagers created hotels by adding a couple of rooms to their mud-constructed homes. Western trekkers were served food in one room at a long wooden table and slept in another room, dormitory style, on wooden beds. The simple accommodations and prices were much the same, but the big difference was the distance between the traveler and the host, whose family now kept mostly to itself in separate living quarters. I missed the participation in Nepali family life as before, but it was replaced with a youthful international social scene that could be pretty interesting. You never knew who you would meet at the table, and conversations were usually in English.

*Oct. 15, Saturday*

I awoke before dawn and went outside to look around. I watched the sun rise over the blue silhouetted foothills beyond the next valley. The atmospheric perspective from the pathways in these Himalayan foothills was breathtakingly vast and beautiful, ridges after ridges after ridges. I sat before this beauty eating eggs at a rough wooden table outside. Other trekkers were sitting at the table. I engaged in easy conversation with Marianne and Gabrielle, medical students who lived in Berlin. We left Noh Danda and walked together all day, talking and talking as the sun rose higher and hotter in the sky. I told them of a couple from California I had met the week before in Kathmandu. They had been rude on a bus, and I felt embarrassed they were Americans. When I discussed this with the two German women, Gabrielle reassured me, "Oh, don't worry, we don't like the Germans either!"

(I didn't know until two years later, in Berlin, that Marianne and Gabrielle had an apprehension of Americans, having to do with the Vietnam War and observations of American conduct in Europe. When I'd described the bus incident with the Americans to them as we walked in Nepal, they considered that I must be an exception to their view of Americans, and were interested in befriending me.)

As we trekked, we discussed our political views at length, discovering many similarities. I was active in protests at home against the US buildup of nuclear armaments occurring rapidly at that time. A week later, on Oct. 22, 1983, in Bonn (German capital at the time), was to be a large demonstration for nuclear disarmament, which they supported.

We were ascending, and the air was thinning. I was walking very slowly uphill and feeling a bit ill. I was touched that Marianne and Gabrielle would wait patiently for me to catch up though they barely knew me.

As the day continued, we met other trekkers who joined us along the way. We called ourselves the international trekking group.

***Journal***

*Oct. 15*

Trekked today with new friends—we are a party of seven now—two German women studying to be doctors Marianne and Gabrielle, a spirited young German woman Rosalinde, a Swiss guy named Willie, a German guy Michael and a Japanese guy Sato who carries his things in a bursting plastic flight bag slung on his shoulder, and I, the American.

I am really pleased with this group I am with—we are in no hurry, take our time, pause as we wish, eat, talk. (Note: Later we were joined by another woman, Mary Angela from Brazil, then living in Germany. I remember her, standing alone on the edge of a precipice saying, "I cannot go on. I will die."

I asked her, "Why, what is wrong?"

She replied, "I am too old, I will have a heart attack." We learned she was forty years old with no known health problems. The medical ones among us assured her and invited her along. She was to become a friend of Marianne and Gabrielle for years afterward, in Germany.)

Lunch in Khare, sweet lady served good dahlbat (rice and lentils, standard Nepali meal). Then, Chandra Ko, great family; they treat their children well at this 'restaurant.' Good pumpkin soup…other Nepalis not so good with their kids, don't give them attention, or swat them. Tibetans are very good with kids. I bought a garnet bead necklace because I'd admired the one Gabrielle had on…. Down the staircase, descending so rapidly our ears popped, very strange to happen on foot. Beautiful river valley, Modi Khola, we followed within ear range (of rushing water) most of the day…and now, Birethanti, much better, gracious and proud people. The hotel owner gave up his own bed for me (in the attic storeroom, over a cache of rolling potatoes) and made two others in the kitchen so we all would have a place to sleep, sweet man! The food is delicious, dahlbat good, ginger tea mmm, mint tea, too, good milk, Mustang coffee a zip (generously spiked with Nepali Brandy)! Will go to waterfall tomorrow to wash after two days trekking and heavy sweating…coleus, marigolds, cosmos and other exotic flowers growing wild everywhere…smoky kitchens (open fires without chimneys) a problem, everyone is coughing…(rambling thoughts…) have definitely been in India before, very familiar, not the same as the first journey, don't miss American food like I did before, in 1973.

At one point, we sat on the patio, all women at the table, all very interesting and self-developed women, two Dutch, three German, one American (me)—yes, I am sure about the women worldwide being in a Renaissance…. I started having thoughts today about my future. Two weeks gone from Portland seems fine. I am glad I am a professional, I miss work but not routine and repetition. I feel my wings!"

(Note: I wrote some unmentionable comments about the toilets and sanitation; one must bear this, paradoxically, to experience the profound Himalayan beauty.)

*Oct. 17, Monday*

We began at Hilli, passed through Terkedhunga 15 minutes away, then climbed up the grueling old stone staircase to Ulleri. It took us the entire morning, and we could look down the whole time at the base of the staircase where we had started. I was out of breath and beat. (Note: Someone counted over 3,500 steps.) We had lunch at Ulleri and continued to Ghorepani (the latter means "cold water" in Nepali). We ended up walking in the dark through the last part of the rainforest.—Rainforest so familiar to me, like home in Oregon, but wilder here. We feared leeches but met with none, luckily. We trekked 11 hours today, climbing 1,400 meters in 8 km (over 4,600 feet in about 5 miles). Then, we had a wild party in the Blue Star Lodge by lantern light, singing again in many languages, English, Scottish dialect, Japanese, German (and Beatles songs in English); dancing on the table and hooting. It was Gabrielle's birthday and we sang Happy Birthday in all of our languages, all to the same tune and then sang Good Night, Sleep Tight (Beatles). After, we went to bed, intending to get up early for our climb up Poon Hill. (Note: Though we sang to each other in our native languages, conversations were in English. I experienced first hand the universality of the English language.)

***Memoir***

*Oct. 18*

All seven of us slept side-by-side in a bed made of four or five heavy wooden, single-sized beds pushed together. Sato, the Japanese guy, had trouble with the altitude in Ghorepani, coughing deeply all night. I was worried for him, thinking of altitude sickness, which can be life threatening.

The next morning, some of us slept in a little later than we meant to, ate a leisurely breakfast, and started walking up the steep path of Poon Hill, about a 1,200-foot elevation gain, anticipating good views. We met others coming down, discouraged, who'd arisen before sunrise and walked in the dark to be there at dawn, only to wait hours in vain for the clouds to move. Hopeful, we kept walking uphill. When we arrived at the top, the clouds parted for us lazy ones! Many trekkers do not have this good fortune and leave without seeing the spectacular white peaks of the Annapurna Range (Annapurna, 26,700 feet or 8,091 meters; Dhaulagiri, 26,951 feet or 8,167 meters). Lucky again, I sat on top of the world in awe of the Himalayan peaks at such a close range, it seemed one could almost touch them. Time disappeared as I sat in pure pleasure with new friends, much the same as I had experienced the haunting Annapurna beauty from the same grassy spot ten years earlier, with other new friends.

(I hesitate to tell you that Poon Hill has become a hot tourist destination for guided tour groups. The grassy knoll now supports a large metal lookout station. I'm glad I have my memories of different times. The timeless Annapurna Range still awaits, though, in all its astounding beauty.)

I spent the rest of the day in the village, relaxing and washing some clothes in a basin. Marianne and Gabrielle were headed to Jomsom. It was tempting to trek with them a few more days, but I was eager to return to India and visit more families before the end of my vacation. Though others may prefer Nepal, India has always been the bigger fascination for me. Ghorepani was a good turnaround point as the next hill station, Tatapani ("hot water springs" in Nepali), was at the bottom of quite a descent, which would have meant a big climb back up. The German medical students and I exchanged addresses, invitations for visits, and heartfelt adieus. Little did I know I would walk with them alongside the Berlin Wall two years later, and further, Marianne and I would become lifelong friends (owing to our shared penchant for letter writing and her excellent command of the English language), with many visits between Portland and Berlin through the years.

In Ghorepani I met Aliza and Gene from America, Washington, D.C. We left together the next morning to walk down the mountains on a newly opened loop trail. They appeared to be a couple, but that turned out to be more his idea. Our international group members drifted apart, each leaving in her or his own time and direction. I saw several of them on the path in the next few days and found out Sato got over his altitude sickness as soon as he descended.

***Journal***

*Oct. 20*

At 1:30 a.m. I went outside the hut. The moon was illuminating all mountains visible. It was one of the most spectacular mountain scenes I saw. Clear skies, stars and ghostly mountains, the Annapurnas and Machapuchare.

Yesterday in the rainforest was wonderful. The easiest day walking. Discovered the Walkman (Aliza's). Listened to her tape of Kitaro's Silk Road, the perfect music for trekking in Nepal. Today, I have painful muscles. I am having a battle with my camera—I want to take pictures of everything…I can't stop, no matter what I resolve. And I know I am running out of film fast. But what if I miss something? Torn between wasting film and regret for not taking shots. Like at this moment, I have taken so many pictures of Annapurna and now is another exquisite view…should I?

Nice hotel, Himalayan Lodge, best food, incredible view of Annapurna. We are just sitting here living with Annapurna this afternoon. Aliza and Gene are really nice companions. The hotel has hot showers (they cut down trees and burn wood for this, not good because of erosion to their environment, but I can't refuse the hot shower when it's so chilly). Weird to see my old bath towel hanging on the line in front of magestic Annapurna.

Aliza has a talent for quickly learning phrases of the many Nepali languages, which vary, amazingly, with each village we visit.

*Oct. 21*

My lunch in Landruk:

Biscuits (cookies), lemon tea, boiled potatoes with salt, one bite swill (my god, this is noodles and eggs?) served with dirty silverware, one Coca Cola, one juiceless green lemon and one delicious yellow cucumber.

Last night we discussed the future of Poland with Bolo and Maria (Polish citizens) under the light of the full moon reflecting Annapurna and Machapuchare ("Fish Tail" mountain), and resolved that each of us makes a difference to the sad state of the world. Bolo analyzed, "the Polish are an 'old people'; Americans and Australians, a 'young people.'" Our Polish friends think Ronald Reagan is the first president who understands the Russians; they like him. We protested. He said, "The Polish are giving up; sad, no hope.'" (Note: If only they could have known how the world would turn six years later, in 1989.) Bolo and Maria were able to leave Poland by

organizing a "tour group," who went their separate ways once
in India, but all will return; if not, no one ever leaves again.

***Memoir***

I realized how precious this trip must have been to them. Hard as it was for me to organize a trip to Nepal, it must have been much more difficult to manage a departure from a Soviet Bloc country. The right to travel and the right to make one's own flexible plans should be on a list of basic human rights.

Later, our host in another village was Sarasoti Dorka. Aliza and I made dinner together in her kitchen, hot spicy curry, and served her, much to her astonishment. She seemed nervous watching us. I wondered if she didn't like the way we wasted water by washing our hands and vegetables repeatedly. Between us, Aliza and I ate a whole jar of fiery hot mango pickle, surprising the locals.

***Journal***

*Oct. 22*

Today, we walked out of the mountains, sadness, have been living in them for several important days and now it's so hard to leave.... A bird is soaring through a valley bowl's rim, descending the basin on air wing...

**Total trek** = 84 km. (52.08 miles), roundtrip Pokhara to Ghorepani:

| Some of the villages | Distance in km. | Distance in miles | Destination Ht. in. meters | Ht. in feet |
|---|---|---|---|---|
| Pokhara to Hyangja | 7 | 4.3 | 1067 | 3521 |
| Hyangja to Suikhet | 5 | 3.1 | 1097 | 3620 |
| Suikhet to Naudanda | 2 | 1.2 | 1443 | 4762 |
| Naudanda to Khare | 5 | 3.1 | 1646 | 5432 |
| Khare to Tirkedhunga | 15 | 9.3 | 1439 | 4749 |
| Tirkedhunga to Ghorepani | 8 | 4.9 | 2835 | 9356 |
| Ghorepani to Poon Hill | one hour | | 3193 | 10,537 |

Total distance (one way) 42 km. or 25.9 miles

***Memoir***

There were several other villages along this route not listed in the distance chart (which I'd hand-copied from someone else's paper into my journal), such as Birethanti, Hille, and Ulleri. Gene, Aliza and I took a different way back, part of a loop, passing through many villages new to us. I did not record the distances or most of their names, but one of the communities was Ghandruk, a larger village which spoke the Garung language, one that Aliza learned several words of, from a couple of local children. Soon after returning to Portland, I went to see a movie that took place in a Guatemalan mountain village, though I can't remember which one, or if it was named. It was astonishing how much the people's facial features of that Central American village resembled those of the Nepali villagers, especially those in Ghandruk.

***Memoir***

*Oct. 23*

We were staying in a new section of Pokhara. Aliza had rented a room for herself and Gene in a small hotel, but for some reason changed her mind and arranged for other accommodations, probably separate rooms, in a different hotel. She gave me their room. I loved that room. It was simple, with walls freshly whitewashed. A straight chair with a woven seat was placed before a window opening into a flower garden. The floor was made of stone. The beds were covered in white cloth. I was really looking forward to being by myself in that pleasant room where I could sit and think.

Aliza, Gene, and I had dinner at the Dragon Hotel and attended a Nepali dance concert. After, we were walking back to our Lodges when we were deluged in a sudden heavy rain. My hotel was closest, so we ducked into my new room, drenched. It was quite a storm, and there were no signs of it clearing. We were all very tired, so Aliza suggested we push the two single beds together and all three sleep across them, the way trekkers often did in the Himalayan villages. It was sort of nice having companions at night, but I was secretly disappointed not to be alone.

I never forgot that room. It often recurred and became a symbol to me, of solitude and beauty. I had a notion that if I had stayed by myself in that room, I would have learned the secret to living an orderly and uncluttered life from that night on. I look back on that stormy night as a lost chance I have yet to find my way to.

*Oct. 24*

We returned to Kathmandu. Gene took a flight soon after that back to the States. I visited Aliza at the Yak and Yeti, a posh Western style hotel with cold air conditioning. We dabbed Aliza's French perfume, Joy, behind our ears. I later learned Joy was valued at $200 per ounce when I asked my mom for it for a Christmas present. Aliza didn't seem that rich in the mountains, where we all wore cotton peasant skirts and hiking boots.

*Oct. 25*

Aliza and I hired a car to Thamel, an area of Kathmandu known for its gem shops, where she wanted to look at rubies. She told me of an older man she'd befriended in Kathmandu who had been a Nazi officer in Germany. She was fascinated by him and encouraged the friendship, agreeing to meet up with him for lunch that day in Thamel.

She recognized him in the street, introduced me, and left us on the pavement while she ducked into a shop. Making conversation, I asked where he was from and when he replied, "Munich," I had a visceral reaction. Without thinking, I observed myself telling him I had visited Dachau and would never forget it and, further, "the world must always remember what happened there." The man turned heel and walked away from me. I wrote later in my journal: "I hate him. It didn't matter to me who he was as a person, I know he was a Nazi official. He symbolized human grotesqueness to me. I hate him, knowing that hate is what his work was about." Even so, I was surprised at myself for reacting so bluntly in the street.

I told Aliza what happened. She said, "Funny, it doesn't bother me like that. And I've never told him I am a Jew. He might feel uncomfortable."

Aliza and I corresponded for a couple of years after Nepal. She married a French man and moved to Europe where they raised a child.

. . .

*Oct. 28*

Making good on my promise to the Indian family, I returned alone to Patna, arriving in the morning. I spent several days with them, fascinating for me. One afternoon we spent four hours sitting in the living room. We took sweet milky tea, fanned flies, and reclined in the heat. We exchanged a few words, but there seemed little need to talk. It was obvious they spent a lot of time in each other's company without conversation. There was a little clacking sound of Vibodh's mother's knitting needles. Flies buzzed around. The young couple lived with his parents, as was common for Indian families. They said I was a good guest, interested in their daily lives and not asking to go out sightseeing. They had a television but only watched it on special occasions. Vibodh told me, "We are learning about your American culture. We are watching *I Love Lucy* shows on our TV." One evening an Indian movie was on and dozens of the neighbors came over to watch it, crowding into their tiny living room, sitting leg-to-leg on narrow wooden chairs.

Vibodh would say to me, "Come!" or "Go!" or "Get on!" the last referring to the back of his scooter when we went to the market.

He told me, "Why are you so formal—always saying *excuse me* if you bump someone? They know you mean no offense, you don't have to say it." I started a discussion about cultural differences, and I learned that *please* and *thank you* were considered very formal and not often used. Vibodh obliged my preference for Western niceties like a *please* following a command, and I tried to be less reactive to his and others' abbreviated requests. One hot afternoon in an area of town where farmers sold vegetables piled in large heaps, Vibodh directed, "Stand over there, not near me. I am not getting a good price with a Westerner with me. They think we are rich."

Vibodh and Nepa had an arranged marriage, typical of many Indians. They were newlyweds in their first year of marriage and seemed to be in love, looking into each other's eyes with flirting admiration. While I was there, they learned Nepa was pregnant. The family was very happy and I got to share their joy.

***Journal***

*Oct. 28*

Early this morning, I watched Vibodh's mother Mrs. D. perform puja (worship ritual) at her altar on the kitchen floor. Behind her a grey rat ran across the room and darted around a basket. A cow ate her meal outside the torn screen kitchen door as a crow hopped up to her back.

***Memoir***

Their house was a two-story concrete structure built by Vibodh. He was proud of his creation and gave me a tour. Stairs and balconies, with their concrete edges chipping off, were unencumbered by handrails and balustrades. Building codes in India seemed to allow the owner many freedoms. The dwelling was dark-grey cement-colored, a basic structure without ornamentation. Family members were intelligent and educated, well-off but not wealthy. From what I observed, they had two servants, a cook and the young boy who waited on them hand and foot.

After the breakfast dishes were cleared and cleaned, the family cook would set to work preparing lunch. He squatted at a large stone mortar on the floor of the kitchen, pulverizing vegetables and spices with a heavy pestle. Immediately after serving lunch, he began dinner preparations. Indian food can take hours to make, with so many tasks of grinding, chopping, and readying many ingredients for several dishes prepared from scratch. It is the same for me when I make it in the US, but I prepare a full Indian meal only for special occasions. Though they lived within the city limits, the family enjoyed fresh milk from their cow tied in the small yard space behind the house. Down their lane, stuck to a long mud wall, hundreds of brown patties dried in the sun, a human handprint pressed into each one. Dried cowdung 'pies,' each about seven inches in diameter, are used for cooking fuel by many, but my hosts cooked on a small two-burner fuel stove.

After visiting the family a few days, I left for Benares. Vibodh and I corresponded by aerogramme for a year, and I learned of the birth of their baby boy.

***Journal***

*Oct. 29, 1983*

Entry written on a train ride, from a monologue 'conversation' shouted at me by an Indian passenger, "I know about your (American) medical system, because I read 'Coma'!" (Note: 1977 American novel by Robin Cook, in which hospital patients are put into a coma and die so their organs could be stolen for profit.)

*Other entries written that same day:*

A woman on the train admonished me: "Young lady, mind your pocketbook. People steal in India. You do not know about this because in your country everyone is rich and there is no crime." She looked surprised and maybe disbelieving when I told her that my apartment had been broken into and my jewelry stolen just before I left for this trip.

"Hello, American friend, I give you good price, anything you want to buy."

Reflections—This trip has been rich, from apocalyptic backstreets of Calcutta to high Himalayan peaks, ghostly in full moon. I arrived today in Benares, the celebrated holy city on the Ganges. I took a picture of a funeral pyre at the Burning Ghats and soon after, an outraged Indian man in a dirty skirt, plastic shoes and dusty legs shrieked, howling and gesturing, running toward me. I fled, frightened that he may seize the camera and throw me on the pyre, managing to disappear into a dark street among big black cows and silk 'saree' shops (Note: Saree is a common alternate spelling for sari.) Now, I am drinking mango shake. I just learned how to wrap a sari. This is another world. Hard to believe I'll be back to business as usual in Portland, Oregon in two weeks. Ciao.

My new favorite drink: Thums Up Cola, with its bright red hand curled into a thumbs-up gesture painted on a six-ounce glass bottle. There are hints of something exotic in its sweet, refreshing liqueur, perhaps cardamom or betel nut.

***Memoir***

Benares—Varanasi, the traditional name—is an ancient and most venerable city on the Holy River Ganges. It is well-known for its many old temples and Ghats, steps leading down a long, steep incline to bathing spots and funeral pyre areas at the river's edge. Hindu religious pilgrims come from far away to bathe in the holy water and obtain blessings. Many people journey to Varanasi at the end of their lives to die there so their accompanying families can light a funeral pyre on the river bank and scatter their ashen remains directly into the Ganges. Often funeral processions wind on foot through the crowded streets to the river. One evening, while walking on a street, I was caught up in one such funeral. I noticed that the evening crowd surrounding me was more animated than usual. Slowly, I became aware of loud, mournful shouting rising above the usual street noises, its phrasing punctuated rhythmically by a resonating *boom* from a big drum. I turned my head to the left and saw a dead body, prostrate next to me, being ferried through the street crowd on the hands of many mourners. It was small, perhaps the body of a woman, bound tightly from head to toe in saffron-colored cloth and completely covered in marigolds.

The funeral pyres were a unique fascination. I went down to the Burning Ghats the first evening I was in Benares. On the bank near the water's edge, I saw three pyres with wrapped bodies laid atop neat cross-hatch piles of wooden timbers, about four feet high. I sat down on the steep steps, at quite a distance above them, to watch the ritual. It was dusk, and I felt that I'd disappeared into the crowd on the stairs. As darkness fell, they lit the pyres. Flames roared toward the night sky. I watched as the round skulls glowed bright red within the consuming flames. My thoughts were on the transitory nature of life. And of my own life. Suddenly, I was roused from my reverie by a man rushing toward me, shouting angrily in Hindi. I knew I should probably not have taken that photograph, but I wanted it, for the memory. The man was gesturing for me to give him my camera so I ran, tripping up the steps with him at my heels, dodging holy cows and mourners. He lost my trail and I still have the photo with the glowing skulls on the wood pyre.

. . .

I had arranged to meet Sunita, an artist in Benares. She was different from other Indians I met—reserved, busy, almost hurried, a trait I was glad to leave behind in the West. She was an intellectual, with art her primary interest. I was not invited to stay in her house because her mother who lived with her was ill. I took lunch there. It was kind of like a business deal. As soon as I arrived and sat down, Sunita set to task showing me photographs of her work and asked me to find her a gallery in the US where she could show. I thought her art was quite good—figurative, fabric paintings in batik with interesting interpretations of Indian life. She emphasized the decorative hands and feet on her figures. I agreed to try to help her and took her art photos with me, along with her resume which showed evidence of being somewhat well-known in India.

When I got home, I took her prints and resume to several galleries in Portland, even corresponded to some New York galleries, but I had no luck and later returned the photos to her.

***Journal***

> Sunita is a very busy person, unusual. I don't see many people working hard here at all—they go to their jobs and sit, moving slowly or sleep.

***Memoir***

Sunita helped me find a hotel near the Ganges, owned by an American "who cleaned the toilets herself" (much to the astonishment of all Indian observers). It was fine. One evening I arrived home to my room. On the floor by the bed was a huge dead insect, three inches long, maybe some kind of roach. It was completely covered with hundreds of busy little ants. Feeling very tired, I stepped over it and got into my bed. The next morning I looked down at the floor. The roach was gone, no sign of it.

At the hotel, I met a friendly local man, Ashok. He invited me to his house nearby where I met his sister. Her teenaged daughter studied Kathak, a classical north Indian dance. I also had studied Kathak in Cambridge, Massachusetts, some years earlier. The dance is so scripted and methodical in its tradition that she and I, from worlds apart, could know how to beat the same rhythms together with our bare feet on the floor of the tiny apartment in Varanasi.

The sister opened her metal wardrobe to show me all her clothes, about five saris. She showed me some colorfully painted wooden bangles, then gave them to me.

I objected, "You must not give me your beautiful bangles."

"It's OK," she assured me. "You can send me an electric mixer when you get home."

Ashok invited me to take a boat ride on the Ganges. We met the next morning at dawn, after his daily Yoga practice. The river was beautiful, misty and still, pink shards of morning sun dancing on the surface. I recalled my 1973 Ganga swim with Louie. Ashok and others told me the Holy Ganges River has no detectable bacteria levels, thought to be a spiritual miracle, as many animals and humans bathe in it and sewage is released into it daily. I did a little research on this and quote George Black from *Onearth* magazine, a publication of the Natural Resources Defense Council, Summer 2009: "By the time the Ganga has passed through Varanasi, the holiest of all Indian cities, the fecal coliform bacteria count is between one million and two million parts per 100 milliliters. The safe level for bathing is 500." (www.onearth.org).

I went by bicycle rickshaw to Sarnath, an archaeological site in the country a short distance from Varanasi. This is the actual location where Buddha lived and first taught the Dharma to disciples after reaching Enlightenment in nearby Bodh Gaya.

***Journal***

*Oct. 30*

I am sitting on Buddha's chair. There may be a lot of bureaucracy and rules in India, but not here at this archaeological sight. I took a time-lapse photo of myself sitting where the Buddha sat.

My guide is M.R. Dass, hired on the spot in the informal India tourist industry fashion—betel-stained teeth and dirty white pajamas, but very kind and seems to know about Buddhist history, a Hindu who studies Buddhism. From Mr. Dass: There were three female and three male disciples of Buddha, 6th century BC. (Note: Other sources describe five disciples, some say men; others, unspecified gender.) They all lived in peace; when Buddha came through the passage, he saw the women teaching the men about karma. He was so happy, he came to sit in this chair and granted each one Nirvana.

***Copied exactly from a booklet, "Guide Album of Saranath Varanasi"***

Betel leaf

There is no locality in Banaras (sic) where there is no betel leaf shop. They can be recognised easily with mirrors facing the customers who see their faces while chewing the betel.

Betel is a heart shaped green leaf on which they put betel nut, lime, catechu and a little tobacco, if someone is habituated to take. Lips turn red and it is a part of ornamentation too. It is just a formality and a habit like smoking. Betel is called "PAN" for which Banaras is famous. Some people get addicted to it but if taken twice or thrice after meals it is never intoxicant but stimulant.

***Memoir***

In a garden on the Sarnath grounds where I took a refreshing tea, I met a group of Indians: Marie, Narain and Ruben, an amazing trio of friends. Marie had lived in Oregon and loved Crater Lake (where I had yet to go). Later the same night, Ruben rode his motor scooter to the train station in Allahabad (close to Benares) to be there to greet me when the train I was on passed through at 2 a.m. I'd told him it was my birthday and the time I was catching the train in Benares. He found the berth I was in (amidst all the confusion of an Indian train station in the middle of the night!) and knocked on the window to give me a birthday present from him, Marie, and Narain. I still cannot imagine how he found me. This, among numerous other kind actions, endeared the Indian people to me.

When the train was just pulling into the Delhi station, a man I'd met in my compartment insisted he would find a suitable auto rickshaw driver to take me to the hotel. He interviewed several drivers lined up outside the station and decided on one. "I've negotiated a good price for you; get in," he said. I got in, but I did not like the looks of the rickshaw driver and would not have chosen him. I thought he looked kind of tough, with a somewhat menacing look. I felt nervous on the ride, but he delivered me to my destination. Predictably, he wanted more for the trip when we got there, but I gave him the agreed-upon price and walked away thinking my apprehensions were justified. Other than this experience, in which I thought I would have been better off had I trusted my own instincts instead of following well-meaning advice, I never felt to be in any danger traveling solo in India. Nowadays, things may be different, as street violence seems to have increased throughout the world.

***Journal***

*Delhi*

The motor rickshaw drivers cheat. This city has many more vehicles than ten years ago. It's definitely a city, fast-paced; the women a fashion parade of silk saris and expensive batik Punjabi clothes. I'm lonely. I talked to some Europeans. It was OK, but I miss my earlier friends Andrea, Gabrielle, Marianne and Aliza. Being here (in Delhi) I feel so materialistic. All I can think about is what I'm going to buy. Have to get out of here, have presents for everyone now.

I am staying again at the Ringo Guest House, same cheap traveler's hotel where I stayed with Louie and Betsy 10 years ago. I met Steve, ashen and morose with dehydration and upset stomach. I told him how to get electrolytes; drink a glass of orange juice and a glass of salt water. He took the advice and when I saw him two hours later, he looked much better, with a bright smile. Low electrolytes can take it out of you.

Many women work in N. Delhi. I saw a woman driving a car wearing blue jeans. (Note: At that time, one rarely saw a woman driver or a woman in blue jeans.) I saw a group of three male cross-dressers in saris and lipstick. I asked them why they were dressed that way, and they said, "Baksheesh!" (street entertainers for mone

***Memoir***

I was fascinated to observe an elderly Indian woman crossing the street as I followed a few paces behind her. She wore an elegant sari and walked with her head held high. Her long grey braid plumbed down her straight spine. Her body movements were fluid and unencumbered. She did not move with the restricted, pained step of many elderly I've observed at home. I resolved to age like she did.

I took a side trip to a town near Delhi for a couple of days to stay with another Servas family. My stay in this home was most notable for three revealing discussions with father and sons, on sexuality in India.

***Journal***

Had lengthy discussions today with the father of the family Suraj and his son Rajiv, an accountant (separate discussions out of earshot of the other) on sexuality in India and America. Each told me there is radical social change in the past ten years, but still everything is very secretive. Almost no women are virgins on marriage but most pretend to be. While sitting on the shaded veranda one day, Suraj told me he and his friends had conducted an informal survey of 100 men, to see how many had slept only with their wives, and it was only about three. I could not get him to say if this was before marriage or infidelity. Not exactly a scientific study, but it was interesting. I remembered my own untruthful, boastful answers on sexual experience at age 18 when given a research questionnaire by a weird university psychology professor required at the end of his course.

In another conversation a few days later, Suraj's eldest son Kumar told me in confidence of his girlfriend. He said, "This is highly secret. The only people who know are my girlfriend, you and my wife. If my father knew, he would throw me out of the house!" When I asked in astonishment about his wife being in on the secret, he told me simply, "She is my best friend; deep personal confidences with my wife are very important to me." He went on to tell me there was "no sexual relationship" with the girlfriend who loved him very much, because, though he was willing, "she hates sex." I was confused by these confidences and wondered just what intimate secrets (or fantasies) I was really privy to. I've changed the names to protect the secret, just in case, and with respect for his wife. One thing for sure, I as an unmarried 33 year-old woman was quite a curiosity to them. At first it was shocking, their frank questions about my sex life, but by then, I'd been familiar with India for awhile and reminded myself how I liked the directness of the culture in other contexts and politely dodged their questions.

*Enroute Delhi to Jindh on a crowded bus, to meet fourth Servas family:*
Traveling in India is miserably uncomfortable.... I am in an endless sea of people in all places. I don't like this. I was surprised on this bus to see women being rude to children. The children take it without protest. The fathers seem better with children here.

It is near harvest time, many vehicles on the road, tractors and plows, combines, (trucks with) big loads of grain, all the way from Delhi.

***Memoir***

*Nov. 3 or 4, 1983*

At last the crowded bus arrived in Jindh, a town in the state of Haryana, north of Delhi. I got off with my luggage at the terminal building (a sign identified it as "The Department of Transportation") and called the number Mahesh Agrawal had given me in an aerogramme letter to Portland several weeks before. The family had decided that one of the elder sons Rajendra Baniya, a medical doctor, and his wife Madhuri, also a doctor, would be my direct hosts for the stay.

Dr. Rajendra was put on the phone to take my call. I heard him shouting through the static of the village phone line, "I am coming in the ambulance!" They picked me up in the family vehicle, an ambulance, complete with Kewpie doll and gold tinsel hanging from the rearview mirror. A servant was the driver. The doctor rode in the ambulance on calls. I extended my hand in greeting Rajendra. He reluctantly took it, later explaining to me, "I understood your Western gesture, but townspeople were watching. It was hard for me to shake your hand because that gesture has a sexual meaning in our culture."

The Agrawals were members of a large extended "joint family" as they called it, all living together in a large house on the main square of the village. The head of household was Mahesh Das Agrawal and his wife, also named Madhuri, a large queenly woman with a broad, gold-toothed smile. Agrawal and Baniya are caste names (Indians have no other surnames), with Baniya branching from Agrawal, part of the broader *Vaisya*, merchant and professional caste. Mahesh, the head of household, used the last name Agrawal, and all of his sons used Baniya as their surname. Their explanation of this never made sense to me. In Hindu tradition, there are considered to be three other broad caste categories, including *Brahmins,* the priestly or scholarly caste, of which my hosts in Patna were a part; *Ksatriyas,* the warrior or royal caste, and *Sudras*, the labor caste. My Portland friend Miten from Bombay explained to me, "Caste is like your DNA."

Staying with this family was very interesting for me. Through a stroke of luck, I was there on November 4 for the Diwali Festival of Lights, an important Hindu holiday comparable to Christmas in the West. (Diwali is a contraction of "Deepavali" and is also spelled Devali). The actual date in autumn varies year to year with the seasons and the Hindu calendar. I was quickly swept up in the Diwali preparations from the moment of my arrival. All family members were busily engaged in activities and the village was in a festive spirit. They took great pleasure in explaining and sharing the holiday traditions and religious stories with me, and I was an eager participant.

The two sons living outside the joint family and their own young families had traveled from other villages to be together in the central home for Diwali. Special foods and sweets were prepared. Outside on the front porch, a young boy, Lalit (about nine years old, Mahesh's grandson), crafted a decorative lampshade from colored cellophane. A whole room in the house was devoted to Diwali, with a brightly colored miniature village diorama set up among lights and candles. Painted figurines of Hindu gods and images were placed throughout the houses. I had brought a small gift to them, a brass candlestick holder, which they set into the scene. In a culminating ceremony, the entire family and I sat together on the floor in the room before the miniature village. The eldest son, Narain (Lalit's father), performed a ritual with Ganges water, colored tikka powder, and rice. Brothers and sisters gave blessings by applying a *tikka* (dot made of vermilion paste) to each other's foreheads. Someone dabbed my forehead, too, with red powder. After nightfall, the fathers and older boys lit long sparklers and set off fireworks from their front porch. With concealed astonishment, I observed Dr. Vaijnath, the ophthalmologist, igniting explosive short-wicked fireworks on the wooden front porch, using a sparkler as the lighter. Life is full of contradictions, especially in India.

Aarti, Narain's elder daughter, was a tall friendly girl with an easy warmth. She painted the palms of both my hands in complex delicate patterns with *mendi,* a thick henna paste. After the artistic application, I had to sit for several hours without moving my hands while the color stain set, luxuriously doing *nothing* and enjoying the gossip and companionship of a group of women in the family. This was a typical pastime of Indian women, often done for weddings or celebratory events, much like the time spent by women of many cultures doing their hair, makeup, fingernails, and toenails before a wedding. When I was a child in the Midwestern US in the 1950s, women did not seek such elaborate grooming preparations before a wedding. I know it is quite common now for an American bride and her attendants to spend hours in a salon.—I wonder if perhaps this is a recent influence of the East?

After the Diwali ceremony, all the women gathered to cook a special meal together in the kitchen, seated on the floor around an open fire *chulha,* a low stove made of two dried-mud sidewalls about eighteen inches high plastered against a brick wall, far enough apart to balance a *karahi*, an Indian wok. Madhuri the grandmother was the head cook and all the daughters-in-law (doctors, lawyers, etc.), her assistants. I had a side conversation in the kitchen about equality of the sexes in India with Dr. Vaishali, a woman anesthesiologist. She summed it up succinctly: "Women are equal in the workplace, but not in the home." This statement was delivered with a characteristic head wag and raised open palm, for emphasis.

Everyone was talkative and eager to explain their traditional joint-family arrangement. They were proud of living together in a large extended family, and I had the impression that although this was tradition, it was already becoming less common in India. I was told in detail of the six sons (of Mahesh and Madhuri), each of whom were wed in arranged marriages. At the time of my visit, four of the sons lived in this large house with their wives and their own children. Each family—husband, wife and all children—lived in one room of the house. No one complained of this, but they told me "intimate relations need to be very quiet, while the children are sleeping." All contributed labor for running the household, and they had no servants. One brother proudly told me they practiced family planning and "most in the family had only two children." Counting, I realized some actually had three or four. The family was prominent in the village, owning and running the hospital, a nursery business selling plants and seeds, and a large farm adjoining a smaller village a short distance from Jindh. All the sons were college-educated professionals, as were most of their wives. At least two sons were allopathic doctors (like American MDs), one a lawyer, and the eldest son ran the farm. Some in the family, including Mahesh, told me they sought ayurvedic medicine (traditional, from herbs) when they were ill.

At one point Rajendra told me, "You are speaking so slowly, we cannot follow you." People of India, you may know, speak English nearly as fast as they speak Hindi and other Indian languages, at a very fast and rhythmic cadence. I told him I thought it could be my regional Midwestern speech rate and possibly a dialect that he could not understand. I wondered if they might understand an American from the East Coast more. I made a forced effort to speak my native language as fast as I could and even imitated an Indian accent to speed up, unsure how that would come across. I felt embarrassed to myself, wondering if an observer may conclude I was mocking them. Rajendra quickly praised me, "Yes! That is much better speaking; now we can follow you!"

I stayed in a room of the dimly lit hospital across from the large house where the family lived. Except for me, the building seemed empty, but they told me usually four or five patients stayed in the hospital. Later I was given a tour of the "operation theatre," and the lab. I was asked to remove my shoes as a sanitary precaution before entering the operating room. Rajendra showed me a horn preserved in a jar of liquid on the top shelf of his laboratory, proudly explaining that he had surgically removed it from a man's head in the village.

***Journal***

We watched an Indian movie, all of us sitting around the small TV set. When an Indian dance scene came on, the young grandson Lalit played the tabla without smiling, his small hands thumping rapidly from thin wrists. He was very good. We ate *gulab jaman* (a confection made of fried reduced milk balls covered with sweet rose-scented syrup) and discussed Indian formalities toward guests and elders. Mahesh (grandfather and head of household) and I sat on the floor, the others in chairs. He is a real character. His typical dress is a traditional white *dorti,* a long skirt suited to the climate made of a light transparent cotton fabric, pulled forward through the legs and tied at the waist, and a dark plaid Western sports jacket. He teases a lot. He oversees the family agricultural business and has a vast seed collection, mostly ones he ordered from the US. His approach is direct and he is a serious business dealer.

Mahesh told me he did not practice religion, did not take it seriously, though he was an active participant in the Hindi Diwali festivities, like I am in Christmas.

Few are interested in peace concerns or nuclear weapons issues. (Note: I thought they would have been, as members of Servas, a defacto world peace organization. Those ideas were very much on my mind at that time, with President Reagan's massive 1980s nuclear armaments buildup.) They see it as 1) quite pointless, 2) a superpower problem only, in spite of my protest about their greatly-feared enemy Pakistan having nearby nuclear capability along with India's, and most importantly, 3) something to do with their religion as set forth in the Bhagavad Gita, that they accept the reality of a situation. (Note: The Gita asserts "the quintessence of cosmic law, renouncing all actions by the mind, not doing nor causing anything to be done." As family members explained to me, "We do not worry nor imagine the worst in life." And another comment of theirs, "If the Gods will that there is a nuclear war, so be it." (A contrast to a Western "work to change it" philosophy.)

I found it ironic that I should attempt to engage any members of the Baniya-Agrawal joint family in a discussion of conflict resolution when they represented a large group of family members living in harmony, and I from conflict-torn America and a discordant family.

In India, it is OK to pick your nose, scratch your balls and belch loudly. Nobody cares, and I really don't either.

The sari pulled over head a symbol of deference and bondage. I am tired!

***Memoir***

Mahesh Agrawal and his wife, Madhuri, had eight children, six sons and two daughters. I do not recall mention of the two daughters when the family was described to me, nor do I remember their presence during the Diwali festival. In India, most sons live with their parents; I assume the daughters lived with their husbands' parents.

There were many family members and I did my best to learn their names in the few days I was with them. These are the names of the six brothers, their wives and some of the children (Brothers 3 and 4, Narendra and Vaijnath, lived with their wives and children in other nearby towns where they held jobs in their professions):

1. Narain, agriculturist; wife Anju; one daughter Aarti; three sons: Lalit and two other boys

2. Rajendra, doctor with local clinic; wife Dr. Madhuri; two sons, Sambha and Vibhu; one daughter Mohana
3. Narendra, advocate (lawyer); wife Payal (also a lawyer?); at least two sons whose names I don't remember
4. Vaijnath, ophthalmologist; wife Vaishali, anesthesiologist, also qualified as a gynecologist; son Vinod plus other children
5. Amit; wife Nidhi 1 (very friendly, gave me gifts); at least two children
6. Santosh; wife Nidhi 2; I can't recall their children

**Marriage**

Family members I spoke to seemed pleased with their system of arranged marriages. Several explained that the parents arrange a marriage on the basis of similar social status, similar education, and "a good character, as reported by the neighbors." They told me it is important that the parents of the girl host an expensive wedding and pay the groom's family a "sum" (dowry); the equivalent in Indian rupees of $10,000 at the time (1 lakh or 100,000 rupies) will "buy" a decent husband, but $20,000 (2 lakh, 200,000 rupees) will buy an even better one, a professional of high status.

Everyone who talked to me, including the women, thought this was a good system, that the parents had the best interests of their children's lifetime happiness in mind. I had to consider that I was staying in Servas homes, where my hosts had an international outlook and were financially secure, well-educated professionals who respected and treated their children well. Arranged marriage may not go as well in other types of families, where there might be less money for dowries, lower social status, or less psychological insight into the needs of their children. They also told me the child seeking a spouse had the ultimate veto power in the arrangement. Though the prenuptial couple did not spend time dating or getting to know one another before the wedding, if either didn't like the looks or something about the other one, the family would not proceed with a marriage agreement with the other family. From my observations in Servas families, it appeared the arranged marriages resulted in happiness.

I was to discuss the topic years later with a colleague in the US who was from India. She had a "love marriage" and though she loved her husband, told me she regretted the marriage years later in America, after his death. Even though she lived a middle class life in the US and had a career, she felt alone and isolated with only her grown children as a family connection. She related having no financial or emotional support from his family in India, as she would have expected if their marriage had been arranged. As time passed, I was to learn more of the marriages of the Baniyas' children.

In former times in the United States, arranged marriages were not uncommon. My maternal grandparents' marriage was negotiated by Heinrich, my great-grandfather, who selected my grandfather for his daughter from an "appropriate" German family in another state where they had family ties. Parental approval and intervention in marriage selection was expected in my paternal grandparents' community in northern Oklahoma.

**Women**

India is a patriarchal society. Married couples live with the husbands' families where the grandfather is the patriarch, with authority in decisions regarding the future of his grandchildren, i.e., college vs. marriage. The Baniya brothers did not speak of their sisters, who had left the family to live with their husbands' families. Yet, as usual with India, there are contradictions: Indira Gandhi was the second-term elected and beloved prime minister of India in 1983. America has never had a woman elected president. And I am fascinated by this colorful story:

In February 1983 prior to my arrival, the fugitive Bandit Queen Phoolan Devi surrendered to authorities, meeting an unarmed police chief at an agreed-upon place and laying down her rifle before the portraits of Mahatma Gandhi and the goddess *Durga*. She was a most unusual Indian woman, joining a band of *Dacoits* after they abducted her from her village and husband in 1979. She found she liked the life, took a new lover from the gang, and learned to use a rifle for subsequent ransackings of high-caste villages. She spent time in jail, but after release in 1996, used her infamy to advantage in pursuing a successful career in local politics.

. . .

Another of the delights of my visit to the Agrawal/Baniya family was an invitation to join Narain on his daily commute on a local village train to the family farm that he ran. On their land, we sat in casual conversation in an unroofed concrete shelter. After he attended chores, we walked into the nearby village to see a one-thousand-year-old temple made only with bricks, no mortar or cement. I attracted a lot of attention in that tiny secluded hamlet. As we were walking out of the village, a man ran up to Narain with a question. He and his male friends had made bets whether I was a foreigner or an Indian. Some thought I was an Indian because I wore silver ankle chains and a headscarf they thought may be characteristic of the state of Himachal Pradesh. They had never been there and had heard the provincials were white-skinned. I was disappointed to find out the bet was for chai.

In conversation with Mahesh Agrawal, I mentioned contacting a Servas host who was a writer in Agra, whose name was given simply as Raavi. We didn't connect because he had not answered my letter of inquiry. Mr. Agrawal said this man was his friend and that he was an ascetic, a writer-philosopher living in intentional poverty. "He did not answer your letter because he has no money, not even enough for a postal stamp." I regretted not making his acquaintance.

I left Jindh on November 6 with Rajendra, Madhuri, and their kids, headed south toward Rajasthan, in the ambulance with their driver at the wheel. After several hours of travel, we came upon an accident on the road. I felt a surge of adrenaline as we rolled toward the scene, thinking, We'll have to be involved in the rescue; we are in an ambulance. The crash had apparently occurred days before, and no drama or victims were to be found. They had simply abandoned the wrecked vehicle and it stayed where it had crashed, in the middle of the road. The driver steered the ambulance around it.

***Journal***

*Nov. 7, 1983*

Now I have journeyed all day yesterday from Jindh to Jaipur (we left Jindh at 6 a.m., arrived Delhi at 10:30 a.m.) to Madhuri's sister's place. I have acquired an Indian viewpoint and was surprised to observe her clean her own bathroom. I asked her about it (Servas visitors are expected to ask questions) and she said, “You can’t trust servants in Delhi.” The family stayed on in the sister’s house, planning to drive to Jaipur later where Madhuri’s brother lives, but I left Delhi at 12:30 pm on the train, arriving Jaipur at 6:30 pm last night.

I am most unhappy at the moment, staying in Hotel Hindi Name. Though nice, private bath and reasonably clean (40 rupees, $4), the people are annoying. The well-locked door is open at the top! The hotel boys wouldn’t leave me alone, shouting through the door, tried to rattle the doorknob and open it despite my protests, even stood on a chair and peered in through the transom above the door. Want to move to the Evergreen Lodge, where I heard young Westerners stay. (Note: This was in the time before I learned to carry a guidebook.)

…Traveling in India is a test of tolerance. Bad smells, shrill shrieking bus horns, motor Rickshaws rolling forward with the pup, pup, pup, pup engine idle and the driver’s mocking “Hallo, Madaaaaaam….” My neck hurts, my back hurts, my stomach is jumpy. I have no enthusiasm and I hope I muster some soon.

And, later that evening…

I’ve moved to the Evergreen Lodge. It’s like Kathmandu, either hippies dressed in colored rags or self-important British superiors who sit around and talk about how awful the Indians are. One woman actually said this: “I made a phone call, it was alright while he talked English, but then he started yammering away in Indian (she couldn’t think of the word *Hindi*, the name of the language)…. “I said to him,” she continued glibly, “ ‘Speak English!’ ”

And it’s remarkable, really, how hard everyone tries to, educated or not. Here is an endearing effort to write English, chalked on a standing blackboard of the restaurant by one of the lodge staff:

*Menu*

| Snacks | Rs. |
|---|---|
| Finger chips | 2.50 |
| Chees pakora | 3.50 |
| Vegetable pakora | 2.50 |
| Banana filter | 3.00 |
| Cold chocklet | 3.00 |
| Cold caffee | 2.50 |
| Cornflax w, milk | 2.50 |
| Rice puting | 3.50 |
| Poridge w; milk | 2.50 |

### *Memoir*

I ordered a snack and sat around for a few hours. I watched a group of colorfully dressed young French people. They seemed unfocused, noncommunicative, maybe junkies. It wasn't like the way I remembered my 1973 trip, with open sharing and easy friendships. It seemed an almost narcissistic self-involvement had set in among the world travelers. In the early evening, I watched an energetic performance of Rajasthani gypsy drummers and veiled dancers in the small hotel's open courtyard. There was no privacy in that hotel. All the charpoy beds were lined up side-by-side in a huge room.

Madhuri had given me the number of her brother's house in Jaipur and I called it. To my good fortune, Rajendra and Madhuri had just arrived in town. I described the Evergreen Lodge to them, and within an hour they arrived in the ambulance to collect me. *Rescue* is a more accurate word. I didn't spend even one night there at the Evergreen. I'll never forget meeting Rupali Mahawar, their lovely sixteen-year-old niece, who hopped out the back door of the ambulance with a bright smile and warm, welcoming greetings. She was a student and eager to practice her fluent English. I observed with interest that I was much more at ease and comfortable with this Indian family than I had been with the unfriendly and aloof Europeans and Americans at the Evergreen hotel.

I, together with Madhuri, Rajendra, and their children, all stayed with Rupali's family in their small home in Jaipur. Rupali's dad (Madhuri's brother) told me in a conversation at the kitchen table that his goal was to live in America, where he could become rich. I told him that he was already rich because his life seemed so good in India. I tried to talk about the stress entailed in living in America, but it's hard to describe it to someone who's never lived in that tension. He was to find out many years later.

Comfortable now in my new home base, I spent a great day seeing the sights around Jaipur on my own. I walked through a mirrored palace and marveled at huge polished silver urns. The City Palace museum featured fabulous costumes from the days of the Raj. I was taken by a shimmering wedding costume made entirely of gold thread, head-to-toe, worn by a Maharani (Indian princess) in old times. It was designed in the traditional Rajasthani style, very similar to what women were still wearing on the streets outside: not a sari, but a multi-paneled, gored skirt which hung luxuriantly from the hips to the floor in a wide diameter, just concealing the feet. A long, fitted blouse was worn over the skirt top. This dress cast a golden influence on the wedding dress I would craft for myself four years later.

I was fascinated by the astronomical instruments of Jai Singh (born in 1688, a Maharaja of the kingdom of Amber, which later became Jaipur). One could walk and climb among these huge pieces outside the palace in his Jantar Mantar observatory built in the 1700s. The tall, sculpturally beautiful black-and-white sundial works as an accurate clock. Jai Singh was an expert in advanced mathematical calculations.

**Trip to Ajmer**

Madhuri's sister's family (including Rupali and her younger brother, Rahul) joined us for continued travels in the ambulance to Ajmer, a smaller town with a temple. As the landscape and passing fields transitioned into drier and sandier terrain, I noticed peacocks walking through scrub trees and green parakeets darting in the branches. I felt relaxed and happy in Rajasthan.

Eight-year-old Rahul could not hold his head upright in the bumpy ride. His small head bobbed back and forth rapidly as we rode. I feared for his obviously weak neck. Rupali told me, "Yes, he has problems. We don't know how he will turn out. That is up to him." Responsibility was clearly assigned to the handicapped individual. I guessed that teenaged Rupali's comments reflected her parents' and India's cultural attitudes. As I was to learn years later, their high expectations for him afforded him some practical opportunities offered by the extended-family network.

We stayed in Ajmer with more of their relatives, who generously accommodated me along with both traveling families. In the morning, all were invited to climb into the bed with Madhuri and Rajendra. I recall many of us sitting together on the bed, yawning, having our morning tea. I thought of my visit to the Indian family in Patna, where Andrea and I were invited to recline on our hosts' bed within hours of our acquaintance.

A fact of travel in India: occasional stomach ailments. Dr. Madhuri cured mine with a pleasantly herbal tasting medicine. She reassured me of its mild and natural properties "because it's ayurvedic." It was effective, with no side effects.

My trip was nearly over. I had worked it out to take a night train from Ajmer to Delhi with just enough time to catch my return flight home. The last train to Delhi was due to arrive at any minute, but we were still in the sitting room of their house. Rajendra remained in relaxed repose on a setee, one leg draped over the arm, unimpressed by my plea to get to the station.

"Don't worry. There is plenty of time," he told me.

I was delivered to the station in the nick of time, boarding a train in early evening in Ajmer. I climbed up to my reserved top berth. Most of the other berths in the compartment, three-tiered, were unoccupied. As the all-night journey to Delhi wore on, I fell fast asleep. In the middle of the night, I awoke, astonished to see many, many people in there, all asleep. All the reserved berths supported comfortable sleepers. Others slumped, snoozing, in every remaining square inch of space: the aisle, the floor, the end of a bench next to someone's curled torso. Apparently they'd boarded in various stops during the night and seated themselves silently so as not to disturb those already in slumber.

**Delhi**

*Nov. 10, 1983*

For my last day in India, I dressed in a sari. It took a few tries to wind it properly, as I recalled my lessons from Benares and Madhuri Baniya. A properly fitting sari should graze the ground in walking. Saris are woven in the width of an average Indian woman's height from waist to toe, but this measure was a good four inches high-water on me. I noticed finger pointing and giggles from women because my skinny bare ankles showed—I must have looked pretty silly by Indian standards.

I put away my camera and walked down the street in my red sari. Everything changed! Rickshaw drivers stopped hassling me and dropped the price in half. Even though I was obviously a Westerner, they presumed I was not a tourist. I wished I'd thought of doing this earlier.

There remained one last task. I took a motor rickshaw to the Safdarjung Hospital to visit an occupational therapist in her rehabilitation clinic. It was a delight to meet Dr. Mrs. Sujata, OTR, who had trained in Los Angeles at the Jean Ayres Sensory Integration Clinic, held in high esteem in my profession. She told me the OTs at her hospital had assumed the title *Dr.* to improve their image and respect. (It did not reflect advanced studies.)

We had nice talks and found much common ground. She commented favorably that I wore a sari. I observed patients highly motivated to do their therapy exercises, not something always seen in my OT clinic in Portland. I mentioned it to Sujata, and she said, "They understand it is a privilege to be here. They live in villages far away and know they must make the most of this opportunity to recover (from strokes or injuries)." She described her work in rural villages helping newly handicapped women be able to work again in their kitchens. At that time, everything in Indian kitchens was close to the ground, the cooking fire, washing things, and storage. She enabled the women to move around the floor on scooter boards. She also worked with children at the hospital. We corresponded for a couple of years after that. I sent her a book that she wanted, and she sent me a beautiful sari. Sadly, the last letter I sent to Sujata, recently, was returned to me from India, "Unknown recipient" stamped in English.

That night I boarded the plane for home and flew through the Pacific night in a Thai Airways jumbo jet bound for the US. As though it never happened, I left my brief but memorable life spent in India those weeks, immersed in Indian crowds and culture, and roared back to Western life, job, supermarkets, rush, rush.

**Return Home to Portland**

A note written to myself on a little scrap of paper I had tucked in a pocket of my lab coat, a few days after returning to work at the hospital:

> Less than one week ago, I was in the Ladies' waiting area of the Delhi train station, watching the women brush their long black hair and fix their saris. I was waiting for dawn, when I could find a motor rickshaw into town. When it was light enough I left, walking down a dirty street of old Delhi, a spectacle, a solitary Western woman with a backpack. Everyone gave me a different story. Finally got some reasonable advice from two European hippies.

Newly home from India, I set to work. I sent letters of inquiry to galleries in Portland with Sunita's art photos. I sent my friends in India duplicate photo prints of themselves. I posted a copy of the Brazelton Neonatal Evaluation that Sujata the OT wanted.

I joined a book order club, as I'd promised Mahesh Agrawal. Through willing Servas travelers like me, he ordered English language books that he could not access in India at the time. His idea was to pay me by sending Indian goods of equal value, no money exchanged. This proved to be quite a task, and costly, as it required I send a box of books to him in India once a month, and I didn't really want or need any trinkets. I wrote to him, politely discontinuing the operation within a couple of months.

***Journal***

***Final Entry Three Months after the Trip***

> *Mar. 1, 1984*
>
> Only in the past few weeks has the full impact hit me, I'm not there anymore. At first, the experience was so recent that it seemed very tangible. Now, I realize, it is so far away, thousands of miles away and in some ways, hundreds of years away. Yet, India is very much touched by the West, not as isolated as it was 10 years ago. The lifestyle here (US) is so different. I feel sad. My memory is still strong, but I'm not there.

. . .

I continued to write letters to Rajendra, Madhuri, and Mahesh for a couple of years. Correspondence was all business with Mr. Agrawal. At one point Madhuri answered a letter, stating she was dictating her letter through Rajendra's pen, because she was waiting for henna to dry on her hands and could not write. Years later, she told me the henna was just an excuse, that she'd asked him to translate because she was not confident of her written English.

Rupali Mahawar and I continued to exchange letters and aerogrammes for several years after the trip, developing a friendship through shared feelings, gossip, and ideas. In observations and reflections, we made an effort to explain our respective cultures to the other. She wrote with concern of "Aarti's misfortune." Apparently Aarti's grandfather (Mahesh) decided that marriage was a better option than college study for her. Rupali told me that her own parents were broadminded and had agreed that, when she was ready and if she wanted, she could have a "love-marriage" rather than an arranged marriage. Aarti's story progressed in several more letters from Rupali: the family found a suitable husband for her, she agreed to go ahead with the marriage, became pregnant, then was raising children, and the final letter of the story, "To my surprise I found Aarti very happy and her husband is also very nice fellow." Fast forward to an email from Rajendra in 2009 with news of Aarti: "She is happy there (in a town where she lives with her husband). Her son is now a computer engineer."

. . .

In reflecting on this second trip, I enjoyed my nostalgic return to the intense sensate experience. I thought of details in an Indian landscape: stunning colors of the women's saris, the sun striking water jugs atop womens' heads, the tinkle of glass bangles sliding down a moving arm. I was able to scratch the cultural surface a bit more through friendships with Indians. I met the German medical students Marianne and Gabrielle in Nepal, another start to a long cross-cultural friendship. I learned to wrap a sari and realized at journey's end that I should have been wearing one. I was most happy spending time with Indian families in daily life. I understood a little more, especially an appreciation for the complexity of the Indian culture. Yet, many mysteries remain. How could the people living on the streets or in the slums of India, destitute, smile so genuinely? Why do Westerners come home from India so happy?

**Calcutta 1983**
*Top:* Attendants on rooftop of my hotel, Sutter Street
*Bottom:* Street vendor and his friends selling Chai
Photos by Marjorie Kircher

Calcutta laundry 1983

Photo by Marjorie Kircher

**Nepal 1983**
*Top:* Center of Kathmandu;
*Bottom:* Pokhara

Photos by Marjorie Kircher

**On the Jomson trek, Nepal 1983**
*Top:* Marianne and Gabrielle taking a rest
*Bottom:* Waiting for dinner in a village

Photos by
Marjorie Kircher

Enroute to Ghorepani, along the Jomsom Trek

Photos by Marjorie Kircher

View from Poon Hill, Jomsom trek
Dhaulagiri and Annapurna peaks

Photo by Marjorie Kircher

Marjorie lending a hand with dinner
Patna, India

**Holy River Ganges, Varanasi 1983**
*Top:* Bathers at the ghats
*Bottom:* Funeral pyres at the burning ghats
Photos by Marjorie Kircher

**Marjorie sitting in Buddha's chair, 1983**
Sarnath, archaeological sight near Benares (Varanasi)

Timer photo by Marjorie Kircher

**Haryana 1983**
*Top:* Madhuri preparing bread at the chulha for Diwali meal
*Bottom:* Marjorie at Narain's farm
Top photo by Marjorie Kircher

**Rajasthan 1983**
*Top:* Sweeper in front of Jaipur City Palace
*Bottom:* Holy Man
Photos by Marjorie Kircher

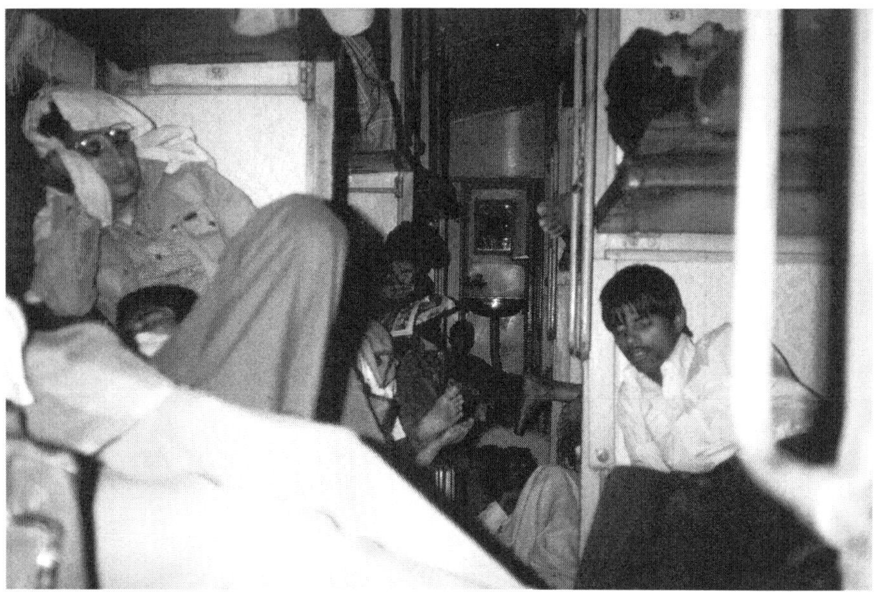

Night Train to Delhi

Photo by Marjorie Kircher

**Delhi 1983**
Movie house near Connaught Circus

Photo by Marjorie Kircher

**Motor Rickshaws, Delhi 1983**

*Top:* Larger, built on a Harley
*Bottom:* Smaller, built on a scooter

Photos by Marjorie Kircher

# Part III

## India, 1997

The year after my return trip to India, I met Mitch, who enjoyed my travel stories. We married in 1987 and developed our shared lives and professional work. We traveled to Europe a few times, always including a visit to Berlin. We worked together on a giant project—building a house designed by Mitch, who is my favorite architect. By the mid 1990s, we were moved in and settling. I had taken a turn to fine art painting, and Mitch was perfecting his licks on the pedal steel guitar. He started a new band he was especially fond of, playing old Western swing tunes. It was a creative time in our lives, and our imaginings turned to broader world travel. I convinced him to travel to India, a part of the world he'd never seen. We traveled for three weeks in December 1997 and early January 1998. The length of my visits to India grew shorter with each return, reflecting my life of increasing obligations and responsibilities at home, a typical human course of maturation, as well as the shrinking American vacation. Business colleagues and friends admonished us for being away for three weeks, about three times longer than most Americans take away from their job and home lives.

. . .

In late September 1997, I contacted Jindh and received this reply in an aerogramme from Rajendra:

> Dear Marjorie and Mitch,
> Thank you very much for your kind letter dated Sept. 29, 1997, received just now. We are all thrilled to know you will be

visiting India and sparing some days for Jindh. We will be waiting for you.

We were busy with celebration of 75th year of birth of my father, 50th year of my birth and 25th year of marriage of Madhuri and myself, all one day celebrated 21-9-97. It was a gala celebration just like a marriage party. About 700 guests were there at dinner. To organize all that was a big job.

There is lot of change after your last visit. Number of new additions, new faces, new set up. I am sure you will find a big change in India as a whole. We will all like to meet Mr. Mitch who must be a good personality. I am sure he must be feeling good to visit India. Might be his first visit.

My daughter was married last year. She has a little baby girl. Everything is going fine with our joint big family. For that we are thankful to Almighty God and well-wishers like you. We are all eagerly waiting for your visit to Jindh. It will be O.K. if you can spare more time for us. Please convey our regards to Mr. Mitch.

With thanks and due regards,
Yours,
Rajendra Baniya

***Memoir***

In September prior to our trip, my good friend Marianne happened to be visiting us from Berlin, on her third trip to Portland. You will remember I met her in a Himalayan village of Nepal in 1983.

She had recently traveled in the south of India, one of many return trips she had taken to the subcontinent after 1983, which included some of the areas we were planning to go on this trip. She spoke fondly of places she'd enjoyed, making notes in the margins of our new guidebook. By now we both fancied ourselves old India hands, and I appreciated her advice.

It seemed fitting that Marianne was with us when we heard the news of Mother Teresa's death in Calcutta September 5, 1997. And just five days before that, together we'd listened to the shocking news that Lady Diana, Princess of Wales, was killed with her Egyptian boyfriend, Dodi, in a high-speed car crash in Paris. As I will always remember where I was and who I was with when I heard the news of JFK's assassination, the memories of Mother Teresa's and Princess Di's deaths will always be paired with my memory of Marianne's visit. It is another point of intersection of our lives, usually spent far apart on different continents.

. . .

Mitch and I both wrote in journals, at least through the first part of our trip, and I relied on these notes to tell this last story. As before, direct entries from the journals are set apart and noted under the heading *Journal. Mitch's* or *Marjorie's* entries are noted accordingly.

Most of the story is told in retrospective under the heading *Memoir.* We both took good cameras and our memories of this trip are much enhanced by Mitch's excellent photography skills.

At the time of our trip, India was approaching a population of one billion people, double the number of people who lived there when I visited in 1973. Prime Minister Inder Kumar Gujral was serving his brief one-year tenure as prime minister. He had been a freedom fighter as an eleven-year-old child in 1931 Punjab, and in 1997, was caught amidst the crossfires of stormy political times and complicated party conflicts. We saw politicians' campaign posters plastered on walls and heard campaign slogans blaring from loud speakers on donkey carts rolling through cities and towns throughout India, the largest democracy in the world.

***Journals***

*Dec. 14, 1997*
*En route, Singapore Airlines*
*Marjorie*
We're in Singapore waiting for our flight to New Delhi and we're pretty travel-weary now. We're up to 32 hours (travel time). Singapore is in the Tropics, 90 degrees F. and thick air. A calm place, very Western. Electronic Christmas music blaring from a keyboard seems odd in SE Asia. We went to a Chinese Taoist temple which was pretty cool. Tables and tables of food prepared for the deities—whole yellow chickens and

ducks laid out. Who takes it away, and at what stage of decay? Squatter loo's are sparkling clean.

*Arrival in Delhi*
*Mitch, on the Taxi Ride into Town*
10:30 pm
Somehow we made it to our hotel in one piece. The guy sitting next to the driver, who picked us up, was hiding his eyes and holding his head in fear as we honked our way into town. (Note: the fearful front seat passenger was sent by the hotel to pick us up at the airport and escort us to our lodging.)

*And his entry the next morning:*
*Dec. 15*
We met some nice Irish folks that arrived early this a.m. at Master Guest House over breakfast. After which we repeatedly braved the traffic in little auto rickshaws. The exhaust fumes were unimaginable. I felt like I had smoked a carton of cigarettes in one day. The drivers are amazing. Driving within inches of each other as they all speed along the little and big streets dodging each other, elephants, cars, cows, beggars, monkeys, buses and trucks. It was much scarier than the Wild Mouse ride (at the Texas State fair). Quite a blast!

*Marjorie, same day*
We spent the day in the streets getting information for our trip to Jindh. The big excitement was five scary auto-rickshaw rides, careening through the streets of Old Delhi like a car-chase scene in a John Woo movie. Poor, desperate humanity looming on one side of the street, near-misses with elephants, other rickshaws, heavy Tata trucks and little Trabbi-like Indian cars to the other. Our eyes, noses and throats are on fire from the Delhi smog.

***Memoir***

The weather in the north was surprisingly cold (maybe 40° F), and the houses and lodgings were not heated. We were always cold. I put on a lot of clothes, two pairs of Indian cotton pants and two shirts under my fleece jacket. The atmosphere was very dark, eerily dark. No sign of the sun, just a choking haze. I lost my voice and was not even sick, probably a result of the pollution from two-stroke engines, then on many of the abundant scooters and auto rickshaws, and many open wood fires on pavements.

On this trip, I wore only saris and Indian Punjabi dress (getting to be known in the West by the Pakistani name Salwar Kameez, a long light-weight dress slit up both sides over baggy pants, tight at the ankles). The sari dress was well-received and commented upon by the Indians, especially the men. They frequently thanked me "for wearing our dress."

***Journal***

*Dec. 16*

*Marjorie*

If yesterday in Delhi was John Woo, today is Mad Max. Took a rusty rickety bus to Jindh (in Haryana state, north of Delhi), to introduce Mitch to the Baniyas, my old friends. The bus left from a parking lot in the old part of Delhi—a worn, grease-stained surface, broken concrete with weeds pushing through. For two-thirds of the journey, the sights along the road looked apocalyptic. Big mud holes in front of junky store fronts with rusting hulls of abandoned trucks and buses leaning against falling down hut structures with huge stacks of old truck tires in between. From this, you might expect children wandering in tattered rags, but not so. Children emerged from this, neatly pressed in smart school uniforms with clean white shirts and neatly braided pigtails toting book bags and smiling eagerly.

***Memoir***

At every place the bus stopped, more and more people boarded, squeezing four onto a seat meant for two and packing the aisles. Mitch's usual calm demeanor and good manners remained just that, as he offered to hold the large baskets of those who stood without seats.

Though it seemed there was less poverty than in 1973, there was also more industrial trash. A stench filled the air, the "acrid smell of burning tires," (as our friend Becky called it on a postcard from her trip to India shortly after ours). We breathed choking black smoke from factories along the way to Jindh, many miles away from Delhi. The road scene reminded me of Mad Max/Road Warrior movies.

***Journal***

*Dec. 16, continued*

*Marjorie*

On this road trip, I saw few signs of the sleepy 18th century Indian villages I remember from my trips to India in 1973 and 1983. The bus ride itself was really freaky! In India they drive on the left side of the road like the British, but this bus driver was always on the right, passing, or in between the lanes, squeezing between a tanker truck marked "highly flammable" and an auto rickshaw or horse-drawn cart with fat bald recycled truck tires. At one point he braked hard to a dead stop in the middle of the road. There was a loud clattering sound as several metal parts fell from the bus scattering across the pavement. Mitch said, "I hope we haven't hurt anyone." I imagined a flattened rickshaw driver and his passenger beneath the wheels. There were hushed murmurs. The driver and some helpers jumped onto the road, gathered the metal parts, threw them on the top luggage rack of the bus, and returned to their seats, without a word of explanation. On we went, speeding along the narrow road, passing within inches of all forms of animals, humans and other vehicles, tailgating more tanker trucks with the skull and crossbone DANGER symbols painted on their back bumpers.

At last we arrived in Jindh. Immediately a huge crowd gathered to stare and discuss us. We managed to locate a telephone and call our friends. Soon Rajendra arrived, this time attired in dark suit and tie. In 1983, his clothing was white loose-fitting Indian pajamas.

> There were other changes. Rajendra told us the town had increased threefold in fourteen years since my visit in 1983. Living arrangements of the joint family had changed considerably. Before, many family members lived under one roof. Now, most of the sons and their families had moved out and set up their own households in separate houses or buildings or had left town. Every wife had her own kitchen, but had to do a lot more work than in the past, when they used to share the work in one kitchen. One son's family still lived in the old house with the grandparents Mahesh and Madhuri Agrawal. Most of the rooms had TV sets now. The teenagers had the luxury of their own rooms in most houses. I think there may be a joint ownership of all the houses and buildings, not sure the terms.

***Memoir***

The larger old family house had been changed in a remodel. They had enclosed the front porch, from where we'd set off fireworks on Diwali, 1983, into a two-story gift shop. The chulha was gone, the dried mud open-wood-fire stove that used to be on the kitchen floor, replaced with a Western-style, Indian-made stove using fossil fuel such as compressed gas. (Traditional chulhas, still used by other people in India, have since been redesigned with a chimney and now hold two pots, for better efficiency and improved indoor air quality.) All other appliances and counters in the Agrawal/Baniya kitchens were now mounted at waist level. This represented a major change in kitchen ergonomics, requiring the cook to stand rather than squat while preparing food. Standing to work is easier on the knees, but probably harder on the back. A natural air-circulation system had also been added to the house structure—a huge open-air well/vent in the center of all floors facilitated air currents moving upward throughout the house. Mitch was fascinated by this. Fossil fuel energy at world market prices has always been very costly to Indians, and where used, comprises a larger percentage of most people's household budgets than in richer countries, so this was a sensible low-cost alternative to Western-style, fuel-intensive refrigerated air.

It was wonderful to see this large family again, to see how the kids had grown up, what they were doing, who they'd married, and to meet the newest generation of little children. Everyone was pleased that we made the journey back to Jindh to see them. They remembered me, and each one in turn greeted us with warm smiles, happy to meet my husband.

The gift shop on the front of the house was patronized by local customers in the town. It was run by Lalit, the son of Narain and Anju and the serious one who, at nine years old on my previous visit, had played the tabla and made a colored Diwali lantern. We met Lalit's new wife, Achla, and cute little daughter, Isha, in their own home. Achla was a beautiful and warm young woman, bright and gracious with intelligent eyes. We were told she spoke several languages.

The weather continued to be cold, with an overcast sky. I felt disappointed, having anticipated pleasant warmth for our winter vacation near the equator, with memories of India heat. I was unaware that we'd been complaining a lot about the cold, but Madhuri noticed. When she asked with slight annoyance, "Isn't it cold where *you* live?" we stopped talking about it. We didn't mention our central heating with programmable thermostat and our high-efficiency wood stove in Oregon.

**Rajendra and Madhuri**

Madhuri and Rajendra had closed the hospital and their medical practice and moved into the building to make their home. No more ambulance. Rajendra regretted not being able to practice state-of-the-art medicine in a village because of shortages of money, equipment, and trained staff. A patient died of a heart attack. Madhuri grew tearful during Rajendra's telling of the story. We were not sure what had happened, but it was clear they thought they should not practice medicine in the village now.

This story seemed hauntingly similar to the state of rural medicine in the US in recent times. I had wanted to believe that somewhere far from my home, like a village in rural India, things still ran on trust and good intentions, considering fate in matters of life and death. This must have been difficult—both Rajendra and Madhuri were proud doctors and had been devoted to their medical careers. Rajendra had served some years before as a high official in the Indian Medical Association. In any event, the doctor couple persevered and carried on with life, as the story will unfold.

They were our hosts this visit. We stayed nights with them in their converted hospital. Madhuri cooked delicious meals and snacks, serving Rajendra and us seated at the table. She would never join us to eat when we asked her to (mumbling something about being too big, pointing to her abdomen) but kept serving each of us more food. We kept eating politely until we realized we needed to say, "Stop," to end the flow of food from the kitchen. We also received invitations for meals in other family homes. It seemed to be normal for the women to serve the men and the guests without seating themselves at the table.

Unfortunately Mitch and I both got sick there. Rajendra gave us a powerful allopathic medicine for stomach ailments that cured us quickly but kept us awake all night, perhaps containing amphetamine-like additives. I reminded him of the milder ayurvedic medicine Madhuri had given me on my first visit. He replied, "We would not have given you ayurvedic medicine, because we are allopathic doctors. This is what we believe." It seemed to me a medical rift may have developed in the family over the fourteen years. They were taking firmer sides on the two medicines, with Rajendra and Madhuri on the allopathic side, Mahesh and Narain taking the ayurvedic cause. Two of Narain's adult sons and daughters-in-law were now ayurvedic-educated doctors. What changes or experiences in the interim could have caused such a now-firm position in Rajendra and Madhuri?

Rajendra was busy at his new business, the Aptech computer school franchises. (Aptech is an IT training organization headquartered in Bombay, with schools located in several emerging countries throughout the world.) He had one set up in Jindh, in the first floor of their old hospital dwelling, and another in a nearby town, which his son Sambha operated. They taught timely computer skills to villagers and rented out computer time for personal use. Their computers were connected to the Internet, bringing their village into the modern digital age.

Rajendra devoted a lot of his time to involvement with the Lions Club International, a source of pride for him. He gave us a silken banner he found in a cupboard, decorated in gold fringe, with a sketch of two Hindu gods, one with a bow and quiver on his back (Lord Rama), having just stepped out of his waiting chariot, bowing before another, maybe Lord Vishnu, who is in a wide stance, giving Rama a blessing with an open palm. The words on the banner, written in English, named him "District Governor of Lions Club" beneath the words "Consolidate and Act."

He also gave us a large metal brooch, enameled red and green with a golden canoe crew rowing under an embossed Lions Club insignia and "Dr. Rajendra Baniya, Distt. (sic) Governor," inscribed across the top and just beneath that, "India, Consolidate and Act," inscribed above the heads of the rowers. I have kept these mementos.

Rajendra told us one of the charitable actions of the local Lions Club was giving blankets to pavement dwellers. As anyone involved in charity work can relate, he had doubts of the outcome of their good deed, suspecting that some of the blanket recipients may have sold them later to buy drink.

**Madhuri, Rajendra's Wife**

Madhuri told us she continued practicing medicine at that time, seeing a few patients on a part-time basis in a downstairs clinic. It was obvious she had more household duties without the women of the joint family sharing tasks. We would hear her up late in the kitchen washing dishes. As an outside observer, I felt sorry for her, then realized this is not so different from my own life at home, doing household duties late at night before going to work the next day. Women the world over seem to have so much more to do, with the complexities of running a modern household consuming precious time we may have had for ourselves. I think all of us who have pursued careers face this conflict of time, especially when raising children. In India at that time, the cook prepared everything from scratch, even foods I buy in store-bought packages and take for granted, such as yogurt, bread, and canned tomatoes.

**Mahesh Das Agrawal**

The family patriarch was waiting for us the next morning, receiving us on his wide bed where he sat cross-legged, busy pulverizing an herbal substance into a fine paste with a mortar and pestle.

"I am preparing an ayurvedic treatment for a friend." He remembered me after all those years, greeting me with a wide smile. He turned to Mitch and said simply, "She loves India."

I was very happy to see Mahesh again, appearing in good health, thin as usual, with a wise, humored glint in his eye. This now seventy-five-year-old man had an awesome presence. I again felt a rapport with him, some fourteen years later. He was a social observer, readily recognizing and commenting on folly, even in some of the activities and obsessions of his own family members. He now openly disdained allopathic medicine, though two of his sons and two of his daughters-in-law were allopathic physicians, the Indian equivalent of MDs.

**Madhuri, Family Matriarch and Mahesh's wife**

I was very pleased Madhuri remembered me. She did not speak English but communicated with warm, welcoming smiles, twinkling eyes, and gestures. A gold-filled tooth flashed in a smile, quickly covered by the extended fingers of one hand as the other reached for the end of her sari to cover her head.

***Journals***

*Dec. 17*

*Mitch*

Mr. Agrawal is very curious and sharp. Everyone serves us tea, all day long.

*Marjorie*

I notice that both Madhuri and Mahesh Agrawal have trouble walking up stairs now; looks like knee problems. I was expecting they wouldn't have these issues, with all the cross-legged floor sitting they do. I thought their knee joints and tendons would be more supple from the constant stretching. Doesn't look much different than couch-sitting knees in the West. They don't get other exercise from what I can see.

In one of the rooms in the main house belonging to a teenaged girl, we sat cross-legged on the bed with its occupant and her grandfather Mahesh Das. She was doing her advanced mathematics homework while watching Indian-style MTV. We all stared at the screen too, watching the music videos. I asked her what her plans were for the math studies. She replied, "I have no ambition."

Amit and Nidhi invited us to dinner. She is such a good cook! I remember her openness and generosity from before. She gave me gifts, little remembrances, in 1983.

***Memoir***

**Narain and Anju**

On the small local train we took with them to the family farm outside Jindh, a heated argument in Hindi (or another regional language*) erupted between a couple of men, heads wound in plaid cotton cloth with the fringed edges hanging over their dark, lean foreheads. I asked Narain what they were shouting about. "Politics; there is an election soon." I appreciated how seriously people in rural India took political issues and their democracy.

*The most common languages spoken in Haryana state are English, Hindi, Punjabi, Urdu and Haryanvi, similar to Hindi.

When we arrived at the farm, some of the hired workers and their wives were squatting around an outside fire. They beckoned us to join them and pulled up wooden chairs for Narain, Anju, and us to sit on. I can still feel the welcome heat. A farmer's wife pulled the edge of her dark-red transparent sari over her head and face, a traditional gesture of modesty not seen these days in the cities. I had a great time walking with Narain through the exotic flowering plants he was growing for his nursery business, now much expanded. Some I recognized, but he had so many unusual ones.

They had built a two-room dwelling there since my last visit, when Narain and I sat talking in a roofless concrete space. Anju placed a little clay bowl with glowing coals in the center of the small bedroom where we gathered. We relished any warmth we could find at all, and ignored the smoke filling the room.

At the end of the day, we walked to the nearby village to catch a train back to Jindh. It was dark, and they did not have electricity. Outdoors, villagers had kerosene camp lanterns and fires going in waist-high-mud-kiln-type stoves that we could warm our hands over. We sipped steamy glasses of sweet milky tea. The air was crisp and clear, with stars visible above the village night. Here I recognized the old India I'd seen in former trips and felt a nostalgic sadness. As before, the trip to the land was one of the highlights of the Jindh journey; for Mitch too.

**Rahul**

Rahul, the unusual eight-year-old boy in 1983 Jaipur whose sister had pronounced his future "up to him," was now living in Jindh with Rajendra and Madhuri, his uncle and paternal aunt. (Rahul's father was Madhuri's brother.) He remembered me, too. Rahul gave up his room for Mitch and me and slept on a couch in the front sitting room. Rajendra had enrolled him in an Aptech course to learn computer skills so he would be employable. Now twenty-two-years-old, Rahul had grown into a polite and engaged person, and there was hope for his future.

His sister, Rupali, told me after our trip (months later on the phone) that he longed for a wife. The family had agreed to do what they could, though it may be difficult to match him, as he continued to be "unusual." And later, "Rahul is married. They found him a simple village girl who knows handicrafts, and they are happy." And much later, twelve years more, "Rahul has two kids, and they are *normal!*"

**Hinduism and the Agrawal/Baniyas, a Few Observations**

Our friends were eager to show us their small temple in Jindh. It was evening, and they pointed out the larger-than-life plaster of paris statues of Hindu gods standing in the shadows of the anteroom portico.

Once I asked Rajendra if he had ever eaten fish (because I had read that Hindus in the south often did), to which he replied, "I have never eaten flesh."

As we were departing Jindh, I went to say goodbye to Mahesh Das Agrawal. I told him, "You have a wonderful family!"

He answered, "We love God, that is all." (In 1983, he had told me he did not practice religion.) He and the rest of the family had always practiced traditional Hindu vegetarianism and observed the holy days, such as Diwali (Deepavali).

Each morning after breakfast Madhuri saw to it that a bucket of warm water was brought for our bath. On the morning of our departure, I told her I would not bathe, expecting a grimy train ride. In my mind, I thought not bathing would also be doing a good deed on two cultural counts: I would be conserving precious water in India and not being such a "clean" American. However, Madhuri was astonished that I would go unwashed through a day. I recalled that ritual daily bathing is important to Hindus and quickly redeemed myself: "On second thought, I'd love that bucket of hot water." She nodded, smiling, and seemed relieved.

In an email to come later, Rajendra signed it "God Bless You."

***Journal***

*Dec. 19*

*Marjorie*

In early morning we rode a bicycle rickshaw to the bus station where we departed from our dear friends in Jindh, headed for a nearby town. Rajendra had insisted we go there as part of his host itinerary for us, to visit their 21 year-old son Sambha and view the family's second Aptech Computer School franchise that he directed. Sambha seemed happy to receive us. Though he told us he worked 12-hour days in the school, he generously took the afternoon off to show us his town, including a University campus and a museum.

***Memoir***

**Arranged Marriage Story**

In the course of the day's conversation, I mentioned to Sambha that I liked his cousin Lalit's new wife, Achla. He told me a story: Lalit was originally betrothed to another girl. The marriage had been agreed upon with her family and his. (They did not know each other but were new acquaintances around the engagement, as is typical in arranged marriages.) The family then learned of Achla's availability for marriage, from a family well-known to them in a nearby village. Sambha and his grandfather (Mahesh Agrawal) were so taken by Achla that they appealed to Lalit to break his engagement and marry her instead. Lalit resisted, expressing an obligation to the first young woman, but eventually his relatives convinced him to change fiancés. Everyone was happy, at the time.

. . .

We had planned to spend the day visiting Sambha in his town, intending to board an evening train to Agra, giving us just two days to see the Taj Mahal. Sambha was late getting us to the train, and we missed the connection. He may have intentionally delayed us to extend the visit. We learned that his landlord, a Lions Club friend of his dad, wanted to meet us and insisted we stay the night in his home. He and his wife were gracious hosts, though I didn't have the energy that evening to be a proper guest.

I didn't feel well after dinner in their house. Luckily we still had some of Rajendra's stomach medicine, but that meant another lost night of sleep, from whatever else was in those pills. Under other circumstances, it would have been interesting to talk more with Rajendra's friends. He was a farmer and had studied agricultural pesticides; his wife had studied English literature and economics. Their son was studying to be a structural engineer.

The next morning we stood on the train platform in the cold smoky mist of the early hours, an hour ahead of the train's scheduled arrival. It was not possible to reserve seats out of this town (reservations were available only for major station departures) and I wanted to be there ahead of time, worried we'd miss the train again. The train finally rolled in two hours late, visibly packed with people. The waiting crowd of passengers on the platform had only minutes to board before it departed. The throng of bodies started inching forward into that compression I'd come to know so well in India, moving with tiny steps, applying increasing pressure, closer and closer together en masse toward the impatient train.

Sambha moved us aside, intending to help us find the best car to board. He walked up and down, looking through the windows at the passengers inside, taking his time to find just the right group for us, as we sweated we'd miss it again. Finally, indicating a car with a motion of his hand, he said, "That one."

Mitch stepped on and the train started to move with me left on the platform! I leaped onto the high metal stair, heavy pack on my back, grabbed a handle and leaned into Mitch's pack as he pressed into the crush of people overflowing into the outside space between the cars of the jam-packed train. A thought about my jumpy stomach and the past night's problem, but never mind that. This was our only chance to see the Taj

Mahal and we had already missed one of our Taj days. A tightly scheduled Western itinerary had smacked up against Indian village life.

***Journal***

*Mitch (on our visit in Sambha's town)*

We saw a very beautiful Krishna museum: NO PHOTOS!!! Air is fresh and traffic is light with only a few horns. I am getting stiff from spending so much time in bed trying to stay warm. India time is unusual. Tomorrow we vow to get up early and get to Agra no matter what. (Note: He had not seen the Taj Mahal and would never have known what he missed. I was burdened with the knowledge.)

***Memoir***

We crowded into the train car selected for us by Sambha. Many teenage schoolboys were sitting on the benches. I saw a narrow open spot on one and readied to sit there, wobbling with the pack still on my back. A chorus of boys told me firmly, "These seats are reserved!" In an instant I remembered something I'd seen before in India and decided to try it: With a pleading facial expression, I looked at two of the boys, entreating, "Please help us?" Immediately, several of the boys scooted together making room on the seat, gesturing for us to sit down. They helped us remove and situate our packs. I thought of Sambha with amazement—could he have known?

Moments later one boy turned to us and asked in English, "Will you talk to us?"

"Of course!" we responded.

They all looked at each other, relaxing and smiling, and set to work with many questions. I loved it! Two of them told us later that other Westerners had refused to speak to them, suspicious of the boys' intentions.

"When we talked to them," one boy said, "they thought we wanted to sell them something."

They told us they were on an organized school outing to a beach, and most of them had never seen the ocean. There were about eighty of them altogether in several cars. They were delightful.

For many years after, at home in Oregon, whenever I hear the familiar resonating tones of an Indian accent, I love to ask, "Where are you from; why are you visiting?" I think of these boys, eager to know about us, trusting my questions will be received the same way.

Before leaving the north of India, I will tell some of the news of the family members, as I have kept in correspondence with them for many years after this 1997 trip.

**Rupali**

I learned from the family that Rupali had married Ram (originally from a village in northern India) and was living outside New York City. Upon returning home I called Rupali, and we talked for a couple of hours. As usual, I appreciated her perspective, now as a mature married woman with children. I remembered her telling me in correspondence from India when she was sixteen years old, that her parents were open-minded—that, if she wanted, she could have a love marriage. Fourteen years later, I pressed her for an update.

"I am really curious—did you have a love marriage or an arranged marriage?"

She replied, "An *arranged* marriage!...because it makes more sense in our culture. I wasn't meeting anyone on my own and I needed my parents' help." I wondered to myself if her father had fulfilled his own dream of living in America (that he'd told me in 1983), by finding her a husband in America.

Through the years, Rupali and I stay in touch by phone and email. I continue to learn about India through our conversations. I consider her a treasured friend, as I do her cousins, the Baniyas.

At the end of May 2011, Mitch and I visited Rupali and her family in New York. It was the first time I had seen her since 1983, twenty-eight years before. We met her husband and two teenaged children. It was a joyous reunion. I'd been in contact with her all day by cell phone as Mitch and I had missed a connecting flight because of a storm and were delayed by a day. Rupali met us at the railway stop when we stepped off. She and I recognized each other immediately. We fell into conversation easily, as we had before in India as younger persons. Through the visit I came to learn more of Rupali's life, successes, joys, and the inevitable disappointments one encounters growing into adult life.

Coming into focus was a picture of the lives of Indian women, living so closely together with their mothers-in-law. I got the impression there was a measure of female discord, perhaps from the profoundly important relationship of the mother and son in Indian culture. To some extent this is one of those issues present in all cultures, but in Indian tradition the mother is completely dependent upon her sons, especially after her husband's death or departure, as was the case of Rupali's mother-in-law, who lived with them. This woman had not much life outside the home, compounded by not speaking English, being somewhat physically disabled, and not driving in the car-dependent suburban culture of the US. A mother's dependency on her sons would likely affect the relationship with her daughters-in-law, and even with her own daughters.

Rupali told me with concern that her younger brother, Rahul, married with two children, is not working. Her parents have since returned to Rajasthan and now support Rahul's family who lives with them. In 1997 Jindh, I'd had hopes for his future, but I'll just have to stay tuned. No one's life is complete, and the stories continue.

Hearing more family stories and struggles from Rupali, I started thinking that perhaps I had tended to romanticize traditional Indian culture. Certainly the lives of women in India are not easy. There is much to be learned from the Indian culture and Hindu religion, but I know that modern women in India also look to women in the West for inspiration in growth and independence. Also, it is difficult to assess the emotional challenges of trying to practice the traditional family system of India within the context of the American culture and values, with our focus on entitlements of the individual.

**Narain and His Mother Madhuri**

It is with great sadness that I tell you of Narain's death (eldest son) in September 2000 after a few months' illness with pancreatic cancer. His mother, Madhuri (Mahesh's wife), died of Hepatitis B a short time before that.

. . .

I was to learn more family news through the years from correspondence with Rajendra. All but two of the six brothers and their children eventually left Jindh. By 2009, all grandchildren of Mahesh and Madhuri Agrawal were married (from Rajendra: "All brothers have married our children," implying arranged marriages); many of the grandsons became computer and biomedical engineers, often married to wives in their same professions. Several of those professional couples emigrated to English-speaking countries—Australia, Britain and the US. Most of the children of the original joint family (offspring of the six brothers and two sisters, grandchildren of Mahesh and Madhuri) did practice family planning after they married, bearing only one or two kids of their own. As far as I know.

Lalit, one of the grandsons, left his wife and the village with another woman, a most unusual turn for an Indian marriage. His widowed mother, Anju, had moved in with them and remained in Jindh with his wife, Achla, and their two children. What could we think of Lalit, a person struggling for identity, less bound by duty than others? I remember him as a child playing the tabla without smiling. His parents were kind, but Narain died when Lalit must have been in his innocent twenties. Who knows what family experiences may have shaped him?

Rajendra and Madhuri left Jindh and their medical clinic in 2002, explaining, "Too much cost for latest techniques to continue profession in Jindh." (Note: This is a similar parallel to the exodus of doctors from small town America.) He added, "None of my children were interested in medicine, who might have eventually taken over the Jindh clinic the moment we both might not be able to pull on with the advancement of age."

They closed down their computer training centers in 2003, "because it was no longer productive for our economy."

They moved to an industrial city closer to Delhi for salaried medical jobs. There, Rajendra worked in a large hospital as a medical superintendent, with a large number of doctors working in various specialties; it had many modern medical facilities, including CT scan, MRI, ultrasound, its own blood bank, ICU, ICCU, physiotherapy, and was adding a cancer unit, a physiotherapy graduate school, and a nursing school with graduate and post-graduate courses. He wrote of "working in the first aid centre of a big hospital run by a heavy industrial company for its 6,000 employees," and of a second job, running a blood bank for the Lions Club.

Dr. Madhuri worked first as a medical officer in a school with six thousand students, then for a while in a polyclinic with ex-military personnel which was run by the Defense Ministry; next, she worked in a "government dispensary" with slum-area people.

Rajendra told me they were happy to return to medical careers, but with their move, they sacrificed traditional life and proximity to family in Jindh. I am reminded of my own extended family's migration from farms and small towns in Kansas and Oklahoma to cities throughout the US in pursuit of careers and economic opportunity during the mid to late twentieth century. In a letter, Rajendra expressed concern:

> It is really a problem in old age when one of the life partners is no more. In India when we used to have big joint families living and working together under one roof with one family business, the old people left alone by one's spouse (dying) was not a problem as there was a social (system) and care and work used to be divided among all family members. Some used to earn only. Other used to take care of family members etc. etc. The division of duties was there. Now like West our country also has small sporadic families. Family members are moving out to earn. Old couples are left alone in their native places and if any one of them goes it becomes difficult for the partner to live with already busy children and adjust according to them.

Rajendra and Madhuri arranged marriages for all three of their children. Their eldest daughter is Mohana, married in 1996 to a computer engineer. They have a daughter and a son and live in a town near Delhi. Mohana cheerfully helped me reconnect with her parents by email after Rupali (her cousin in New York) connected me to her. Mohana told me she has a master's in Food and Nutrition. Her younger brother later told me she is also an accomplished artist who shows her paintings in public spaces. (Her father had not mentioned her advanced degree and artistic talent, emphasizing only the male family members' achievements in his emails.)

Sambha was married in 1998, one year after we met him. He and his wife have two children, a son and a daughter; now this family lives with Rajendra and Madhuri, within a smaller version of the traditional joint family. Sambha runs a showroom of computer laptops. Rajendra and Madhuri's youngest son, Vibhu (one of the modern teenagers with his own room in Jindh, 1997), was married to Rohana in 2005. Both are computer engineers in Bangalore, and they have one child, a young son.

In summer 2012, Vibhu stayed with us in Portland for two weeks while he attended advanced training seminars for his work as an engineer in Bangalore. We learned family news, and had the chance to spend time with a member of the younger generation. I was surprised when he ordered a mango marguerita in a restaurant. Vibhu said, almost with pride, that he ate chicken and lamb now, but I noticed after a few days that he really preferred vegetarian cuisine to eating meat (I knew better than to serve cow). He told me that his cousin Lalit had set up a new life with his girlfriend, who assisted him as an artist (painter) and *Swami* (a publicly recognized Hindu spiritual teacher who lives in service to mankind). Vibhu told us Lalit's advice was sought by many and he presented a lot of seminars. He quickly accessed his cousin's website to show me his paintings and Swami wisdoms.

Another cousin, Vinod (son of doctors Vaijnath and Vaishali), is a computer engineer who lives in California with his wife Anagi, also an engineer, and their young son. His cousins Vinod and Anagi flew to Portland to meet Vibhu for a weekend and spent an evening with us. We had a great time viewing slides of 1983 and 1997 Jindh. The cousins were astonished to discover I had photos of them as four-year-old boys in their village in India, tucked away in my upstairs closet in Oregon. Vinod and Anagi were both energetic, happy individuals, easy to engage and eager to learn of Mitch and my personal interests and concerns. In our conversations, I learned they enjoyed life in California but felt nostalgic and missed India. They planned to move back eventually but had reservations of giving up their lives in the US. I quoted Gabriel García Márquez, "two nostalgias facing each other like mirrors," as their eager nods affirmed. Anagi made chai for us in my kitchen, the best I've ever had. After they left, Vibhu told Mitch and me of their love marriage. They had met in their mutual workplace in India. Their extended family life was challenged by their different religions. Vinod's family is Hindu; Anagi's, Christian—an alliance that would not occur in an arranged marriage.

Vibhu and I discussed aspects of India's changing society in several conversations. His own marriage to Rohana had been arranged by their families (they'd been matched with careful consideration of caste, education, profession and astrologic compatibility), though it was apparent he'd noticed his rebel cousins. He confirmed that arranged marriage was a topic of much discussion for younger adults. Many of his cousins had moved away from their birth village (Jindh) seeking opportunity, the same as many others of his generation. They had more money, but he discussed with regret that a way of life had been lost. He and his wife typically worked eleven-hour days as corporate engineers for a US-based multinational firm, leaving them limited time for family life. (Though I envied the hired "chopper" who worked in their kitchen each morning, cutting up vegetables in preparation for the couple to cook dinner upon their return from work later in the day.) Vinod and Vibhu had grown up as close as brothers in the same joint family in Jindh. He realized that two cousins growing up in his modern Indian world would not have an opportunity for that kind of close relationship.

We discussed living in proximity to aging parents, as his dad, Rajendra, and I had discussed in emails. Many older Indian parents have started moving in with their children in new cities or countries where the young people work, a reversal of the past when the adult children moved into the parents' home. Vibhu expressed concern for the older ones. They've moved away from their home communities where they had long-time relationships and established routines. And they may not drive, like Rupali's mother-in-law and many other elderly people in the US and communities around the world. This is an issue we can all ponder.

***Email***

*A group email from Rajendra on January 5, 2011, sadly announced the death of the patriarch:*

We are sorry to inform that our dear father Sh. Mahesh Das Agrawal departed for Heavenly Abode on 1.1.2011. He was 88.

A Shanti Path (Peace Meeting, a mantra for truth, harmony and love) will be held for him on 9th Jan, 2011 from 2 to 3 pm in the C.R.K. College, Jindh.

Grief stricken family
Dr. Rajendra Baniya Son
Narendra Baniya Adv. Son
Dr. Vaijnath Baniya Son
Amit Baniya Son
Santosh Baniya Son
Savitri Devi Daughter
Sangeeta Devi Daughter

(Note: All living sons were listed in their descending birth order; daughters were named last, despite the birth order of Savitri as second and Sangeeta as fifth. Though both daughters are married, they are listed with the surname of Devi, the Sanskrit word for "goddess.")

Rajendra sent me a touching personal letter expressing his grief for his father, who died in his arms:

As you know my father is no more.... I was just lucky to be with him at his last time. As being eldest in the family I was to perform all the rituals. I have seen number of deaths in (my) profession. But once it is your own person it is quite painful and unbearable to see one not breathing in spite of all your trials; you are helpless to see your own family member dead....

He taught me everything. I used to share all my happiness and worries with him. Now I find myself alone in this vast world. Time is a big healer so I will also be normal with passage of time....

> He had peaceful death. He lived in his own style and way. We are no match to him.

And my reply to him and Madhuri:

> Thank you for writing this wonderful letter sharing your feelings on your father's death. It is so painful. I too was with my mother when she took her last breath eleven years ago. It is a profound experience I will never forget. Also the loneliness afterward, of knowing you can never talk to the person again in this life, to learn and get counseling from him. It is like a huge final silence in the place of that person. Mahesh Das Agrawal was an unusual and a wise person; I could tell that across our cultures. You are right, time is a big healer and you will be normal. It is a melancholy joy to mourn now, with the comfort of others and to miss the person. It will take a full year, all the seasons, but it's OK. I will write more later.
>
> Best to you,
>
> Margie

***Memoir***

*Dec. 20*

*Agra*

It was a pleasure to step onto the train platform into bright sunlight upon arriving in Agra, the first time since our arrival in India that we saw the sun in a natural atmosphere. We seemed to have escaped the thicker smog and pollution. I felt well, fortunate to have recovered from the previous night's ailment. We stood a few moments in the golden light on the platform, above the old British-laid tracks. Families clad in white cotton garments sat cross-legged on the concrete surrounded by their leather-strapped luggage. Nearby stood stacks of huge wooden crates loaded with Asian cargo, brass and aluminum cooking vessels, textiles, pottery, and the like.

Inside the station, we joined the usual crowd of bodies pressing toward the ticket counter without an assembled waiting line. Not eager to repeat the uncertainty of getting on another train without a reservation, we waited for a reserved seat on the Taj Express back to Delhi the next evening. Gradually we noticed a quiet Indian man in white pajamas standing near, observing us and waiting to speak. He was offering to be our guide, conversing politely in perfect English. We were struck by his quiet, non-obtrusive manner, quite different from the approach of many other local touts hoping to sell us something. His name was Moin.

We asked him to take us to our hotel and to the Taj Mahal before dark. He showed us to a waiting taxi. Moin was too poor to own a vehicle. He handled all the negotiations smoothly, and we arrived quickly to our hotel, the Lauries, a shabby old relic from the British days. We liked it. Our spacious room was comfortable, and looked out onto a large weedy garden. The place was unkempt, but had a private bath and was cheap, less than ten dollars a night. There was enough decaying evidence to imagine its glorious past. Moin kept the taxi waiting and ushered us quickly to the Taj. We arrived at dusk and slipped inside the gate.

There she was, the queenly Taj Mahal, as I remembered, though I hadn't seen her in more than two decades. Her white dome glowed through the chilly evening mists rising from the river below. Mitch was taken aback with his first glance of this beauty, ghostly in the waning light.

We padded on bare feet across the cold marble surface outside the central mausoleum, fascinated by the perfect geometry of the elegant minarets and spectacular dome, prominent in every view, now silhouetted in the evening twilight. I studied the Arabic calligraphy and flowers inlaid with gemstones on the arches of the outside walls. Mitch wrote, "The workmanship is magnificent."

We took photos as long as we could with the last light. At the end of our visit, the shoe keeper easily found our shoes among the hundreds of others left in rows at the entrance—he had a mysterious method of organization and retrieval.

Talking to Moin, we learned that he was a university graduate, having searched for a position in his field for many years. As typical, he was married and lived comfortably with his parents. He was Muslim. I am not sure how long he'd been doing the tour-guide business. His story is an example of the course of the many unemployed in India—educated men waiting among crowds of rickshaw and taxi drivers in stations to find business. Many of the guides and drivers spend days waiting for one customer.

He gave us advice: Don't go into the craft shops near the Taj when they beckon. They are known to offer spiked tea, drugging unsuspecting tourists and stealing their money. As we walked down the lane, sure enough, a tout approached us to invite us into his shop for tea. Mitch hesitated, then started to go with him. I looked behind us at Moin who was gesturing and shaking his head, "No!" We didn't go in, but kept walking.

We hired Moin to guide us for the whole next day. After touring, he escorted us into craft shops specializing in inlaid marble. They used the centuries-old inlaid marble craft used to decorate the Taj Mahal itself. Those shops offered better quality than the ones near the Taj. As Moin got commissions from them, we'll never know for sure about his warning of the drugged tea in other shops. In certain countries of South America, criminals have been known to use the drug burundanga on people they want to rob. A person affected by this drug becomes compliant with handing over credit cards and identity information, without even losing consciousness. I think Moin probably intended to protect us.

Mitch bought a small inlaid marble elephant, paying about $5 in rupees. We took a few close-up photographs of some beautiful inlaid marble art pieces, but we made no big purchases, probably a disappointment for Moin.

Moin took us to a restaurant. He thought we might like a place filled with Westerners. The violin and classical tabla music were the best part. We felt our American egalitarian tendencies when he declined to join us at the table for dinner. After our nagging, he finally agreed to sit with us after we finished our meal, but we could sense his discomfort.

***Journal***

*Dec. 21*

*Marjorie*

Got a good night's sleep. Moin picked us up at 10 am with a taxi hired for the day, an old Premier Padmini with scratchy wool couch-like seats. We never saw any seatbelts in India. We motored along a long straight road headed for Fatehpur Sikri. Traffic moved slowly and we got a good look out the windows.

I took interest in the outdoor barber lathering up, shaving and cutting the hair of men seated in front of a mirror in full view of the road. Mitch watched the dancing bears, trained to prance on their hind legs alongside the road while their masters yanked a chain on their necks and held out a cup for coins from motorists stopped in traffic. We photographed construction materials—long metal pipes, lumber, rebar rods—being transported alongside our taxi by bicycle rickshaw and other very different vehicles than one would see at home moving commercial goods.

***Memoir***

We toured Fatehpur Sikri, the famous fort town built of red sandstone by Mughal Emperor Akbar the Great and occupied as the capital of the empire between 1570 and 1585. It was mysteriously abandoned, probably because it lacked a dependable water supply. Akbar, a Muslim, was a progressive, scholarly ruler who embraced other religions and incorporated signs and symbols representing several beliefs into his buildings. One of his wives was a Christian. There was an intriguing small white marble mosque at one end of the town. Only women were allowed to enter, so Mitch could not see the inside of the marble screen, carved with a bevel in such a way to allow the interior occupants full view of the activities of the outside. And from the outside, the carved filigree screen allowed no view of the interior. This screen design can be found covering the windows of traditional Islamic houses so the women could look outside without being seen.

***Journals***

*Mitch*

The abandoned city was amazing with many buildings of varied architecture around a big plaza. We were constantly hassled by boys selling wares and finally Margie bought a couple of necklaces for 300 rupees (approx $12, at the time.) SSSSS! says Moin. Should have been 30 rupees. (Note: I loved those cheap necklaces, chip-glass set like gems in loose bevels, and wore them during the rest of the trip. I still have them.)

*Marjorie*

We returned to the Taj Mahal, now really crowded with mostly Indian tourists. Glad everyone is enjoying more affluence and on the move, but miss the old days, when tourist sites the world over were just not that crowded. Groups of women in colorful saris, Indian kids wearing sunglasses and headphones, festive. Moving inside beneath the dome in another body-to-body forward-pressing crowd, I heard a man speaking American English behind me. I turned around to see who it was but saw only Indian faces. After a moment I realized my error, the American behind me from Chicago was of Indian descent. We shared a laugh.

***Memoir***

On the porch outside the dome, we met Bill from Canada and Andreas from Poland, young men who met while traveling across the Middle East overland, on my old route. I was surprised they could travel this road with the hotter political tensions, even in 1997. They said it was easy; then, on second thought, "Oh wait, well, *you* wouldn't be able to do it, not on an American passport."

Moin was a great guide and interesting conversationalist. After a good day of sightseeing, he escorted us to the station on time for the evening train to Delhi and accepted our agreed-upon payment without argument or bare-rib display of poverty.

On the train, I observed two teenaged Indian girls of about the same age sitting with their families on either side of the middle aisle. The facial expressions and gestures of one of the girls seemed oddly familiar. Both girls were dressed in the usual style for young women, Punjabi pajamas, their mothers in saris. Stealing glances, I observed the girls and the families to figure out what I had recognized. One girl met my eyes with a brilliant smile showing many teeth; the other girl covered her smile with her hand, shyly casting her eyes downward. The two families were conversing in English, and I learned the family of the girl with the wide smile and fearless gaze lived in America. They returned to India every year to visit family and try to keep their children connected to India.

Mitch and I returned to our Master Guest House in winter-cold Delhi. We spent an ice-cold night huddled together in our little bed in an unheated glass room built on the rooftop, surrounded by a potted garden. We marveled how much we would have enjoyed this room in pleasant weather. We woke before dawn to catch a plane to Kerala, thinking of warmer weather. At breakfast we heard the temperature in Delhi had gone down to freezing in the night. I was excited to travel again, on what would be my first trip to the south of India. I'd heard so much about it through the years. Anticipating comfortable travel within India by air, a first for me, I felt older and more affluent. On my other two trips, I only imagined the comforts of this type of high-style travel.

**Delhi to Cochin, Kerala State (in the Far South of India)**

We arrived with time to spare at the Delhi airport, with reserved and prepaid air tickets to Cochin in hand. I felt smug with my trip planning from home, knowing we'd fly instead of spending several days on a crowded Indian train, as I'd done on long distance trips in the past. We went to the ticket counter and waited in a long line to check in. When it was finally our turn at the counter, the agent said, "Foreigners are not to be checking in until first checking your bags."

OK, we went to the baggage check area and waited in another long line, by now getting a little nervous about the departure time. We got to the front of the line. Almost predictably, the second agent proclaimed, "What is this? I cannot accept your bags until you have first checked in at the ticket counter! Go back in line."

Loop to loop, next thing I remember was running for the tarmack minutes before the plane was to take off, with our unchecked bags in tow. The flight attendent told us curtly we'd have to stow our backpacks in the overhead. They didn't fit. "Then you must hold them in your laps!"

What a flight, with our backpacks wedged in front of us between the seats, literally no room for our legs and feet. I stretched my legs up over the backpack in a kind of yoga pose, held for the duration of the flight. Yet another chapter in the old story "Travel in India." I can laugh now.

***Journal***

*Dec. 22*

*(All journal entries from this point on are mine; Mitch had stopped writing in his journal.)*

Ahhh, finally warmth and pleasant air to breathe, sunshine, blue skies. We enjoy walking around the streets of Cochin (Note: Traditional name Kochi, situated on the tip of a peninsula between the Lakshadweep Sea, an inlet of the Indian Ocean, and large Lake Vembenaad). Here I feel an ease, a lack of the pressing tension palpable in most other Indian cities and towns. That vacation letting-go feeling at last. The native language is Malayalam, which has a very musical tongue-trilling sound. People give more space and move slower here. The men dress in short lungis, which can be converted quickly into long lungis. They lower their lungis into long skirts, dropping the cloth to their ankles whenever Mitch raises his camera.

***Memoir***

We stayed at the Hotel Seagull on the waterfront. I remember a bad smell coming from a drain in the floor. Mitch put a water-filled plastic bag over it, which helped some. In the morning, I got up and walked toward the promising dining room I'd spied the night before. The room faced the sea, with breakers visible through a glass wall of small-paned windows. I was too early; no one was breakfasting. All the dining tables were occupied, though—sleeping hotel boys, rolled tightly in their blankets, were stretched out on the long tables. We went out.

Returning from breakfast, we noticed an entry door ajar in a newly whitewashed high wall of the Fort House Lodge next to the Seagull. We pushed it open and ventured inside. What a hospitable place! The courtyard was lovely—fascinating tall clay statues, archaeological in appearance, were placed among the tropical garden plants. It was a modest hotel with simple rooms, very clean with red mosquito nets hung decoratively above the beds. We changed lodging immediately. It got even better, with delicious spicy local food served under an open-air thatched-roof restaurant. We found out it was owned and run by a Westerner, often the case when the bathrooms are that sparkling. It was to be our only hotel with mosquito nets on the trip. We marveled at our lucky discovery.

**Cochin, Kerala, Exploring the Backwaters by Boat**

Kerala is known for its backwater life: people living in small villages in houses built on the banks of narrow canals, rivers, and lagoons. Lush tropical vegetation grows in thickets close to the water's edge. Meandering down a lane our first morning in Cochin, we saw a handwritten note tacked to the post of an outdoor café, offering cheap backwater boat rides. Though a little dubious, we bought tickets and showed up for the ride at a canal the next morning. A humble, flat wooden boat (called a *wallum*) awaited its passengers with six blue metal folding chairs set up in a row along the bottom. We stepped on the small boat and took our chairs. A polite family from New Zealand with two young kids held the other places. The boatman was a very thin, dark-skinned man clad only in a lungi skirt. He was barefoot and held a long pole. The captain, our tour guide, wore a white shirt with his lungi and flip-flops. The boatman plunged his pole into the soft mud and pushed off from shore. We spent the morning gliding through shallow by-way channels. We ducked under vine-covered tree branches. The smiling captain pointed, unexcitedly, to a long black snake swimming in the water near our low boat: "Keep hands inside of boat. Deadly poisonous snake there."

My glass bangle broke, falling from my wrist and landing with a shattering tinkle, scattering colored glass pieces between the ribs on the bottom of the boat. One of the New Zealander boys responded, "Hurry, I'll help you gather the shards so you can remember!" He was eight years old, fair-haired, and his name was Angus.

We stopped in a tiny village, deeply shaded in dense jungle foliage. People squatted in sunlit openings on the water bank pounding coconut shells with mallets into a fibrous pulp that would be made into durable coir mats. The coconut industry there is remarkable, nothing is wasted and coconut palms are easily grown. We stopped in another village where women in teams of two spun coconut fiber with handheld spinning wheels. Working outside beneath the palm trees, each stood at one end holding a wheel between both hands. The fiber strands were held in tension about fifteen feet apart from the two women. They would spin the wheels and the fiber while walking toward each other, meeting at the center.

In that same village, we were offered green coconut drinks. When we agreed to buy one, a man held a small machete between his teeth and tied his ankles together with a rag. Then he passed a cloth sling behind the trunk of a coconut palm tree, held an end in each hand, and pulled the cloth tense as he shimmied straight up the trunk of the tree to reach the coconuts. He cut several loose with his knife, letting them fall to the ground. His waiting coworker retrieved the fruits, and with a machete, lopped the outside shell from a coconut, punched a hole in the top and inserted a straw. Green coconut milk made a delicious, refreshing drink on that warm day. I much enjoyed that backwater excursion.

**Alleppey (Alappuzha), Kerala**

The next day we made a short train trip to Alleppey, where we spent Christmas Eve. We'd come to this town expecting to find passage on a boat to travel to our next town via another Kerala backwaters trip. Our hotel here was a little fancier, with a swimming pool. They'd decorated for Christmas with large colored-paper stars hung from the ceilings, each constructed three-dimensionally in a folded paper configuration, ornamented with perforated designs. A few small ornaments dangled from a potted palm tree in the lobby. Kerala is the only state in India which has a lot of Christians, comprising 20 percent of their population; only 1 percent of the whole of India is Christian. It was a pleasant coincidence that our plans landed us in Kerala for Christmas. The hotel gift shop had some nice old-India antiques where Mitch and I bought gifts for each other. Mitch gave me a braided silver bracelet, and I gave him a carved wooden box that smelled of roses. At Christmas Eve dinner around the pool, we watched Indian women (other hotel guests) walk into the pool wearing their silk saris. A middle-aged American man approached our table, saying he'd seen us in another town. I imagined him to be some kind of spy, an agent of the State Department.

The "nicer" air-con hotel was too cold and had little cockroaches in the bathroom. I don't usually mind bugs that much, but something about roaches...the ickiest of the bugs, skittering across the floor furtively to conceal themselves, as though they're aware of their human reputation as shameful filth.

It was a sunny Christmas morning in Kerala, kind of a low-key holiday for us, very pleasant. I thought of the contrast to home: the solemn stop-the-day empty streets, families staying in behind closed doors in a culmination of elaborate, exhausting preparations and Christmas shopping. Backpacks on, we walked down to the water to find the boat we'd booked tickets on, moored on the bank of a wide canal. It was much bigger than the first backwater wallum boat, motorized, with a covered area and a top deck. A smiling Indian man in heavy spectacles took our tickets and welcomed us aboard. He wore pressed pants and a clean white shirt. This was a kind of charter ride, and he was our guide. We settled our luggage in the first level. I had decorated my backpack for Christmas with a string of tiny colored stars. Two American women, Nancy and Mary from Los Angeles, were already on the boat. Other passengers included a young American man living and teaching English in Bombay and a young Indian family with two kids—all pleasant people, easy to talk to. Those days in India, it was unusual to find ourselves in the company of Americans, for reasons I am not sure. The water sparkled with sunlight, and the temperature was on the pleasant side of hot. On this larger boat, we had to stay on the deeper central waterway of the long Lake Vembenaad, though the boatman steered as close to shore as possible. We observed village life as we glided by. Children stood on the front steps of their property, half immersed in water, washing lunch dishes and cows. Two boys with radiant smiles stood in water up to their necks, filling large brass water jugs. Boatsmen in lungis poled large flatboat wallums loaded with bananas, coconuts, and unfired clay dishes to market. A young girl in a bright red dress and hair ribbon sat upright in a straight wooden chair at the water's edge.

Soon the boat was guided into a cove and tied, though we were far from our destination. The plank was put to shore and the guide in thick glasses beckoned for us and the other Westerners to get off. "Something for you to see." We followed him into a Catholic church near the water. "Today is Christmas, and I am thinking you are wanting to come here," the man said with sincerity. We thanked him for his thoughtfulness and Christmas wishes. The quiet church housed many brightly painted plaster of paris statues of Jesus and Mary, reminding me of the Hindu gods and goddesses in nearby temples.

Kerala's Christian population has apparently been there since Christians appeared in Europe. It is said that Saint Thomas, one of Jesus's twelve disciples, sailed to the coast of what is now Kerala, India, where he introduced Christianity in 52 AD. We also heard a story many times in south India, a theory that Jesus himself had traveled to India and earned followers in Kerala, that he even married and fathered children there.

We arrived at the end of our boat journey to Kottayam and found lodging in the Hotel Aida, patronized by Indian businessmen and their families. Our room was simple, large, and bright. I liked this place. We set to work decorating it for Christmas with our large colored-paper star and string of bright cellophane stars. I did some laundry in the sink and strung it across the room too.

The hotel had an adjoining restaurant. The front wall was made of a series of old heavy wooden door panels carved in geometric patterns and hinged together. The next morning, it was hot by nine and breezeless. All the door panels were folded back, open to the street. From our breakfast table, we had a fine view of Kottayam's morning commuter traffic: auto rickshaws, bicycle rickshaws, Ambassador cars, and scooters, one with a family of four whose slim bodies all fitted neatly onto the seat. Elephants lavishly decorated with painted designs padded between big trucks grinding their gears. Alongside of them walked white Brahmin bullocks with little bells bouncing from the tips of their blue-painted horns, pulling two-wheeled wooden carts outfitted with wide, bald tires. A cacophonous pageant, but slower and less noisy than such streets in the north.

As I watched the morning traffic parade each day, I got in the habit of enjoying a typical south Indian breakfast of masala dosa, a large, flat, crispy pancake (made of rice and black lentils) folded in thirds with a dab of spiced potato with black mustard seeds in the center and peppery cumin yogurt sauce on the side. No Indian restaurant in Portland could match this fine breakfast experience. I lazily brushed away buzzing flies, all of us languid in the heat.

**Old Coconut Plantation Estate**

Mitch and I had intended to treat ourselves to a room at the old Baker coconut estate in Kumarakom, then owned and run by a ritzy Indian hotel chain, but we were unable to connect with the hotel from home. When we finally reached them by phone from Alleppey, they were booked up with foreign tour groups. Lucky for us, as we would have missed the local very Indian Hotel Aida with the elephant traffic view. And we didn't miss out on the old British coconut plantation after all. We traveled by taxi to dine in the resort on Christmas night, which was decorated for Christmas simply (as the others) with paper stars hung from the ceiling and a few ornaments gracing potted plants. We returned the next day to the beautiful grounds, taking a long tea in the shade of the wide verandah. We sipped from delicate porcelain teacups and saucers placed on an antique Victorian table. Exotic birds played amidst the orchids hanging from tropical trees. It was very pleasant, no tension; admittedly, a brief pause from our "trip to India." I enjoyed an ayurvedic massage: I lay nude under a blue cotton sheet, supine on a long wooden plinth with two-inch rails along the sides. Two Indian women applied ayurvedic oils liberally to my skin and worked in synchrony on both sides of my body. My oiled skin was so slippery that I would have slid off the plinth if not for the rails. They sang in unison as they worked, in mirror image, on both my hands, both arms, both legs, both sides of my trunk. A most unusual massage, sensory saturate, followed by a steam bath. At sunset, Mitch and I strolled along the lagoon, and after, we enjoyed another delicious Indian dinner in the formal restaurant.

***Journal***

*Dec. 25, 1997*

Mitch is so sweet about Christmas. We had a beautiful, luxurious dinner at the Taj Garden, I in a red sari. We enjoyed the plantation so much we went back the next day. We now have a regular cab driver named Sonny who taxies us back and forth between Kottyam (where we sleep) and the relaxing coconut plantation in Kumarakom, about a 30-minute drive.

***Memoir***

The hotel concealed a family history of British India enacted on the historic Baker coconut estate. Begun in 1878, the plantation estate had been home to four generations of Bakers spanning one hundred years to around 1977. The Bakers' original immigrant ancestor, Henry Baker of Essex, England, had journeyed to India in 1818 to work as a Church Missionary

Society priest. Henry and his wife, Amelia, worked as missionaries for nearly five decades in the area now known as Kerala. Their work focused on educating the native people; they are credited by some for originating the foundation of the current high literacy rate in Kerala, between 90 and 100 percent, depending on the source, though there are other reasons. The Maharajas in this region (Travancore and Kochi) of the past Raj princely states had an admirable reputation for providing education and services to their people; following that, Keralans elected several Communist governments who provided public education. One of Henry and Amelia's sons, George Alfred Baker, eventually cleared Mangrove swamps, planted coconuts and rice, and in 1878 built the beautiful bungalow house where we spent the day after Christmas. In the early times, all the water used on the plantation for drinking, cooking, and bathing had to be transported from five miles away in wooden wallum boats. The luxuriant-appearing tropical life had not been easy for the occupying British pioneers, but it definitely was the life of Riley for us tourists.

Reference: The Country House that Became a Garden Retreat by Peter De Jong

**He Is a Very Good Driver; He Is a Christian**

During the night taxi rides in the dark, Sonny would turn off the car lights "to save the battery." He would turn the lights on briefly at intervals to see what might be out there, such as people who frequently sat on the edge of the road. Most cab drivers drove this way at night.

We started discussing the possibility of Sonny driving us across the Cardamom Hills when we were ready to leave Kottayam. One evening, in an effort to persuade us to travel into the hills in Sonny's taxi, his assistant turned to us from the front passenger seat and presented this argument: "Mr. Sonny is a very good driver, he is a Christian." We looked at each other, puzzled.

Back in our room at the Aida, I said to Mitch, "Could be that he thinks he has only one life."

***Journal***

*Dec. 27*

Long car ride with Sonny through astounding mountainous Cardamom Hills, headed to Tamil Nadu…

***Memoir***

Sonny took lunch with us at the table without the protest Moin had given in the north. The menu was printed in Malayalam, so we asked him to order for us, and we liked the meal he chose. It was simple, well-spiced dal, air-puffed puri breads, rice, chai, and a bottle of my favorite ThumsUp Cola. Though he spoke English, Sonny was quiet, taciturn, not conversing or even making eye contact at lunch. His assistant had not come on this journey, and I think he depended on the sociable man to keep the talk going in Kottayam. Most cab drivers we hired in India work with an assistant sitting in the front passenger seat—perhaps to keep them company, or for safety?

The drive was pleasant as we wound down the road through the lush hills, fragrant and green with cultivated tea and cardamom plants. Cardamom is native to southern India and grows in leafy clumps of tall shoots, each five to twenty feet high with small fruit along a three-foot stalk. We stopped at a roadside stand and bought a packet of the aromatic green pods. At another stand, we ordered chai and watched the attendant pour the sweet brown liquid in a two-foot stream, foaming as it collected in three small glasses.

Taxi drivers hired by tourists in India often take on the self-appointed role of tour guide and so did Sonny. We noticed he'd pulled up to an entry gate. A swinging overhead sign announced in cartoonish lettering, "Periyar Wildlife Sanctuary." In we rolled. We watched two monkeys scamper through high branches of a gigantic tree. No tigers in sight, but there were rumors of sightings around the lake hours before. I looked around and was fascinated by sleeping Indian tourists, lined head-to-toe in repose around a stone ledge ringing a large shade tree. The silken end of a lady's brightly colored sari cascaded over the stones, touching the ground as she slept. Ah, that's the life.

We drove out of the cool hills and motored across a hot plain, eventually arriving in a village near Madurai, where we were expected by new Servas hosts.

We'd returned to India, so to speak. The heat and dust hung on you. The noise and general tension were more intense than in Kerala. Spice, hot oil, and smoke from street cooking blended with the scent of burning incense and faint open sewer into a familiar smell. Sonny searched the streets for the address of our hosts.

***Journal***

*Dec. 27*

Now we're in Tamil Nadu, much poorer and crowded, compared to Kerala. Sad to leave. Our new Servas Hosts Kabir and Maaya Jayarama are most gracious. They presented us with a wrapped Christmas gift with a Mickey Mouse gift card attached. The handwritten note said "Best Wishes." Very sweet and thoughtful open-mindedness, as they are devout Hindus.

However much we like them, both Mitch and I got serious heebie-jeebies today. Their house looks like (the unoccupied apartment where we boarded in) Prague, doubt they live here much, it's in disrepair. They are cardamom growers, with their main house on an estate up in the hills. They arrived here this morning to host us. Walls in kitchen stained with brown oil, afraid of getting sick again and we have no more of Rajendra's instant cure medicine. We refused the 'pure' drinking water they offered us from a bucket on the kitchen floor, felt impolite.

***Memoir***

Fortunately, we did not get sick there, despite the worry. The house was large and airy with a covered porch in the front. They'd made a temple in a small enclave near the kitchen. We were given a large room near the front porch with a private bath nearby.

Maaya spent hours in the kitchen preparing food for us. They were strictly vegetarian. As in other Indian homes, Kabir sat with us at the dining table, but Maaya would not. Once I approached the threshold of her kitchen, intending to enter. She gestured frantically, but I didn't understand her language and she didn't speak English. Then I realized I was wearing my shoes and removed them, knowing this would have been a serious violation of the sanitation code. All kitchen equipment and preparations were done on the floor, so there was some realism to this. She cooked with a portable two-burner metal stove supplied by bottled fuel.

Kabir asked us what we wished to see in nearby Madurai; the main attraction, of course, the Sri Meenakshi Temple. We were really pleased they wanted to host us for sightseeing the next day, immediately arranging to rent a taxi for the trip from their home. En route, we realized that a recent monsoon flood in the area had washed out several main roads. This happened while we were traveling in northern India and had made international news, though we were unaware of that until it was pointed out to us when we returned home. By pure luck, we missed big rains during our whole journey. The taxi driver had to take a long winding trip through rutted back roads to get to Madurai, about seventy kilometers from their village. It took us over two hours to get there, so we had lots of time for long interesting conversations with Kabir, discussing world peace, Gandhi, economics, and other topics. We had similar political views. They were wonderful people, conversations were easy. It was a good day, and the temple was fascinating.

The Sri Meenakshi Temple was built within the center of the city, largely in the 1600s, surrounded by gardens, a reflecting water tank, and an outer wall. Twelve high *gopurams* (ornate tower gates) are visible from the surrounding countryside. It is a massive temple of stone and wood, very impressive, especially with its recent restoration. One major gopuram gate faces each of the four directions on its large, fifteen-acre grounds. The towers contain thousands of brightly painted wooden statues of Hindu gods in many incarnations. The statues of varying sizes are placed closely together among short wooden columns and carvings, on tiers of ledges representing porticos of household dwellings within the tall structures. A closer look at the gods reveals live monkeys sitting comfortably among them on their ledges.

Inside the cool, dark interior of the old temple among a thousand stone pillars, large statues of important gods stood in gated enclaves. I realized this was not a sight-seeing museum experience for Kabir and Maaya. They were worshipers in a much-revered temple, among thousands of other pilgrims on that day. We walked slowly and spoke little. Kabir bought fragrant white flower garlands for Maaya and me to wear in our hair.

An elephant gave me a blessing with his trunk on the top of my bowed head. The fee was one rupee, which he collected with his trunk. Mitch took our picture. I was wearing a sari from 1983 I especially liked, iridescent mauve trimmed with lush gold embroidery.

Kabir and Maaya took us to an incredible vegetarian restaurant in Madurai. Its furnishings were modest but well-appointed, not the typical heavy décor of Indian-Western luxury style. They ordered a fine *thali* meal for us. This was served traditionally on a large metal plate with an enormous serving of rice mounded in the center; about six different vegetarian preparations were served in small metal *katori* cups placed around the rice. A thali dinner includes *dal* (varied types of fragrantly spiced lentils and beans, also known as *pulses*), *raita* (yogurt, lightly seasoned with spices and salt), and varied vegetable preparations such as spiced okra, eggplant and tomatoes, or many others. Pickles and condiments with Indian flat breads such as *puri*, *chapati*, *roti* or *naan* are always served plentifully on the side. The drink is always water, followed by chai with a sweet after the meal. The food in this restaurant was wonderfully delicious with complex flavors, superior to food in good Indian restaurants in US cities where I've eaten.

We had made arrangements by aerogramme in the weeks before our trip to stay with another Servas host in a nearby Gandhi rural cooperative. Though we looked forward to this with curiosity, Mitch and I decided to cancel that visit—I can't believe I am reporting this missed opportunity, but at the time, we felt too exhausted. Though the visit would have been fascinating, it takes a lot of energy to converse, get to know new people in a more intense in-home stay, and neither Mitch nor I felt up to it. There is a limit to how much one can experience and enjoy in a given amount of time. True for travel, same for life.

***Journal***

*Dec. 28*

*On the Road to Madurai*

Need to slow down…We are moving so quickly, intense experiences become a faded memory as, next day, we're on to some strange new experience and I'm still feeling sad about giving up the day or week before. Trying to reflect on this trip as it unfolds—I am remembering Agra—only a week before but it seems like it was months ago. Thinking of our house and our life in Portland really seems several centuries away. Went through a time warp back to India, slowly realizing it.

After our day in Madurai with Kabir and Maaya, we drove through small poor villages in the dark of night. They're still working at 9 pm; all little stalls are open to the street with fluorescent tubes on. Somebody buys that chai and cola and it's not foreigners. Road work also continues at night. It seems like people are working a lot more than in 1983. Bridges were washed out with the Monsoon. I'm feeling fortunate at this point to have had safe journeys with good drivers. The road trips are sometimes scary. Mitch has a bad cold but seems to be recovering. The weather is now perfect, thankfully.

***Memoir***

We took our leave of Kabir and Maaya; they returned to their cardamom plantation in the hills and we headed back to Madurai for more sightseeing. We agreed to meet up with Kabir a few days later in Madras (Chenai) where he was going to meet their children at their private boarding school. They promised to visit us in Oregon and we vowed one day to return to India and visit their cardamom plantation for a longer stay.

***Journal***

*Dec. 29*

Mad Madurai! The streets are impassable but everyone and every vehicle passes through. The only way this is possible is due to enormous patience on everyone's part (except mine). Two overwhelming impressions—everyone has so much tolerance and patience and I don't see cruelty or anger displayed, no one strikes or curses another. The Indians keep asking us, "Why so many divorces in America?" I finally am telling them, "Because there is so much cruelty in relationships and people won't stand for it." I am sure there is much I am missing (of the realities of life in India); now Kabir is telling us of family lawsuits "because of greed."

I am remembering conversations with Kabir—he was surprised to learn that we have many handicapped people in the US—"with your advanced medicine?" I tried to explain how it works. We don't have a lot of disabilities that are easily correctable by surgery such as clubfoot or cleft palate, both clearly visible in the streets of India, causing marked impairments with inability to walk (clubfoot) or speech, eating impairments and social stigma from radical facial disfigurement (cleft palate). Children born with Down's syndrome or spina bifida in India, for instance, may not survive without the extensive life-saving serial surgeries they can get in America. (Note: These procedures are usually available to children in the US through programs like Shriner's and to those lucky to have health insurance.)

***Memoir***

I have pleasant memories of those days we spent on our own wandering around Madurai, our trade for giving up the Gandhi rural cooperative.

We were fascinated to watch a hand weaving operation set up along the street beneath shade trees outside the long red-and-white-striped wall of a temple tank: the colored threads of partially-woven saris were stretched to long lengths between loom-racks made of cross-braced bamboo poles. I stopped to take a photo. When I looked up, Mitch was taking a photo of me, now surrounded by a herd of about twenty-five water buffalo. It was unnerving! I must have missed sounds of their approaching arrival amidst traffic noise, but shortly I was hearing their snorts and felt their imposing energy, quite different than the shy Brahmin cows. I slowly picked my way through them and gave them some distance.

Inside the Mariamman Temple Tank, an old man looked up from filling his water jug. He greeted us unashamedly with a broad smile, toothless save one snaggletooth. He was bare-chested above a short lungi, standing in water up to his knees on the submerged granite steps. On the temple island, boys in their underwear jumped off a tree-lined promontory, making big splashes with half-cannonball water landings. Each held his plaid cotton lungi, tied in such a way that it filled with air and buoyed him up in the water. I wondered if they could swim. This deep tank is fed through subterranean pipes from the Vaigai River, usually filled with water only in preparation for the January Teppam Float Festival; it was near that time, and we were fortunate to be there.

A temple tank, usually stepped and often geometric in design. is an essential part of the architecture outside a Hindu temple. As actual wells or reservoirs, tanks provided the water supply for the temples in older times. The clear reflecting water offers a visually pleasing element in the landscaped environment and a refreshing place to cool off on a hot day.

On the same promontory beneath the trees, I met a friendly woman banker who declared her idea of American life with a spark of envy: "In your country, men and women are equal; you share the housework fifty-fifty!"

I was amused and explained a few things to her. She replied, smiling with a head wag, "So you are telling me we have an international problem?" We laughed together, two women strangers.

We went back to the Sri Meenakshi Temple and were again awed by the massive towers, about 150 feet tall, housing brightly painted wooden figures of deities in playful poses: Rama, Krishna, Ganesha, Hanuman, Lakshmi, Durga, Kali, and many others I cannot name. The Hindu gods are believed to be avatars or angels of Almighty God, born on earth in human form to help guide people through their struggles. Hindus entreat certain avatars during worship, depending on needs, such as Ganesha, remover of obstacles to success, and Hanuman, who embodies strength and perseverance. There are similarities to Christianity, but Christians have only one avatar of God, who is Jesus; some await a second coming. The name of Almighty God to Hindus is best represented as the Trinity of Creators—Vishnu, Shiva, and Brahma—who were not born but exist as powerful energy.

Many vendors lingered on the temple grounds, trying to sell us sunglasses, necklaces, shoes—many small objects. They would nearly hang on us, desperate in their attempts to earn pennies for the day. We reacted with politeness, "Yes, those are nice, but we don't want to buy any." That was interpreted as potential interest, and they became more forceful in their sales pitch: "Yes, madam, only looking, very nice, try this on, I give you good price, two for the price of one, three for the price of one, my best price, you like it, pleeeeease, just try this on...." Though we felt bad for their poverty, their sales pitches were constant and hard to take. I figured out that if I said these words, "Leave us!" the vendors fled us rapidly, but they also would hang their heads and seem ashamed. To this day, I am puzzled about this and still do not know an effective, amiable way to refuse a street vendor in India.

Back in our hotel in the evening, I lay reading in bed when a large animated silhouette appeared on the windowsill, just inches away from my shoulder but on the other side of the glass. It ran away quickly, squealing as I tapped on the window. I did not lift the curtain to see what I imagined to be a huge rat; the shadow and the sound effects were enough. I imagine I would have lifted the curtain at home, feeling more secure in familiar surroundings. I do have to add, however, the classical Indian music concert we were about to hear two days later in Madras more than made up for the squealing silhouette. I have since noticed large rats about in Portland, and the experience in Madurai helped temper my reaction to such varmints. But at the time, the windowsill rat in Madurai factored big on the heebie-jeebie scale.

A few days later, we headed to Madras on the train. I felt traveler's envy in a conversation with a well-spoken woman from Australia. She had just departed Trichy (Tiruchirappalli), a nearby temple town, and Thanjavur (Tanjore), where she'd visited an architectural temple. She was astonished we had not thought to go there. Oh, that old familiar feeling, typical on a trip to India, that my journey fell short! I wrote the names down for next time. With a sigh, I looked out the windows of the train. It was a warm, clear morning, and the sun shone on bright-green rice paddies; a woman bending forward at the waist reached down with brown arms stretching long to harvest the grain, her back straight in a kind of Yoga pose. Her vermillion skirt was girded up above the water, ankles sunk in soft mud.

Researching those temple places, I have to admit the good traveler was right—we certainly must visit these one day, lots of fantastic history going back to times BC, tales of Chola emperors, Pallavas, Pandyas, Cheras, and Nayaks, with Trichy having Sri Ranganathaswamy—the largest temple complex in India—and Thanjavur having the World Heritage Brihadishwara Temple, 270 feet high. Now obscure objects of my desire.

**Madras (Chennai)**

We knew our visit to Madras would coincide with the classical music festival going on there, but we needed to find out about tickets. As we were checking in to our hotel, we saw a man in the lobby carrying an instrument case and asked him what he knew. "Yes, I am a musician performing in tonight's concert at the music academy down the street. Just follow to my room and I will give you two free tickets." I love India.

The entire concert was mesmerizing. I've seen many concerts of sitar, other Indian instruments, and voice in US cities, but a thought during this concert was, This is over my head. We marveled at the performers, which included Ustad Allah Rakha's son Zachir Hussain on the tabla. His star performances in the US always draw a crowd and enthusiastic cheers, but on this stage in India, he was just one of many masters. His playing was even more complex and impressive in India. Mitch and I were fascinated with two instruments we'd never seen: the *Kanjira*, a small, seven-inch tamborine-like percussion instrument, the sound of which filled the auditorium; and another percussion instrument, the *Ghatam*, a big clay pot played by a guy with a big pot belly, sounding the way you might guess—huge, hollow, bass, and resonating.

The audience was filled with spectacled music scholars, keeping time with their hands and forearms rotating back and forth in a measured counting pattern.

On the next day, we called Kabir and met him, now accompanied by his teenaged son and daughter speaking perfect English and dressed in Western clothes. He took us to another good vegetarian restaurant, where we continued our conversations and became acquainted with his kids. Pleasant hours.

Auto rickshaw drivers start price negotiations with foreigners by asking four times the local going rate for a ride. Mitch finally decided he'd settle for double the rate, as none of them would bargain beyond that with us. When we were with Kabir, he managed to settle on the local rate. An Indian man from New York we met told us that he had the same trouble we did with the fares: "They know I'm a foreigner." Oddly, I felt better and less discriminated against.

Just walking around the block in Madras was fascinating. We observed people carry on their activities outdoors, reflecting a highly socially interactive culture and perhaps, underlying that, a temperate tropical clime. We saw a big group of boys playing a lively game of marbles on the street. Women in those gorgeous colored saris gathered for water at the public spigot. An old, wrinkled tailor man foot-pumped his treadle sewing machine outside his shop. Children played nearby on a portable Ferris wheel, set on wheels so it could be moved from one neighborhood to the next. A man turned the Farris wheel with a hand crank. In front of a store under a big sign lettered "Snow White Pin Men," a shirtless, bare-ribbed old man ironed shirts with a large iron heated with burning coal embers, visibly glowing red through vents on the iron's sides.

With everyone working or playing together in the streets, a lot of social interaction went on that sometimes included us. People gave us a nod and a smile; we exchanged greetings in Hindi; sometimes conversing in English. A big factor in this social work and play scene might be a limited amount of electricity and running water. Imagine if every household in the block had plenty of electrical outlets: Pin Man and the tailor would go inside to plug in the iron and the sewing machine, switching on the lights. With running water and electricity, the women would not gather at the pump, and they'd have less excuse for socializing, perhaps preferring to watch television alone in their homes. The weather outside was pleasantly warm, but they may prefer it cooler inside air-conditioned homes, and the kids would probably prefer to play computer games and search the internet indoors, forgetting the marble game, as it has been long forgotten in American culture. My dad used to play marbles in rural Oklahoma. He was born in a farmhouse in 1919.

Our hotel seemed to be near the action and the heart of Madras (music festival, marble game, water spigot, etc.), but we were also within walking distance of the beach. Women and men walked into the ocean waves clad in their street clothes: colorful saris or rolled-up trousers. Mitch and I walked barefoot on the soft sand, dancing along the foam of the breaking waves. Vendors roasted corn on the cob over wood embers on metal grills set up along the beach. Though we were on the edge of a major Indian city, the shore was clean, almost no litter save a few discarded corn cobs and flecks of charred wood.

Large mandalas drawn in white chalk suddenly appeared on many public sidewalks and concrete surfaces. We learned this was a celebration for New Year's. Each mandala, about three to four feet across, was drawn with one continuous line, impressively complex and symmetrical. Some were filled in with multi-colored chalks.

**Mahabalipuram**

It was near the end of our three weeks in India. We stored our luggage at our hotel in Madras and with one knapsack packed with toothbrushes and a change of clothing, boarded a public bus for Mahabalipuram (Mamallapuram), a small town on the Bay of Bengal. This was to be another mini-vacation within the India journey.

I was thoroughly relaxed. En route to the ancient beach town, I remember gazing out an open window of the bus at a row of palm trees on the horizon, aglow in the sunset. I had a feeling I'd known before, as if time had stopped. Everything was perfect and as it should be. I realized the soft undulating rhythms of India had penetrated me. If I thought of fast-paced home, it seemed so very far away, in a different dimension.

In Mahabalipuram we found a lot to see and think about. We went first to the Shore Temple from the late seventh century of the Pallava Kingdom. It is literally on the shore, with the front walls close to the breaking waves. Centuries of eroding sands had softened all features of the chiseled stone statues of animals and gods; the edges of the stone temple halls were softly rounded. One had the sense that even this ancient stone temple, having endured for many centuries, must eventually surrender its temporal existence, dissolve into the sand, and be washed over by the sea. A sea wall had been erected in front of the temple in an effort to delay this.

We spent a pleasant, quiet morning strolling through the old temple grounds. Though it is a World Heritage sight, few people were around, which was just fine with us. There were signs that a few worshipers had been there before us—inside their enclaves, statues of Vishnu and Shiva bore smudges of colored chalk on their foreheads and a few flower petals placed at their feet, puja offerings left earlier in the morning. An old woman in a faded sari walked barefoot between a stone elephant and a smaller temple structure. We may have seen one or two Western-appearing tourists aside from ourselves, but hardly anyone else was there.

Walking away from the temple on the beach, I saw two tiny dung beetles hard at work on the ground. I watched them for some time as they coordinated their efforts to transport a tiny ball of dung, bigger than the two of them. Later, I found out we have dung beetles in Portland, but I had never seen them. It takes patience and time to see the small world all around, both of which are in short supply in the West. You learn that in India. I am reminded of the old sixties poster: "Stand still and look until you really see." The trick is to remember.

Massive stone boulders abounded around Mahabalipuram, many carved remarkably in varying ways. Whole temple portico rooms (*mandapams*) were carved within the lower portions of eight of the boulders—huge amounts of stone had been chiseled away to create a void for each room space—supported with many stone columns, each cut from the boulder in a solid vertical cylinder continuous with the ceiling and smooth floor. No two columns were alike, so it took a while for us to examine these. Entire walls of some of the stone temples were sculpted in relief, the most remarkable being the Krishna Mandapam. Long, winding stairs would often be carved into the rock all the way up the outside of a boulder, leading the visitor to a grand vista of the ocean from the top, perhaps a religious site in the past.

Two large boulders, joined by a rocky cleft in between, provided an enormous surface for the sculpting of a magnificently detailed relief, a World Heritage site, depicting Hindu epics of the Descent of the Ganges (the goddess Ganga). The boulder's carved surface measures about 90 feet across by 30 feet high, but sources vary. Prominent interpretations of stories illustrated in stone include the Ramayana story, in which Bhagiratha stands on one leg doing austere penance to bring down the sacred waters of the river Ganga from her origins in the heavens or, in earthly location, the high Himalayas of the Tibetan Plateau. Shiva consents to protect earthly creatures by breaking the flood force of Ganga's fall. The Mahabharata epic tells of Arjuna's Penance to receive a boon (power) from Shiva for fighting a war. We took our time looking at the detail of this beautiful, intricate carving from the seventh century. The large elephants were so well-crafted that their skin looked leathery real.

This carved rock panel served as a backdrop to a night performance of an exceptional Bharat Natyam dance we attended, a part of the Mamallapuram Dance Festival, held to concide with the music festival season of Madras.

The next morning, our last in lovely Mahabalipuram, we awoke to the ching-ching, ching ringing of stone carvers working in the same precise manner as their ancestors did in this very place for more than a millennium, as the marble inlay craftsmen work in Agra near the Taj Mahal. Mitch chose a small chiseled stone Ganesh, reclining blissfully as he reads a book resting on his crossed knee, the sole of his bare foot upturned. Little Ganesh, to this day, is blissfully reading his book in our home.

Any fantasy of the West having receded from our consciousness was about to be put aside. Our jumbo jet was due to leave from Madras that night, carrying us back to the late twentieth century, come what may to our mental state of India-induced blissful relaxation.

In a whirl, we bussed back to Madras, retrieved our luggage, and called Kabir, who wanted to meet us at the airport for a send-off. We took our last ride in an Ambassador taxi to Chennai International Airport.

Some thirty-six hours later, we made our re-entry to the US at LAX, January 4, 1998, only one hour earth-time after we'd left India. We were hungry and, in a jet-lagged fog, went to eat a big salad and drink iced tap water at the giant spaceship restaurant on stilts. We felt just like the Jetsons.

. . .

***Journal, After Return to Portland…***

*Jan. 6, 1998*

One morning, standing in the staff room two days after returning to work, I found myself curious to observe a woman grinning ear to ear, exposing rows of teeth and exclaiming in a loud projected voice, discussing a soap opera she'd seen, or been in. Everyone was appearing to me to be high-pressured and anxious, even manic! (I feared I would join them as time wore on.)

I am already missing Indian people, in returning to the socially cold, yet manic West. (Their) intense interest in other people, which in my first trip was off-putting, has now become for me an endearing trait of the Indians.

As told me by my Indian friends or maybe it was a stranger on a train: "India is self-sufficient in agriculture, does not import basic food, all without the use of pesticides." I am thinking about a country half the geographic size of the US, with a billion people: Using any method of agriculture, how can they continue to feed the ever-expanding population? Things may be OK now, but what is going to happen?

*Jan. 18, 1998, Sunday afternoon*

It is raining heavily. At 4:00 p.m. it is nearly dark in Portland, Oregon.

It's hard to find the words to express the feelings we have traveling across cultures so rapidly; we'd barely begun to be accustomed to the ways of India, when we jetted ten thousand miles halfway around the world, plopped back into our Western lives and immediately tried to resume our work schedules. I felt oddly displaced! I actually carried drinking water with me for several days afterward; a reassuring habit I'd gotten used to.

The first day back I was shocked by the news that a man I work with, Ken, a psychologist, was killed suddenly with his wife in a car crash. There is a terrible irony to the story and how it relates to our trip. The accident occurred in Portland at the time we were taking our first auto-rickshaw rides in India. I remember thinking we could lose our lives, racing through the streets of Old Delhi, tail-gaiting huge petrol-trucks in our three-wheeled tin-cased rickshaw built atop a small motor-scooter. Once we nearly rear-ended the backside of an elephant who occupied one of the amorphous converging lanes of traffic. We never saw any seat belts in India. And I know I was thinking of my Toyota at home and the safety implied by its good crash test rating. Ken's car was a bigger, safer Toyota than mine. One just never knows one's fate, no matter how careful the attempt to make life "safe," reducing the probability of disease and accident. Americans (and I among them to a certain extent), have an obsession with "safety," much more than Europeans for instance. Not sure exactly why this has permeated our cultural thinking—it's an odds game, an illusion, probably creates new markets and boosts profits somehow, and there is a concern for liability, but never mind that. Ken was an elder whom I had looked forward to discussing the trip with upon return, reflecting on life with him as I like to do upon return from India. I know he would have been especially interested in this trip. Instead, at my work, there was an empty space and silence where Ken had been.

Last night we were invited by a Sri Lankan friend Joseph to attend a harvest time Pongal celebration of several groups of South Indian and Sri Lankan cultures. There was a cultural program with about fifty performers of South Indian arts, music and dance, mostly well-schooled children of all ages. Joseph organized it and told me it was the first time all the groups of Oregon and Washington were together. He told me he was inspired by living in America with its recent multi-cultural emphasis in schools. His group, the local Tamil Sangam sponsored the evening; we'd attended their events before. They invited the Telagu group and the Kabir and Malayalam groups. There were hundreds of families in attendance, and, as usual, we were nearly the only Westerners of Euro-descent there, but it was a familiar situation to us. As in India, everyone was kind and friendly and accepting of us. The food, made in home kitchens, was also familiar and delicious.

Even now, we continue to slowly recover from jet lag and reverse culture shock. I haven't quite finished washing all the clothes yet; I'm down to the delicate saris which must be hand-washed and elaborately draped across the room, to air-dry. This washing also serves as my own purification ritual, to be finally finished with all that Indian dirt. One who has lived in or traveled to India and returned to the West might relate to this.

I drew a paradoxical comfort in India when I was ill, reminding myself of various illnesses contracted occasionally by friends at Portland restaurants and barbeques that resulted in greater illness than I actually had in India. And of much-publicized serious illnesses resulting from eating food in the US tainted with bad ecoli bacteria. Also, the antibiotic-resistant bacteria that have become prevalent in US hospitals; some say from over-use of antibiotics.

Our journey back to Portland was long, almost 48 hours if one considers that we started the journey in Mahabalipuram many hours before the plane left from Madras, but otherwise reasonably pleasant and not turbulent. The food on Singapore Airlines was great. They served us Indian breakfast after take-off, then switched to Japanese meals with seaweed as we flew through Tokyo. Friends Phil and Terry met us with welcoming greetings at the airport. It was cool and raining the night we arrived and it never felt so good. After weeks of sweating in the humid tropics, I was glad to be back to winter (with our central heat and wood stove, that is). Five days after our return, deep snow fell on Portland and shut down the city for two days. I did not mind staying tucked in by the fire, not driving on the icy roads. That was last week, but now it has all melted. The weather is balmy at 50 degrees and it's drizzling and wet again, as usual.

. . .

***Correspondence***

*From a letter sent to Kabir and Maaya shortly after returning to Portland from the trip:*

*Jan. 12, 1998*

Thank you so much for your kind hospitality to us in your home in India, our trip together to Madurai and our visit with Kabir and the kids in Madras. Thanks for coming to the airport to see us off. For sure you must come to Portland to visit us, whenever it can be arranged. For any or all of the four of you.

*From a letter sent to Rajendra, Madhuri and all Joint family members: Jan. 12, 1998*

Words cannot describe the feeling I had returning to Jindh after 14 years. It was only our second day in India, and for us and our comfortable American ways, the bus ride to Jindh jolted us with an intense culture shock (that went away after several more road trips). When we finally arrived in Jindh, it was touching to be warmly received by people who knew and remembered me. I had no trouble remembering the personalities of each family member who I had got to know in 1983. You are all members of a very special family; I thought of this many times on our recent visit. I consider you lifetime friends, and invite you to visit us in Portland, whenever you can come, this year, or 14 years from now. We are looking forward to Rajendra's visit this July if he can arrange this. (Note: Rajendra did not make that trip to Portland.)

*From a letter sent to Marianne in Berlin: Feb. 8, 1998*

We are back from India one month now, but it's taken us about that much time to reconstruct ourselves back into the frantic pace of the Western lifestyle. And we cling to the memories of the journey, trying to sort out everything across the cultures and the centuries, editing our 1000 slides when we have time, whisking from the Taj Mahal and rural roads of Agra to a gig of Mitch's band in a Country Western bar scene, back down to Kerala and memories of sweating in the tropics and lazy boat rides on the beautiful backwaters to falling out of bed at 6:30 a.m. to speed up the Interstate, crossing bridges over two rivers to work, late to another 8 a.m. meeting. From the ancient temples and worshipers before those large painted plaster of paris Hindu gods to the blazing lights of the superstores, "what-should-I-make-for-dinner?"—I'm so tired after working, driving and shopping for 12 hours! Well, that's how my life seems to me at the moment.

...Mitch was really great to travel with, because he's very patient with the Indians. I think the Indians are among the most patient, tolerant people in the world. And I think they are *not* cruel. We in the West can be cruel, in the ways we sometimes relate to each other, the sarcasm, judgment, all the subtle and not so subtle ways that start with childrearing habits, ending in military strategies and news featuring cruelties and sensationalism, including movies that glamorize violence, unfortunately now catching on in India.

Seeing my friends in the village in Haryana state was really amazing after 14 years. To travel 36 hours halfway around the world, then five more hours on a shaking jam-packed bus, leaning from the weight of the men hanging on the outside, arriving to Jindh where hundreds of people gathered to stare at us; there, a large family knew me and was waiting for us, where we'd shared fond memories of each other, having spent time together traveling to Rajasthan in 1983, shortly after I met you for the first time!

*From a postcard home, sent to Amanda S.:*

*Dec. 30, 1997, Madurai*

*(On back of a photo of a Kerala backwater boat)*

We spent peaceful times in these backwaters, in a boat like this, but that was last week and seems like an eternity ago. Now we are in Tamil Nadu, in the thick of humanity, big trucks grinding gears, auto rickshaws, bullock-drawn wooden carts, scooters, buses with men hanging on the sides (pulling them into an angled lean around a turn), wandering cows and bicycles, blaring horns—just walking down the street is a carnival, but you have to watch out for all the vehicles.—you wouldn't believe how we've been forced to throw caution to the wind. We just returned to our hotel for a "fresh lime soda" after spending the afternoon at an ancient Hindu temple tank.

**Thinking of India, Many Years Later**

Lots of questions: I read they've cleaned up the pollution a bit and improved engine efficiency on the motor rickshaws and scooters in Delhi, with the former two-stroke engines now using compressed natural gas. Indian engineers are moving back to India with ideas and Western educations; India is becoming more affluent, but how will they cope with increasing emissions and air pollution from an expanding middle-class consumerism? Yet, they just might lead the way for all of us, with their admirable practicality and ingenious solutions for alternative energy I've been reading about, such as their use of solar lanterns, powered in a rural community by a solar collector and charging station; villagers pay a fee to rent and recharge the lantern, comparable to the previous cost of kerosene for the same hours of light (*Onearth*, Summer 2009, www.onearth.org). And villagers' use of biogas digester home apparatuses for converting cow dung efficiently into methane fuel to power small gas cooking stoves, reducing indoor smoke and carbon dioxide emissions from the burning of scarce firewood (or unprocessed dried cow patties) (*Solutions*, Fall 2012, www.edf.org/about/solutions). Maybe they'll make new products and sell versions of them to us, as some of our energy corporations are busy looking the other way, putting their efforts into lobbying against viable alternative energy solutions.

Will they finally give in to Western values, or can they hold on to the "real" India the way they did with 350 years of British occupation? Will they keep themselves apart from Western models, advancing themselves with their own economic ideas as the West potentially recedes under its own vacuous greed and corruption? However, India too, is notoriously corrupt.

I sense there is an unstated requirement that you need children to be fully accepted in India. I am not sure if a Hindu religious belief is attached to this, but I suspect superstitions are attached to childless women and couples, confirmed by my friend Joseph from Sri Lanka, a childless Christian. When I was younger, I felt pressured about having children from everyone I met in India. This topic was actually discussed in a Christmas letter from a friend, also without children, who had just returned from her fourth or fifth trip to India. When I became older, returning in 1997 with Mitch, still childless, it seemed there was a subtle distancing in the relationships with old friends, especially with the women.

There are millions of Indians living outside of India; they retain their religion and culture, though many have never been to India. How do they do this? I've observed they create close-knit sub-societies, with the women wearing saris on special occasions, cooking complicated Indian food, sponsoring Indian music and dance for their children, and sharing this with our communities, enriching the cities where they've settled. Yet I still think I am missing something important about how Indians retain their culture within other cultures and how they managed to hold on to it during the centuries of British occupation. Indians learned to speak English fluently in India while retaining all of their other rich languages. I'd venture to say that British cultural influence is limited within India now, perhaps only in the drinking of milky tea. I think India is an incredibly strong and resilient culture, but there seem to be secrets. Indians participate in public life wherever they have immigrated (or were born), don't really isolate, yet they remain apart. Perhaps it is a quality of resilient flexibility combined with a mysterious something-else.

. . .

There is something I acquired in India: the feeling of comfortable anonymity in crowds, to be a person in a crowd of many, many humans. You may feel alone inside your thoughts, but you are really not alone. You might feel as though you are disappearing into the mass. In India, the crowd envelopes you, holding everyone up and gently moving all along in a human wave. No fistfights break out, no kicking or unkind words. No defense of personal space, but a sharing closeness.

It is the people of India—and the wonderful warmth, compassion, patience, and absence of cruelty—that always draws back the Western traveler, despite the discomforts.

And very importantly, I've learned to rely on the kindness of strangers. One will grow into a treasured friend.

*Top:* **Delhi Traffic 1997**, viewed from auto rickshaw
*Bottom:* Margie on scooter, small town in Haryana state
Photos by Mitch Gilbert

Bicycle rickshaws in early morning

Town in **Haryana state 1997**
Photo by Mitch Gilbert

Photo images of the **Taj Mahal** by Mitch Gilbert, 1997

Photo images of the **Taj Mahal** by Mitch Gilbert, 1997

Photo images of the **Taj Mahal** by Marjorie Kircher, 1997

Photo image in **Fatehpur Sikri**, Mitch Gilbert, 1997

Photo images of **Fatehpur Sikri**
*Top:* Small mosque only for women, Exterior, by Mitch Gilbert, 1997
*Bottom:* Interior, by Marjorie Kircher

**Election campaign in India, 1997**
*Top:* Campaign posters; left & right
*Bottom:* Stumping from a horse cart
Photos by Marjorie Kircher

**Kerala backwater 1997**
*Top:* Boatman, by Mitch Gilbert
*Bottom:* Mitch, by Marjorie Kircher

**Kerala backwater, 1997**
*Top*: Photo by Marjorie Kircher
*Bottom*: Photo by Mitch Gilbert

Washing dishes and cow on backwater's edge
Photos by Mitch Gilbert, 1997

*Top:* Fort Lodge in **Cochin, 1997** Marjorie Kircher

*Bottom:* Antique statue in lodge courtyard Mitch Gilbert

**Kerala, 1997**
*Top:* Margie on Christmas day with star, by Mitch Gilbert

*Middle:* Movie Poster (MK)

*Bottom:* Street cow
Marjorie Kircher

**Kerala, 1997**

*Top:* Women in Alleppey, by Mitch Gilbert
*Bottom:* Mitch, having tea on the veranda at Kumarakom, day after Christmas, by Marjorie Kircher

Road drive through **Cardamom Hills, 1997**

*Top:* Thums Up for Margie, by Mitch Gilbert
*Middle:* Sonny, by Marjorie Kircher
*Bottom:* Afternoon Nappers, by Marjorie Kircher

**Tamil Nadu, 1997**

*Top:* Brickmaker, by Marjorie Kircher
*Bottom:* Bullock cart, by Mitch Gilbert

**Tamil Nadu, 1997**
*Top:* Vegetable vendor, by Mitch Gilbert

*Bottom:* Street bath, by Marjorie Kircher

**Sri Meenakshi Temple, Madurai, 1997**
Photos by Mitch Gilbert

**Sri Meenakshi Temple, Madurai, 1997**
Photos by Mitch Gilbert
Find the real monkey in top photo, with Ganesha

Elephant blessing Margie,
Sri Meenakshi Temple, Madurai, 1997
Photo by Mitch Gilbert

**Madras street scenes, 1997**
*Top* photo by Marjorie Kircher; *Bottom* photo by Mitch Gilbert

**Madras street scenes, 1997**
*Top:* Portable ferris wheel by Marjorie Kircher
*Bottom:* Bus hangers-on by Mitch Gilbert

**Madras street scenes, 1997**
*Top*: Construction excavation workers by Mitch Gilbert
*Bottom*: Homespun service vehicle by Marjorie Kircher

**Madras beach, 1997**

Waders, by Mitch Gilbert

**Madras street, 1997**
Mitch with new friends, by Marjorie Kircher

**Mahabalipuram, 1997**
*Top:* Ancient Temple on beach by Mitch Gilbert
*Bottom:* Cow detail, ancient temple by Mitch Gilbert

**Mahabalipuram, 1997**
*Top:* Temple carved into boulder; photo by Mitch Gilbert
*Bottom:* Margie with boulder temple column detail, by Mitch Gilbert

**Epilogue**

In October 2007, Mitch and I were traveling in Andalusia, southern Spain. We had just checked in to a little pension in Cordoba in the Jewish Quarter near the Moorish Mezquita Mosque and were catching our breath in our warm room. Our window was open to the central patio where tables were placed inside a verdant potted garden. We overheard an animated conversation in English between a Canadian couple and a British woman comparing travel stories in the garden. It was hilarious, so similar to our own recent misadventures trying to find vegetables on the menu dominated by sausage cuisine and navigate through Granada in a rental car where no street names were signed. We stifled our knowing laughter and moved closer to the window for a better earful, trying not to make our presence heard. Finally we had to leave for dinner with no choice but to pass through the group in the courtyard. We admitted our eavesdropping and joined the conversation briefly. Days passed as we nodded to the couple from Toronto when we passed them in the courtyard or noticed them in a nearby restaurant.

On the morning we planned to leave for Sevilla, we sat in the courtyard eating our breakfast, bags all packed and zipped in the room. The Canadian couple was finishing at the next table.

"Where are you headed?" the woman asked.

"Sevilla."

"Oh, so are we. …Want a ride?"

"Well, sure. We're all packed."

"You have backpacks? Good, because our rental car is parked five blocks away."

And off we went with Judy and Rick to Sevilla by way of Carmona. Great day and easy conversation. Said they, "Oh, by the way, we'll be driving through Portland next February on our way to Lake Tahoe."

"Here's our address. Thanks for the ride. Bye."

Off we went separately. We ran into them by chance on the street at least three or four more times in Sevilla. We returned home, and they were off to Morocco. We corresponded by email. They came to Portland in February (four months later). Sadly, Mitch's father died and he had to leave the day before they arrived, but I stayed for them and joined him a day and half later. Judy and Rick were very sympathetic and helpful to me, cooking dinner while I packed for the trip, taking me to the airport and caring for our dog before the housesitter arrived. Staying in our house gave them time to see more of Portland.

While they were visiting, Judy read the very beginnings of this manuscript, not much more than the 1974 journal reflections, and related to it as a world traveler. She encouraged me to keep writing. We parted. Over more emails, she asked me to send the story so Rick could read it. Empowered by Judy's comments and those of other friends, I kept writing and writing, and here it is.

Serendipity is why I love travel! You never know who you will meet and how they will figure in your story.

# ABOUT THE AUTHOR

MARJORIE KIRCHER is an avid traveler far and near, a searcher for the underpinnings and the missing details. She is an occupational therapist working with children and adults and has been awarded the Cornelia Myers Writer's Award for her article on perceived exertion, appearing in the *American Journal of Occupational Therapy*. Kircher also enjoys pastimes of painting and photography. She lives in Portland, Oregon with her husband, Mitch, and almost-literate dog. *The India Traveler* is her first book.

4273309R00146

Made in the USA
San Bernardino, CA
07 September 2013